STUDIO

STUDIO
STructured User-interface Design for Interaction Optimisation

Dermot P. Browne

KPMG Management Consulting

Prentice Hall

NEW YORK   LONDON   TORONTO   SYDNEY   TOKYO   SINGAPORE

First published 1994 by
Prentice Hall International (UK) Limited
Campus 400, Maylands Avenue
Hemel Hempstead
Hertfordshire, HP2 7EZ
A division of
Simon & Schuster International Group

Typeset in 10/12 Plantin
by Goodfellow & Egan, Cambridge

Printed and bound in Great Britain by
Redwood Books, Trowbridge, Wiltshire

Library of Congress Cataloging-in-Publication Data

Browne, Dermot.
    STUDIO : STructured User-interface Design for Interaction
Optimisation / Dermot P. Browne.
        p.   cm.
    ISBN 0-13-014721-4
    1. User interfaces (Computer system)   2. Human-computer
interaction.   I. Title.
QA76.9.U83B76   1993
005.1′2—dc20   93-12402
                                                           CIP

British Library Cataloguing in Publication Data

A catalogue record for this book is available from
the British Library

ISBN 0-13-014721-4

---

2 3 4 5 98 97 96 95 94

Contents

6 Conclusion *247*

Preface

User expectations of Information Technology (IT) have risen dramatically in recent years. Exposure to personal computing and the ease of use that this offers has raised hopes that business applications will become appreciably more accessible and usable.

Commerce expects business benefits from its investments in IT. Promises of ease of use raise these expectations, yet the benefits often remain unrealised.

Advances in information technology, especially Graphical User Interface technology (GUI) have exposed the limitations of data driven and function driven approaches to interactive system design.

Taken together, user expectations, commercial interests and technological advancements have brought the issue of *usability* sharply into focus. There is an acceptance that usability is worth striving for, even though the meaning of usability and how it can be achieved is not widely understood.

How usability can be achieved is the subject matter of this book. A method for user interface design that delivers usable interactive systems is presented. This method is called STUDIO, which stands for STructured User interface Design for Interaction Optimisation. STUDIO bring together the best of the available techniques and notation, along with new techniques, to provide a comprehensive industrial-strength method for the design of user interfaces to business applications.

This book is a primer, albeit a detailed one. Its purpose is to inform the reader fully as to what is required for the development of high-quality usable systems. As a consequence it is anticipated that designers will be better equipped to plan for and provide quality interactive systems, procurers will be better positioned to demand usable systems from suppliers, and professional user interface designers will find it a valuable practitioners' guide.

Those who have a background in application systems design but are not familiar with the issues of user interface design, as well as inexperienced user interface designers, will hopefully find this book educational and enlightening, but should not treat it as a self-sufficient or self-contained training course. While the adoption of a systematic approach to design is a prerequisite for improved usability, user interface design is an applied skill that will only be developed fully with practice and training. To assist in this development, anecdotes and examples from projects that have applied STUDIO are included within the text. It is hoped that these, together with a worked example, will help the reader to appreciate the scope of user interface design concerns and how these can be addressed.

STUDIO as documented here has been developed with window-based technology in mind. This does not preclude its use in the development of conventional systems or, indeed, its employment by projects utilising the very latest technology, such as pen-based interfaces or multimedia.

STUDIO is largely independent of both technology and specific structured methods. None the less, it may be practised in tandem with other system development methods. A companion document, *STUDIO for SSADM*[1] *Projects*, describes how STUDIO is to be employed in concert with one such structured method.

STUDIO continues to be developed. A manual, *STUDIO Stylising Guide* has been produced to deal with the issue of providing consistent interfaces that permit users to transfer their skills easily between applications. STUDIO will be developed further in response to changing business requirements.

The motivation for documenting this method has been KPMG Management Consulting's many years of experience in developing bespoke interactive systems, including systems that employ windows technology. Experience has shown that such developments are not well supported by established practice. STUDIO seeks to correct these deficiencies.

The contents of this book are based on the experiences of the author, gained directly from striving to provide usable IT solutions and largely while working within the 'IT Practice' at KPMG and previously at a major systems house. My gratitude is extended to all the persons I have worked with, and sometimes warred with, in the pursuit of usability, and to all the reviewers of this manuscript, particularly Professor M. A. Norman.

---

[1] SSADM: Structured Systems Analysis and Design Method. SSADM is mandatory on Government IT development projects.

Introduction

This chapter begins with a discussion of why user interface design is an issue for the 1990s. STUDIO is then introduced. The need for a method-based approach to user interface developed is then elaborated. Some of the myths surrounding user interface development are discussed and, hopefully, dispelled. A brief case study is presented towards the end of this chapter.

I.1 User interface design: the issue of the 1990s?

Historically, the provision of viable IT solutions was risky. A survey conducted in 1979 by the US Government Accounting Office (Cox, 1987) indicated that less than 5 per cent of systems commissioned were actually used as delivered. Nowadays, there is far less risk associated with the commissioning of IT. Developers now have the tools at their disposal to be far more confident that they can deliver systems that meet functional requirements. This has made it possible for developers to broaden their horizons. As the following quote suggests, the emphasis of systems development is moving away from the provision of elegant technological solutions to the provision of systems that are effective in practice:

> *In meeting the challenges of automation, each company must rely on three sets of skills: engineering the technology (getting the machines to work), managing the technology (getting machines to work with people) and managing the organisation (getting our people and machines to work more efficiently than their people and machines). Twenty years ago just getting computers to work was a challenge, and companies rightly stressed engineering over management. But the priorities are shifting.*
> *The Economist June 14, 1990.*

Unfortunately, the application of IT has not provided the business benefits expected, certainly not with respect to white-collar workers. The following quotes suggest that IT, at a significant cost, has provided no national benefit in thirty years:

> *Mr Stephen Roach, an economist with Morgan Stanley, calculates that the average output of an American information worker has not budged since the early 1960's. Mr Roach's studies make sobering reading. They indicate that*

computers have so far failed to boost productivity even on the most generous measure, output per worker. Including capital costs, as any truly accurate measure should, would make the picture look even worse.

Analysts at DRI, a firm of economic forecasters, estimate that the share of office equipment in America's stocks of fixed capital (excluding property) has climbed from 3% in 1980 to 18% in 1990. All to no avail.
Both quotes taken from *The Economist*, June 14, 1990.

The end-user population for IT products is more diverse than ever, and is still growing. The Institute for the Future, a Californian think tank, predicts that by 1995, '90% of American white-collar workers will have a screen' (*The Economist*, June 14, 1990).

This growing population of computer users is also becoming more demanding. Managers and executives often have their own personal computers (PC) sitting alongside a dumb terminal connected to corporate applications. Comparisons are easy to make and often result in criticism of the dumb terminal interface. Users now want the data access capabilities, offered presently through dumb terminals, to be integrated with the usability offered by PCs. Integration is achievable but will pose a significant overhead for user interface designers. True integration will require the creation of applications that retrieve data transparently from diverse sources, possibly distributed across different databases or even different hardware. To achieve true integration and avoid the potential pitfalls will require skilled user interface design.

Today a far greater percentage of systems code is designed for the provision of user interfaces. Advances such as WIMP (Window, Icon, Mouse and Pointer) style interfaces offer greater design options, both good and bad. Surveys indicate that upwards of 50 per cent of the code for a system can be utilised for its user interface (MacIntyre *et al.*, 1990). For instance, where centralised corporate computing provides the required functionality, then benefits may be sought from the provision of a new user interface alone.

International bodies are now championing the call for usable systems. The Department of Trade and Industry in the United Kingdom has been running a campaign entitled 'Usability Now' with the twin objectives of raising awareness of the benefits to be gained from well-designed user interfaces and educating industry as to where advice can be found. A recent European Commission directive on the 'minimum safety and health requirements for work with display screen equipment' (Directive 87/391/EEC) demands a response from each European member state. These responses must include procedures for establishing working practices that include assessment of how well systems support their users. In response to this directive the Health and Safety Commission in the United Kingdom has published a document entitled 'Display Screen Equipment Work: Guidance on Regulations'. The British Standards Institute is also producing a set of standards (BSI 92/35512 DC) with respect to the provision of usable systems. In Europe the ISO (International Organisation for Standardisation) body and the CEN (Comité Europeen de Normalisation) are producing standards covering similar issues. Standards and legislation will be forced upon IT procurers and they in turn will expect suppliers to provide systems that meet the standards.

The standards mentioned above will certainly raise awareness within the business community of the need to design for users. This awareness will lead to an increased demand for skilled user interface designers and supporting methods.

I.1.1 User interface design acceptance

Many user interface designers wonder why it has taken so long for their trade to become widely accepted and practised. After all, for many years there have been quality journals, conferences and publications addressing the subject of user interface design. Even so, there has been a lack of uptake in the IT industry of the techniques underlying user interface design. It is important to consider the reasons for this in order that further progress is not delayed. Two possible reasons are proposed below.

Resistance to new techniques

Many persons view structured methods as burdensome. As a result they are resistant to any proposals that seek to add new techniques or methods to the system development process. This is an understandable yet untenable view. Method-based approaches are necessary in order to streamline and rationalise activities that would otherwise be chaotic and high risk. Unfortunately, existing methods are inadequate with respect to some of the more recent developments in IT, particularly Graphical User Interfaces (GUIs). STUDIO addresses this inadequacy.

Belief that the techniques are being practised

There is no doubt that some of the techniques advocated by user interface designers are being practised. Unfortunately, they are often not practised in the way intended. Prototyping is a prime example. Prototypes are often developed and used to guide design even though they are never tested with users. In addition, the techniques that are available exist like islands with no bridges between one and the next. STUDIO provides the necessary techniques and bridges.

I.1.2 What is a system?

When developing any system, two essential and obvious facts should not be forgotten. A system is nothing without the people who use it, and system development necessitates design activities.

IT alone does not make a system. Until technology is placed in the hands of users and is employed in anger it cannot truly be called a system (Figure I.1). Many effective non-computerised systems exist. Technology must only be considered as an enabler for better systems. IT is not a solution in itself. While data analyses, functional analyses, business analyses and process analyses are all necessary to varying degrees on different projects, the designs that result all fail if that essential system component, the user, is not taken into account adequately. IT solutions always have

Figure I.1 *A system in use. [Translation: Speak Norwegian!]*

shortcomings for which users are expected to compensate. Unfortunately, users have failings too and IT should compensate for them. For instance, users forget, some thrive on structure, some apply well-proven strategies to their work, they make decisions, they may be information hungry or susceptible to information overload. Users may be short of time. Users are fallible. All users have experiences which can help or hinder them in the pursuit of their duties.

The abilities and limitations of users must be taken into account if usable systems are to be developed. Users are employed to perform duties. If they are to be supported appropriately by IT, then their duties and tasks must be understood and taken into consideration during user interface design.

The second point is that the interactive aspects of systems must be designed. Structured methods have evolved and been successful because they have concentrated on understanding those aspects of a system which are most stable and finite: the data and functions. Such structured methods are inadequate with respect to the interactive aspects of systems. Specialist design skills are still required. The skills of professional user interface designers will become an essential component of project teams as the user interface accounts for increasingly greater portions of systems and as users become more demanding.

User interface design is frequently left to the whims and best intentions of various parties including analysts and programmers. While these parties may work with the best intentions, their priorities are usually guided by project deadlines and ease of implementation rather than by the requirements of that essential system component: the user. This is not a criticism of analysts and programmers but, rather, a sad reflection on the IT industry.

It has been commonplace for the industry to generate accurate and complete functional specifications that procurers endorse without full understanding. Subsequently, possibly even years later, a fully functional and accurate system, according to the specification, is delivered only to be met with the response 'that is not what we wanted', or 'that is not how we thought it would be'. The poor communication of requirements (Browne et al. 1992) may explain some such scenarios. This communication problem is depicted in Figure I.2 by analogy with a transport requirement. A buyer requires a vehicle that will allow him to traverse central London quickly. He also wishes to be shielded from the elements. In addition, he would prefer it if excursions in the vehicle did not necessitate a change of clothing. Unfortunately, the analyst only elicits from the buyer the requirement that the vehicle provide a quick mode of conveyance across central London. As a result he provides a bicycle and thus meets his contractual obligations. Unfortunately, he fails completely to satisfy the buyer. The conclusion to this story would likely be disuse of the product or an expensive maintenance exercise involving the addition of covers, fairings, panniers and a motor for the bicycle.

The problem of communication is well known. In response there has been an upsurge in prototyping activities with the intention of giving procurers an early and realistic sighting of the analysts' understanding of what is required. Unfortunately, prototypes are not the complete answer. All too often prototypes are not seen by

Figure I.2 *Requirements capture.*

actual users, but, rather, by user representatives who are not very representative. Prototyping is often planned in such a manner that the prototype itself becomes a *fait accompli*. Prototypes may not be tested in a sufficiently rigorous manner to ensure that design inadequacies are trapped. Users viewing a prototype may genuinely agree that it is a vast improvement over what went before, but because they are not IT specialists they may fail to identify or convey how the design could be improved. It is for these reasons that user interface provision must be regarded as an iterative design activity. Adequate user requirements must be afforded to designers who can then apply their experience, and best practice, to produce designs that are well suited to their purpose. Such designers should at least be aware of what is possible with the technology at hand, what the limitations and abilities of the user population are and the use to which the technology will be put. Thus user interface designers are a specialist band, knowledgable in the field of user interfacing technology, trained in task analysis and educated in human behaviour.

I.1.3 Summary

No longer is the IT industry preoccupied with making IT work. The problem now is getting IT to work effectively with users. To support the growing population of increasingly demanding users, appreciably more resources are being directed towards providing quality user interfaces. While there is international recognition that this shift in effort needs to be supported by better practices, there is presently no accepted method for the design of usable systems.

I.2 **STUDIO**

STUDIO provides a framework and accompanying techniques for the development of user interfaces displaying high-quality usability. STUDIO provides a method for planning, managing and conducting development in a manner that ensures the ultimate usability of interactive systems. To achieve this, a range of relevant techniques have been brought together to form a coherent industrial-strength method.

STUDIO stands for STructured User interface Design for Interaction Optimisation. The words that compose the acronym STUDIO are discussed in turn in order to introduce the method.

STUDIO is **STructured**. It provides a method composed of sequential stages and steps. This STructure facilitates planning and estimating and hence managerial control of a project. Because it is a fully documented method its application reduces re-invention and rationalises documentation. It offers a basis for shared understanding between the various roles on a project team and by so doing improves communication and accountability.

STUDIO delivers the **User interface** of computer systems. A User interface is everything that impacts a user's interaction with a system. A User interface includes, documentation, training materials, on-screen dialogues, help systems and hardware, including peripherals. It is the User interface of a system that permits the communication of task requirements to the computer, the assimilation of information as presented by a system to users and the delivery of the products of a user's interaction with the system.

STUDIO is a method for the **Design** of the structure and form of the user interface to a system. STUDIO provides a framework in which design can be performed in an orderly manner. Where it is possible to be prescriptive STUDIO provides guidance based on best practice.

STUDIO is concerned with a dynamic process, namely the **Interaction** between the user and a system. Technology is redundant until a user interacts with it to some purpose. Therefore, STUDIO's prime concern is users, specifically supporting them in accomplishing their aims through interaction with a system.

The objective of STUDIO is **Optimisation** of the interaction between user and technology. This is often referred to as usability or, more colloquially, user friendliness. To this end STUDIO quantifies usability using metrics such as **P**roductivity, **L**earnability, **U**ser satisfaction, **M**emorability, and **E**rror rates. STUDIO delivers systems that demonstrate quantifiable usability benefits.

Structure of STUDIO

STUDIO is composed of five stages as depicted in Figure I.3.

Stage 1 (Project Proposal and Planning) has two steps. The first of these is 'Cost-benefit analysis' as applied to user interface design. This step provides a means of justifying an investment in user interface design. The second step has the general title 'Quality planning'. It stipulates how quality assurance is to be addressed when applying STUDIO.

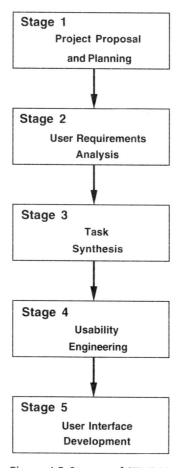

Figure I.3 *Stages of STUDIO.*

Stage 1 of STUDIO answers the question of whether user interface design expenditure is not justifiable. Where various disciplines will be competing for resources on a given project it is essential that user interface designers can justify their involvement.

Stage 2 (User Requirements Analysis) bears many similarities to systems analysis. User requirements analysis has the specific aim of collecting data or evidence pertaining to the design of user interfaces as distinct from purely functional or computational components of a system. User requirements analysis is divided into five steps beginning with 'Preparing the groundwork'. This step prepares for the analysis of planning activities and timetabling sessions with prospective users. The next step is 'Evidence collection', during which analysts gather user requirements data. STUDIO describes a number of techniques that can be used during evidence collection. Next comes 'Task analysis', during which the results of evidence collection are documented in various notations. These notations are used in later stages of STUDIO for design. The task analyses are validated during the next step: 'Validating the evidence'. The stage is completed by 'Reporting the findings'. User requirements analysis, unlike traditional systems analysis provides the necessary documentation and understanding from which user interface designs can be generated informatively and later evaluated.

The techniques of systems analysis are largely unsuitable with respect to user interface design. Stage 2 of STUDIO addresses this inadequacy by providing suitable techniques and concentrating on user concerns and requirements rather than on data or functional requirements.

Stage 3 (Task Synthesis) takes the results of user requirements analysis and delivers an initial user interface design. There are five steps in this stage, some of which can be performed in parallel. The step entitled 'User support' generates the necessary documentation such as user manuals that will form a part of the user interface. STUDIO offers much guidance with respect to providing effective documentation. The 'Style guide' step delivers a document stipulating rules that must be adhered to by the user interface design. In essence, this step ensures that a consistent user interface is developed. 'Task synthesis' is the step during which designers begin to generate user interface designs. Interface specification notations are introduced at the 'Design specification' step. These notations permit designers to perform 'Formative evaluations' before any prototyping is performed. In this way, potentially expensive design inadequacies can be identified and rectified in a cost effective manner. User involvement during this stage is largely in the role of reviewer.

User interface design demands a set of skills not normally practised by IT designers. It is for this reason that STUDIO provides extensive guidance on topics such as the production of user documentation, consistency at the user interface and user interface specification.

Stage 4 (Usability Engineering) combines prototyping and impact analysis to provide a manageable approach to iterative prototyping. This stage takes the design(s) produced in Stage 3 and submits them to evaluation through prototype testing. This begins with a step for 'Usability engineering planning', which includes the time-tabling of user involvement and production schedules for evaluation materials. 'Prototype build' is then undertaken. Prior to user testing of any prototype a 'Design audit' is undertaken. This audit identifies flaws in the design through the application of simple diagnostic tests. In parallel with building the prototype, the evaluators 'Prepare evaluation materials'. Following the successful completion of these steps 'Prototype evaluation' takes place. The results of this evaluation are submitted to 'Impact analysis', which prioritises the desirable modifications to the prototype allowing valuable development resources to be deployed to best effect. Prototype evaluation and impact analysis may be repeated iteratively. Having concluded all evaluations and prototype modifications this stage is completed by 'Update documentation'. Usability Engineering (Stage 4) delivers a usable prototype and supporting specifications.

Prototyping is rarely performed in a manner that takes full advantage of the opportunities afforded by rapid prototyping environments. STUDIO ensures that prototyping is both a manageable and an effective means of testing designs.

The involvement of user interface designers during a project is largely complete once usability engineering is concluded. None the less, their work must be handed over to, and integrated with, the work of other developers. For this reason STUDIO includes a short stage entitled 'User Interface Development' (Stage 5). This stage begins with a step entitled 'Hand over specification'. The main purpose of this step is to ensure that the deliverables from the work of the user interface designers is properly understood. During 'Integration/interfacing', the user interface designers work with other development team(s) to resolve issues of integration. 'Acceptance testing' will subsequently be performed during which user interface designers have a role in verifying and validating the final user interface. Finally, 'Termination reporting' ensures that lessons learned during a project are not lost. Such lessons should include data on effort expended so that future projects can be planned accurately.

The good work of user interface designers can be undermined during the latter stages of a development due to lack of communication between different roles within a project team. Stage 5 of STUDIO helps avoid such disappointing scenarios.

STUDIO needs to be adapted to suit the requirements of particular projects. For instance, on projects developing a new user interface to existing functionality, STUDIO has been shown to be the only method required. Individual steps of STUDIO have been used in isolation to fulfil specific project requirements such as the production of corporate user interface style guides. STUDIO has also been used in tandem with structured development methods where the latter are used for data analysis and database design.

Subsequent chapters introduce and explain the five stages of STUDIO in detail. For those readers who are unfamiliar with the subject of user interface design, the remainder of this chapter provides a discussion of many of the issues central to the subject. This discussion begins by responding to the question 'What is required of a user interface design method?' 'What does the term user interface actually mean and what constitutes a user interface?' is a question that, surprisingly, does not obtain a consistent answer. The meaning of the term 'user interface' is discussed. It has been suggested that style guidelines, when adopted unerringly, are all that is required for the development of quality user interfaces. This assertion is questioned. This is followed by consideration of the philosophy of the user-centred approach advocated by STUDIO. Discussion of the term 'usability' and how it is measured is then provided.

Having discussed the terminology of user interface design and provided answers to some basic questions, the relationship between STUDIO and traditional structured methods is discussed. A brief case study is then provided followed by an outline of the structure of this book.

I.2.1 **What is required of a user interface design method?**

Methods are adopted for many reasons. Methods assist with project planning. Time and resource estimates are made easier when planners have a clear understanding of each of the activities that need to be undertaken during the life of a project.

Methods identify deliverables and milestones at which project progress can be monitored by client and supplier alike. By so doing, projects may be re-planned or resources re-deployed as deemed necessary.

Proven techniques are crucial to the success of any method. They permit analysts and designers to work confidently in the knowledge that they are applying themselves constructively.

A method must be sufficiently well documented that training can be standardised and common understanding in its application assured. This minimises the dependency of any project on particular human resources and reduces the risks associated with such dependencies.

User interface design makes further demands of a method. End-user involvement is essential to user interface design and thus any method must promote user involvement throughout the project life cycle. Interface designs are judged in terms of usability and thus support for cost effective usability testing must be provided. In addition, a user interface design method must promote the application of good user interface design practices.

STUDIO supports project planning by being highly structured: deliverables from each stage are clearly defined; training courses in STUDIO are available; STUDIO demands user involvement throughout; and the method offers much advice on best practice.

I.2.2 **What is a user interface?**

A user interface is any aspect of a system that impacts a user's interaction with that system. When contemplating the phrase 'user interface', an image of a computer screen, possibly filled with windows and colours, often comes to mind. While this image is accurate it is also incomplete. User interaction with a system does not happen through a computer screen alone. A user's introduction to a system rarely begins with the user viewing a screen and being expected to fulfil a job function. Most users will have already gained experience of a computer, experienced the predecessor to the present system, completed a training course, or possibly been party to the development of the new system. As a result, user interfaces must be considered as including all training materials, input devices, workplace furniture, the workplace environment and other users.

A new financial dealing room opened in the late 1980s boasted many technologically advanced features. Unfortunately, shortly after going live it became apparent that the system's users had become quite de-motivated and lacklustre. A retrospective analysis showed that the room lacked the basic atmosphere to which the users were accustomed. The dealers could not perceive market moves; their adrenalin didn't flow; and they were left depleted of triggers on which to base their 'gut reactions'. The old system had grouped dealers trading different commodities in one room. The ambient noise generated in the old room had provided a source of information on market movement. The dealers in the new room did not trade frenetically and, as a result, their room was now comparatively quiet and lifeless. To remedy the situation the rather expensive remedial step of piping noise from the old, but still operational, dealing room into the new room was made. This is an example of how the social and physical attributes of a system can determine its effectiveness.

1.2.3 Style guides

One of the most talked about topics in the computer industry is the issue of *style guides* or *look and feel guidelines* to be employed for user interfaces. A number of these now exist, including 'CUA'ᵗᵐ from IBM (1991), the Apple Human Interface Guidelines (1987), 'OSF/MOTIF'ᵗᵐ from the Open Software Foundation (1990), and 'Open Look'ᵗᵐ from AT&T and Sun (1989). The advantages of such guidelines are that they determine a certain style and consistency for user interaction. For instance, all commands might be chosen from pull-down menus, the *close* window function is always performed by clicking on a certain part of a window's frame, etc. Such guidelines can offer benefits, particularly where users are expected to move between and use different applications in the course of their jobs. A knowledge of the *in-house style* can be transferred to many different applications without necessitating extensive re-training.

While it might be thought that the usability of products will inevitably improve through the provision of graphical user interfaces (GUIs) and the application of look and feel guidelines, a paradox exists. The greater flexibility for design afforded by GUIs actually means that there is more opportunity for creating poor designs. Standards do not resolve this problem; they merely provide a framework and a set of constraints within which it is suggested that any design should fit.

Where a set of guidelines is adopted, for whatever reasons, it is still necessary to perform analyses to support interface design. For instance, no guideline can dictate appropriate literals (i.e. command names) and, determine the appropriate positioning of windows or, in fact, their content. Appropriate dialogue sequencing, format of information, content of warnings, error messages, help texts, etc., have to be determined as a design exercise.

Guidelines do not provide design solutions. They only constrain the design space in order that consistency can be achieved. While consistency is a good design principle, it alone cannot guarantee usability.

Users of transaction processing style interfaces often suffered the problem of not being able to view two related sets of data simultaneously. The advent of GUIs has circumvented this problem through the use of windows. In many applications users are at liberty to display any two sets of data they wish, juxtaposed on a screen. What is often forgotten is that the user pays a price for this capability. It has become the user's responsibility to perform window management activities. For instance, the user is required to move windows so that they do not obscure data of interest, close windows so that the screen is less cluttered, size windows, etc. None of these operations are related to a user's immediate task requirements and thus such overheads tend to be forgotten. The guidelines mentioned previously provide advice on how to support window management operations. None of them offer assistance on how to develop a system so that the user is not required to perform window management. This is not a fault of the guidelines but it is a consequence of the fact that they are generalisations that cannot take account of specific task and user requirements.

The assumption that the adoption of GUI technology will ensure usability is a fallacy.

GUIs and interface standards are not a panacea for usability. GUIs offer greater bandwidth for interaction and consequently more opportunity for poor design. Adopting guidelines helps to identify the design issues. Resolution of these issues can then be achieved through careful consideration of end-user requirements and how they can best be supported.

A demonstration user interface for a major police system was completed in early 1990. Most of the tasks undertaken with this system require the viewing of documents and database records simultaneously. As many records and various parts of the documents are viewed frequently, the designers (Browne et al. 1990 and Woods et al. 1991) decided that all window management would be under system control rather than user control. Because the users' tasks were well understood it was possible for a set of rules to be generated for window positioning, opening and closing. As each operation was invoked, the rules were applied. A formal evaluation of the user interface showed that the users benefited from the use of windows. On debriefing, the users had no complaints regarding the approach to window management. In fact it was not an issue, presumably because the system operated in a task supportive manner.

I.2.4 User-centred approach

The ethos of user interface design is twofold. Firstly, those responsible for a system's development are not the most suitable designers of that system's interface. Secondly, end-users, or at least the legitimate representatives of prospective end-users, must be involved in the design process to ensure the usability of the final system.

System developers tend to create engineering models. One example is offered by the carburettor (Gentner and Grudin 1990). An engineering model of the carburettor would include the choke valve and the throttle valve. The former controls the strength of the air/petrol mixture while the latter controls the amount of mixture leaving the carburettor. In the not too distant past, car controls included a lever connected directly to the choke valve giving the driver mastery of the air/petrol mixture. Given that, nowadays, drivers usually only want control over the speed of a car's movement and do not wish to be bothered with the efficiency of the engine, this control should not form part of the driver's interface with the car. Modern cars now put the onus for efficiency on the car and leave the driver to drive. Similarly, database management systems made the users aware of the data structures being used for data storage. Thus users of relational databases had to perform operations, such as the joining of tables, and found this extremely cumbersome, difficult to understand and an overhead that they would happily forego.

Engineering models can impair interaction with a system when they pervade the user interface. Unfortunately, engineers can usually provide cogent arguments for why the engineering model exists. In addition, the engineers usually find it difficult to accept that users have no appreciation for, or desire to understand, these models. Most users, whether they are driving a car or accessing data, have no desire to understand the functionality of the system; they simply wish to perform some tasks. It is these tasks that should provide the basis for user interface designs. In the above example, users wished to direct a car and control its speed. How this is achieved at an engineering or technical level is an irrelevance to drivers. (On occasions, engineering models can be a valid starting point for the design of an interface. For instance, an appreciation of, and the opportunity to work with, relational data structures might be crucial to database administrators; their jobs and, consequently, the tasks they have to perform, dictate that this is so.) The point being made is twofold. Firstly, engineering models (i.e data structures, and functions) should not be the bases for user interface designs. An understanding of what people wish to achieve with a system should be the basis for design. Such an understanding is captured by task models. Secondly, developers are not likely to be the most suitable personnel to perform user interface design work. They are too influenced by their knowledge of underlying engineering models.

User interface design should begin with an understanding of the tasks that the system is going to support. That is, what are the requirements of the end-users of that system? What are the capabilities of those users? Which functions should remain under user control (throttle management) and which under system control (choke regulation)? In what sequence are tasks to be completed? What does the user require (i.e. information) in order to progress each task? What method of interaction will best support these tasks? These are just a few of the questions to which a user requirements analysis provides answers in order to establish a task model from which user interface design can progress. By performing task modelling early in a development, an outline user interface design can be produced. By so doing, it is quite possible that requirements will be identified that will need to be addressed by the engineering model of a system as essential functionality.

A user-centred approach is required to user interface design.

I.2.5 **Usability**

The quality of a system can be assessed on many dimensions. Typical of these are reliability and maintainability. Such 'itys' are often given great emphasis by system procurers. In 'invitations to tender' they may be ascribed absolute values for suppliers to attain. For instance, the deliverable must be 'available 99 per cent of the time during normal office hours and never be unavailable for a period longer than five minutes during these hours'. Such criteria can be made contractually binding. Where the supplier fails to meet such criteria the system has to be re-worked, otherwise a financial penalty is incurred. For many years such functional issues have dominated quality assurance practices during system procurement and development. Recently, concern has grown over the subject of user interaction with a system and how this communication channel is a major determinant of system quality. This concern has been fuelled by experiences of increased staff costs resulting from user dissatisfaction and the realisation by hardware and software suppliers that usability is a strong market force. Many a marketing campaign has been launched on ideals such as *user friendliness* and *ease of use*. While such terms are vacuous, usability is still important.

In designing a system for issuing books in a university library a structured system development method was adopted. The analysis stage of this method identified the need for a function to update book records as those books were issued. The analysis identified the *issuing of a book by the librarian to a reader* as a task. A function to support this was specified and implemented. Unfortunately, this analysis was incomplete. A second and better task description would have been: *issuing of multiple books by the librarian to a reader until the reader and librarian are satisfied that the transaction is complete*. The difference between the two descriptions may appear trivial but the ramifications of realising that the task is the issuing of *numerous* books has many implications.

A reader comes to the issue desk with five books under her arm, puts them on the desk and presents her membership card to the librarian. The librarian then begins to issue these books one at a time. It is also the case that this reader already has three books on loan and her loan limit is six books. Thus the reader is only going to be allowed to borrow three of the five books. Taking the first task description, the system might be implemented such that once three books have been issued the loan limit is reached and the librarian informs the reader to that affect. The reader might be quite upset by this as the book of most import to her is one that has not yet been issued. To satisfy the disgruntled reader the librarian now has to go through the remedial tasks of de-issuing one of the just issued books and issuing the important book. The improved task description would not have led to this situation. As soon as the reader's membership number had been input to the system the librarian, and in turn the reader, would have been informed that she could only loan three books. The reader could then have chosen the books she wanted, avoiding the need to issue and immediately return a book. A further alternative suggested by the second task description would be only to commence the issuing of books once all books being requested by a reader have been made known to the system. The choice between these latter two designs could be made on the basis of other task analysis information, for instance the frequency with which book issuing is refused because those books are reference only or are reserved by another reader.

Usability addresses how well users can make use of the functionality of a system. This is distinct from utility, which refers to whether the functionality of a system can do what is needed. A system can have potential utility while being less than useful operationally. Usability refers to an operational quality whereas utility can be assessed non-operationally.

It is not sufficient to state that a system offers 'improvements in interaction' or that 'it is friendly' or 'easy to use'. These are unqualified statements that do not help to assess the relative merits of a product or deliverable. The purchaser of a car would not be impressed by statements such as 'this is a nice car' or 'it will not give you much trouble'. A car buyer is far more likely to be influenced by top speeds, petrol consumption figures and boot capacity. Similarly, when purchasing software the procurer requires some means of stating the criteria that the deliverable should meet and therefore what the acceptance criteria will be. These criteria should include measures of usability.

Usability is the degree to which users can exploit the potential utility of a system.

While it might be thought that usability is not quantifiable, closer inspection has shown that usability can be measured. It is possible to state usability criteria in a quantifiable and then testable manner. For instance, 'a trained user shall be able to produce a twenty-word message, save it and send it within fifty seconds'. Now, of course, the criticism could be levelled that it is still necessary to state what is meant by trained user and yes this would have to be qualified. Indeed, exceptions such as the user spending an inordinate amount of time composing the twenty words would have to be excluded, but the general tenet of the statement still holds and could be used as a benchmark. The same sort of questions might be asked of the road test figures for cars. For instance, an acceleration of 0–60 miles per hour in 5.7 seconds might be stated and accepted without question. In actuality, readers might not be able to replicate such a figure unless they attempted the feat on a flat road, with no passengers, an almost empty fuel tank, and could assume the psychomotor skills of Nigel Mansell. Even then they would only be successful on 51 per cent of occasions. Notwithstanding such caveats, usability criteria can be set and are important to system procurers.

The challenge to system developers, striving to provide quality products, will be to establish the procedures and means to assess whether usability criteria have been met. Invitations to tender are beginning to include such criteria. Requirements are likely to include statements regarding usability that cannot easily be ignored. No longer will users be content with stating that a database query should take less than x seconds to complete; they will extend this to include a time for the query to be composed. After all, what is the point of a sub-second system response time when it takes a trained user thirty seconds to generate the query and then it is inaccurate on 20 per cent of

occasions? Usability criteria will create concerns for developers who are not prepar
for dealing with usability issues.

I.2.6 **What are usability criteria?**

Usability criteria or usability metrics are quantifiable measures of an interactive
system. They are dependent on a user interacting with that system. That is, they
cannot be obtained from observation of the system developer's interaction with the
system or by having the system simulate interaction. In essence, the end-user cannot
be eliminated from the system during usability assessment.

Within STUDIO, five categories of criteria are repeatedly referenced. These are
Productivity, Learnability, User satisfaction, Memorability and Errors, together
referred to as the **PLUME** measures.

Productivity

Maximum system response times are often stipulated, even though these may be
negligible in comparison to user request times. The reason for this appears to be some
deep-rooted belief that users will adapt in some optimal fashion that renders the user
request time optimal. While it may be the case that users do perform as efficiently as
the system will allow, there are often ways in which the system could be designed to
help the user perform more quickly.

Examples of productivity, when used as a usability measure, are how many invoices
a data entry clerk can complete and how many decisions an executive can make and
action in a fixed period of time.

Productivity is quantifiable but it does need careful qualification against tasks and
user populations. A user who has recently completed a training course is not likely to
be as quick as a user who has performed a task in earnest five hundred times. Subtle
changes in tasks can also alter time to complete. It is often worth adding the caveat of
error-free interaction. A further factor that can confound assessment of this measure
is situation specificity. For instance, in any safety critical system, *alert* situations are
likely to impact task performance.

Learnability

Learnability is a temporal measure referring to the investment in training required of
the user. To set a criterion for this requires the establishment of a level of proficiency
or throughput, for instance how long it takes a user with no prior system experience,
to be able to process forty transactions per day. Such a criterion provides procurers
with sufficient control over suppliers to limit their risk, for instance the risk of a major
overhead in terms of increased training costs or a loss of productivity during system
introduction. On occasions, minimum bounds on learnability might be set so that the
procurer can ultimately earn revenue from providing training courses. It is important
to bear in mind, particularly from a supplier's standpoint, that such criteria must be
well qualified and not open to interpretation. The two main dependencies will be the
user population and the tasks to be accomplished. For instance, different absolute

criteria might be justifiable depending on the age group of the users and whether they are expected to 'type a piece of text', or 'align a crosshair and target'. Younger users would be expected to be quicker at the latter task.

User satisfaction

Where user acceptance and staff turnover are major determinants of a system's usefulness, then the satisfaction of users should be taken into account. It is not easy to stipulate acceptable user satisfaction levels or, indeed, how they will be achieved or measured. None the less, where a procurer is particularly concerned with this issue, then efforts may need to be made to quantify this aspect of usability. A common method of assessing satisfaction is by a battery of rating scales. One such rating scale might have seven points ranging from completely satisfied (1) to complete dissatisfied (7). The timing of any assessment of satisfaction is important. Users who have spent considerable time on a difficult training course and are presently attempting to put their learning into practice might not provide a reliable source of data.

Memorability

An attribute of humans is their forgetfulness. An absence from work or simply a period during which a task has not been practised can result in a reduction in a user's ability to interact effectively. Design decisions can contribute to the memorability, and thus usability, of a system. Office systems such as electronic mail and timekeeping applications that are used infrequently are examples of applications for which memorability is a desirable quality. Under controlled conditions memorability can be quantified. For instance, it could be stated that 'a user who has sent ten mail messages over a two-week period and is then on leave for one month should, on returning, be able to send a new message successfully within one minute and without recourse to any system documentation'.

Errors

Where the costs of inaccurate operation are high, then error rate will be of importance to procurers. While errors can appear innocuous at the time of commission, they may prove expensive in due course. In the financial business sector an error that introduces an extra '0' in a data field can be very expensive. Again, error rates must be stipulated in the context of users and tasks. Less experienced users can expect to make more errors and some tasks are more error prone than others.

A few other categories of usability criteria might be important on occasions.

Accessibility. This refers to the percentage of a potential user base that can make use of a system. For instance an automatic teller machine that can be used by 70 per cent of current account holders is more accessible, and more usable, than one that can only be used by 50 per cent of the current account holders. The reasons for accessibility not being 100 per cent can be numerous, including techno-fear and physical inaccessibility.

Accuracy. In some application domains it makes more sense to measure accuracy rather than error rates. Accuracy is easily thought of as the converse of error rate but this is not always useful. For instance, in a combat situation real interest is not in how many errors (wasted missiles) are made but, more specifically, on how many targets are 'downed'. One system might encourage the user to employ a scatter strategy while another might encourage a 'whites of the eyes' strategy. Error rate is likely to be higher with the first strategy but it may still be the better and more accurate system if more targets are hit. Similarly, with information retrieval it may be appropriate to quantify usability in terms of the number of accurate retrievals per unit time rather than the number of mis-retrievals.

Transferability/interference. In a business setting advantage may be gained from the expendient transfer of skills from one job to another. Interaction with one system may affect the usability of another system indirectly. Incongruent systems may affect usability adversely.

Various usability criteria have been described above. Different projects will place different emphasis on different usability categories depending on the objectives and context of the system in question. For instance, financial institutions might place great emphasis on the accuracy of deal capture systems, while speed of task performance might be paramount for dealer support systems. The following quotation demonstrates how important one business at least considers usability to be to the success of its systems:

> *A system which has a high degree of reasonable usability is a system that is 'normal to use'. A 'normal to use' system incorporates language and procedures that are familiar to specific users performing specific tasks under specific conditions. It blends in so well with the user, the user's tasks, and the user's work environment, that it almost 'fades into the background'. The user can concentrate on the task at hand instead of having to concentrate on the tool being used to perform the task.*
>
> *When they work with highly usable systems, people make fewer errors, fewer incomplete, inappropriate, or inefficient actions. They work better and faster. At the same time, they will be less likely to tax the training and support resources of the area that developed the system they used. But most important, highly usable systems have better user acceptance. If people are comfortable with a tool, if they are confident that it can help them do their job better, then they will be willing to use it more extensively and more creatively. Given two products of equivalent functionality, people will prefer a product that has greater usability. In fact, people may even prefer a product with slightly less functionality if it has significantly greater usability.*
> Aetna Life Insurance Co., The Aetna Casualty and Surety Co., 1986.

I.2.7 **Summary**

This section has introduced STUDIO the method. It has then discussed many of the issues faced by user interface designers. These discussions included explanation of the attributes of a user-centred design method, a definition of the term 'user interface', the limitations of look and feel guidelines and what is meant by usability. Hopefully, these discussions have helped the reader to appreciate the issues of concern to user interface designers.

I.3 User interface development and the software life cycle

Code to support the user interface of systems usually accounts for a major percentage of the whole system code. Smith and Mosier (1984) estimated that 30–35 per cent of code was for user interfaces. More recently, a figure in the region of 47–60 per cent has been offered by MacIntyre *et al*. (1990).

In 1989, Rosenberg estimated that 29 per cent of all software development expenditure was spent on graphical user interface development projects. As the complexity of user interface components increases and users become even more demanding, it can be expected that this figure will rise further.

Analyses have shown that upwards of 60 per cent of the total cost of a software system is incurred during the maintenance phase of the software life cycle. In addition, it has been estimated (Leintz and Swanson 1981) that 60 per cent of maintenance costs are for changes to the user interface.

Taken together, these figures suggest that improvements in user interface design practices could bring major productivity gains to the IT industry. The application of STUDIO offers a means of realising these productivity gains.

The attitude that user interfaces do not need to be designed but can simply be created towards the completion of a project is naïve. Unfortunately, this attitude has prevailed for many years and has contributed to the software industry's reputation for delivering unusable systems.

The success of any method depends on having procedures for checking correctness and completeness. For software, such procedures are often referred to as validation and verification (V&V) procedures. Verification refers to whether the deliverables at any stage of a project conform to their specification as produced at previous stages. Validation refers to the assessment of whether a deliverable meets the top-level system requirements. Software engineering practices can have many checkpoints at which V&V take place. When such plans are adopted it is rare for any of the V&V procedures to take account of usability issues. They are almost exclusively directed at functional considerations, even though a major percentage of a system's code can be for the purposes of user interfacing.

A typical life cycle is shown in Figure I.4. Traditional practices of systems analysis and specification may be performed with little or no regard for user interfacing issues.

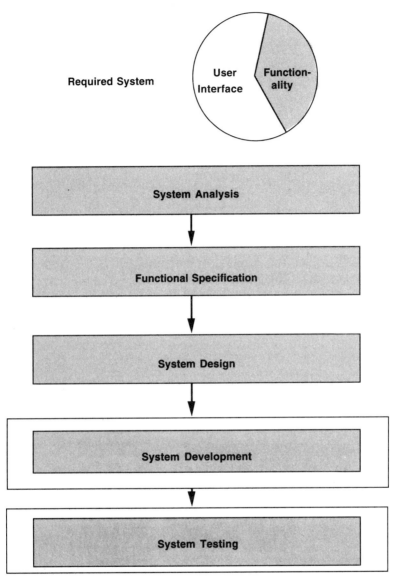

Figure I.4 *Traditional system development life cycle.*

Only when the system is nearing completion will effort be expended on developing a user interface. Paradoxically, it is far easier to build a user interface at this stage. Why? Because in meeting the functional requirements decisions will have been made (regardless of users or usability) that limit the degrees of freedom for user interface design. The result? A fully functional system that meets all contractual obligations but is of poor quality in terms of usability. Side effects? The client is penalised in terms of an unnecessarily large training overhead, the productivity of end-users is poorer than is desirable, the life expectancy of the system is foreshortened, etc:

> *Usability and functionality are of equal power and importance; both must be achieved.*
> Shackel 1986.

Why are user interface considerations so readily ignored? The reasons are straight-forward. The procedures have never been established for the V&V of non-functional requirements. This is changing. Clients are beginning to stipulate usability requirements. Once this becomes common practice, then changes to the system development life cycle will take place. It may not be the case that the stages change, but simply that the practices at any one stage will be more appropriate. Figure I.5 conveys the fact that these extra practices do not necessarily add to the stages; they are simply directed at those stages of development to which they are most appropriate. The development life cycle depicted in Figure I.5 suggests that many systems can be divided roughly 60 : 40 per cent between user interface and functionality. With such a life cycle, V&V for non-functional or usability requirements can now be performed. For instance, usability requirements can be set and used as a basis for making technical decisions that were previously based on purely functional grounds. Similarly, the results of the task synthesis can be verified to check that the design addresses the usability requirements and non-functional requirements.

These additions to the development life cycle can be appreciated with reference to developments in system architectures. There is a move towards providing user interfaces on PCs that are networked to database applications resident on hardware acting as a server. The software resident on the server(s) of such an architecture is primarily functional and its development is well addressed by existing structured system development methods. Software resident on the PCs is primarily, although not exclusively, supporting user interfacing requirements. Thus the practices for user interface design are particularly appropriate to the development of the PC resident software:

> *. . . client/server computing. In this computing model, the processing of an application is split between the front-end portion on a PC or workstation, which handles local data manipulation and maintains a user interface, and a back-end portion on a server, which handles database and other number-intensive processing.*
> *Datamation*, July 15, 1990, p. 54

The system development life cycle could be presented as a parallel cycle as shown in Figure I.6, best practices being adopted for the client and server portions of the architecture with the software interface between the two components being estab-lished early in the life cycle and its veracity being checked as the life cycle progresses.

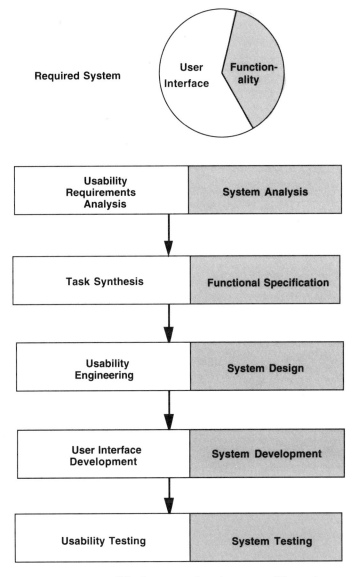

Figure I.5 *Modified system development life cycle.*

The upper portion of Figure I.6 provides a conceptual view of a client–server architecture. The clients, either personal computers or workstations provide user interfaces while the servers often mini-computers or mainframes act as data repositories and computational engines. Under the client side of this architecture is depicted the typical stages of a structured method. Such methods are often ideal for the analysis and design of the server aspect of modern systems. Under the client side is depicted

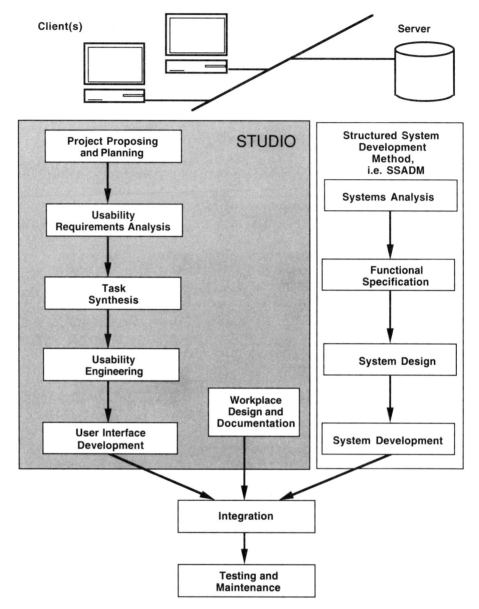

Figure I.6 *Alternative system development life cycle.*

the stages of STUDIO, which provides a suitable method for the design of the user interface that is resident on the client hardware. On the basis of the stages and deliverables required by parallel analysis and design, points of contact and interaction between the two methods can be established. By so doing, the smooth integration of the deliverables from the two methods can be assured. Together, STUDIO and a structured method can support the design of complete client–server solutions.

1.4 **Case study**

STUDIO is suitable as the sole method for projects developing only a user interface. Such projects are becoming more commonplace as businesses wish to assess for themselves the merits of employing graphical user interface technology or wish to provide a new user interface to existing applications. Such projects are often conducted by prototyping the user interface. The case study which follows is an example of such a project.

The project was undertaken on behalf of the Home Office in 1989–90. It was entirely a user interface design exercise employing state-of-the-art technology and a user-centred approach to design. This case study is reprinted with minor changes from Browne *et al.* (1991), with gratitude to the Home Office.

Case Study

Helping police with their enquiries

Overview

The Home Office Large Major Enquiry System (HOLMES) was developed to assist the police service in the United Kingdom (UK) to administer the investigation of major crimes. All fifty-two UK police forces use HOLMES. This represents a significant national investment in terms of hardware, software and manpower training.

Whilst users are generally satisfied with the facilities that the HOLMES system provides, there are known to be a number of problems with its use. The most common complaint is that HOLMES is manpower intensive. The input of information requires considerable effort by trained personnel, and there is often insufficient time remaining for thorough research of the database and related documents. HOLMES training requires attendance at an intensive four-week-long course and refresher courses at intervals thereafter. These courses cover all HOLMES procedures including the use of the HOLMES database. There can also be long queues of documents waiting to be indexed (indexing is the translation of textual information contained in statements, messages and other documents into a structured HOLMES database). As a result there can be pressure on indexers to work ever faster, in turn causing a reduction in the quality of the stored information.

History

The combination of issues about the existing HOLMES system and the development of new computer technology prompted the Home Office's Scientific Research and Development Branch to carry out a feasibility study (Boyle and Mylam 1989), the aim of which was to determine whether some of the practical difficulties faced by indexers could be mitigated by the application of new technology.

The study identified that indexing is a bottleneck in all incident rooms. During the feasibility study it was realised that by placing the emphasis on providing an enhanced user interface rather than concentrating on functionality *per se*, significant benefits in the amount of time spent on indexing might be achieved. To this end a Demonstrator system was developed.

This Demonstrator enabled the testing of various techniques such as the on-screen annotation of documents and the evaluation of different displays and graphics.

Scope of the Demonstrator

The Demonstrator supports three roles within HOLMES incident rooms: statement reading, indexing and researching. Statement readers are usually senior officers who review documentation entering an incident room and indicate any of the information that should be entered on to the HOLMES database. It is the responsibility of indexers to update the database. Research can be a dedicated role for the purpose of identifying lines of enquiry from information available. The flow of information in an incident room and the roles associated with activities is shown in Figure I.7.

Underpinning the Demonstrator's facilities is a simulation of sufficient functionality of the HOLMES system to allow meaningful evaluation by users. The Demonstrator supports the basic HOLMES database structure and allows cross-referencing of information between all indexes and documents.

The HOLMES database is structured into a number of indexes. The nominal index, stores details pertaining to people; the vehicle, telephone and address indexes are as one would expect. The category index holds information of particular relevance to the enquiry which is not covered by the other indexes, e.g. details of weapons and property. The sequence of events index contains time-

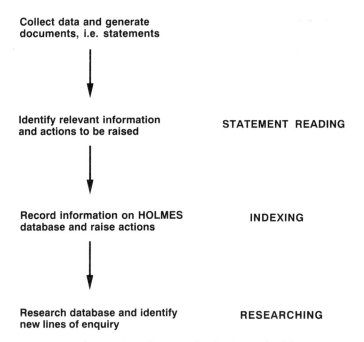

Figure I.7 *Information flow and roles in an incident room.*

dependent lists of events relating to certain aspects of the crime, such as the movements of the victim prior to the incident.

The statement reader module allows documents, previously typed on to the system to be *marked up electronically*, using a mouse and keyboard. Statement readers indicate the information to be entered on to the HOLMES database. Statement readers may further annotate documents by typing notes in the margin as to how the information should be represented on the database. The statement reader will also indicate where actions are to be raised to further the enquiry, e.g. for an officer to trace and interview a person mentioned in a statement.

Each document ready for indexing retains the annotations supplied by the statement reader and, consequently, information is already in the system which allows it to provide short cuts and to prompt indexers as to the next task to be completed.

The Demonstrator provides explicit feedback as to the state of indexing of any particular document. An example of a screen depicting a *state of indexing graphic* is shown in Figure I.8. It is common for documents to contain significant amounts of complex information, for instance descriptions of a group of people, their relationships to one another and links with addresses and phone numbers. With the current HOLMES system it is easy to lose track of the records and links which have been created. An oversight of this nature could seriously degrade the quality of the information available to the enquiry.

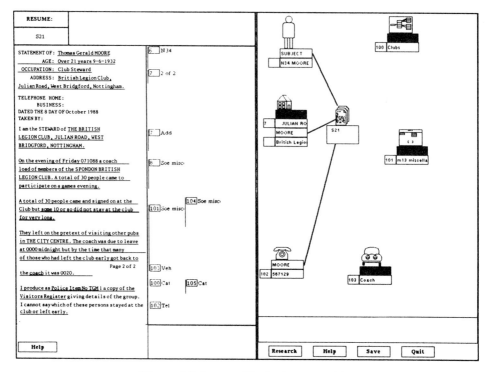

Figure I.8 *State of indexing graphic.*

The principal objective of indexing is to update the enquiry database quickly and accurately with new relevant information whilst ensuring that none is duplicated. The Demonstrator provides an enhanced database enquiry module.

Demonstrator development

Project team

An experienced HOLMES indexer from the Metropolitan Police was seconded to the Home Office to assist in the design of the system. Specifically, he provided advice on the practicalities of indexing and usual procedures, provided liaison between the project team and HOLMES users and prepared material for use during evaluations. Members of the HOLMES Support Group of the Home Office Police Requirements Support Unit were involved as users in reviewing the design documents, gave advice and liaised with the police forces to arrange for participation in the evaluations.

Analysis phase

The design of the Demonstrator was conducted in a user-centred manner giving continuous opportunity for critique. It began with a short familiarisation phase during which the design consultants visited incident rooms accompanied by the police secondee. On each visit statement readers and indexers were interviewed using ready-prepared questions. The topics covered included 'problem areas' and 'desired improvements'. Where possible, statement readers and indexers were asked to perform their jobs while being observed.

Design phase

Proprietary user interface look and feel style guidelines promote consistency in interface design. However, the interaction requirements of this complex application could not be satisfied by any such guidelines. To promote consistency a bespoke user interface style document was produced. This document covered issues such as defining terminology, the operation of menus, the use of windows, etc.

The first pass design provided a number of user interface designs for selected tasks. It documented the way users could navigate through the dialogue. This document evolved into a fully fledged design document for the three modules of the Demonstrator. The design document contained many diagrams illustrating snapshots from the dialogue.

The project employed statecharts as the notation for specification (Harel 1988, Browne *et al.* 1990). The initial design was implemented as soon as possible so that it could be reviewed and criticised by the design team. This design process was iterative with the fine detail of the design not being established until the latter stages of development.

Prototyping phase

Prototyping was performed in the object-oriented development environment, Smalltalk-80[tm].[1] In addition, code from The Analyst[tm],[2] a set of tools and application packages implemented in Smalltalk, was re-used for the production of user interface components.

Evaluation

An evaluation was performed to test the following hypotheses, with regard to indexing:

■ Indexers feel they perform better using the Demonstrator than the existing system.

1 Smalltalk-80 is a trademark of Parc Place Systems.
2 Analyst is a trademark of Xerox Special Information Systems.

- Indexers are able to perform faster using the Demonstrator than using the existing system.
- Indexers prefer using the Demonstrator to perform specific tasks.
- Indexers feel confident in using the Demonstrator after one day of training.

The Demonstrator was intended to be sufficiently robust and to support sufficient functionality to allow experimental subjects to perform realistic tasks. To promote this the system was primed with data prior to evaluation. A training database developed by Nottinghamshire Constabulary, based on a real incident involving a rape, was used. The documentation was entered on to the system and a proportion indexed to create a realistic database. This contained of the order of two hundred records.

Fifteen indexers from eight different forces participated in the indexing evaluation, eight using HOLMES and seven using the Demonstrator. Members of each group had a wide range of experience of using HOLMES operationally.

Each group was required to complete a pre-evaluation questionnaire which assessed attitudes towards indexing using the standard HOLMES system. The Demonstrator group were subsequently required to complete a post-evaluation questionnaire concerning their experience of indexing using the Demonstrator.

Having completed a period of familiarisation the subjects were asked to index six documents. During this period they were observed by Home Office staff who identified the constituent tasks and timed performance.

A check on the quality of the indexing was carried out by examining whether actions had been raised correctly and ensuring that no important information had been omitted from documentary cross-references.

Questionnaire results

Analysis of the pre-evaluation questionnaires showed mixed opinions on HOLMES. Whilst there was agreement that HOLMES search facilities are not too complicated to use, there was also a feeling that they could be improved. The post-evaluation results from the Demonstrator group suggested that the Demonstrator went some way towards improved searching.

All but one indexer found the Demonstrator easy to learn and all subjects felt confident using the Demonstrator by the end of the session.

Most of those who expressed an opinion felt that it would be possible to do a better job using the Demonstrator than using standard HOLMES.

Most subjects found the display of the marked up document preferable to the pen and paper version. The on-screen display left less room for ambiguity and ensured that annotation text was always legible. The actual functionality of annotations was not so consistently well received, two subjects feeling that it was too complex.

Access to index records was regarded as an improvement in the Demonstrator.

The sequence of events display was either loved or hated by indexers. There was general agreement that the graphical display was a significant improvement but that the associated functionality made it cumbersome to use whilst indexing.

Observation results

No statistically significant difference between the times taken to index documents on the two systems was found.

The quality of work across the two groups was found to be comparable. It is, however, important to note that the Demonstrator group had only had a single day's training on the system.

Hypotheses

In commenting on the effect of the system on the quality of their work, almost all users felt that it had the potential, in regular use, to enable them to do a better job. They were divided as to whether they felt they were working any faster. In reality there was found to be no difference in the speed of the two groups.

However, after only one day's training the Demonstrator group were indexing at the same rate as the HOLMES group. There seems to be little doubt that with more experience they would be able to do the job quicker.

The use of graphics in building the indexing list and keeping track of tasks were popular with the users. The intrinsic attractiveness of a graphical display must be borne in mind when interpreting these results. However, observers noted that the state of indexing graphic (Figure I.8) was learned quickly and subsequently used effectively by all users. Particularly important was the indexers' positive reaction to the format of the marked up document on the screen. This was fundamental to the interface's design. Their attitude was that provided they could see the document being indexed at all times, or at least cause it to be displayed easily, then they would be happy to do away with the paper version.

The indexers in the Demonstrator group all responded that they felt confident using the Demonstrator after the relatively brief period of familiarisation. This fact is particularly significant given the large-scale investment in training which has been committed by the police service in recent years.

Conclusions

Graphical user interfaces are not a panacea. They allow considerable design freedom and thus, paradoxically, provide more opportunity for poor user interface design decisions.

The evaluation of the Demonstrator system illustrates the success of approaching interface design in a user-centred manner. It is important that future work on operational and intelligence systems (including HOLMES 2) for the police service, and indeed on other highly interactive systems, builds on the lessons learned in this study.

There is no substitute for the experience of the actual users of a system. Without such involvement early in the project, inappropriate design decisions would have propagated through the development cycle and would have been expensive to rectify. It is important that users participating in the design process are provided with as much reviewable material as possible as early as possible. The experience of this study suggests that example screen layouts are a suitable format for this material.

The production of a style document was a worthwhile undertaking. The consistency it provided underpinned all subsequent design decisions and was a significant factor in ensuring usability.

The Demonstrator proved to be an excellent way of testing design ideas. The best method of testing the adequacy of design is by hands-on interaction. However complete a design document may appear to be there is always the opportunity for errors to be introduced or shortcomings to be overlooked.

The benefits of user-centred design was demonstrable. After one day's training users felt confident using a radically different design for a familiar application. Indeed, they acknowledged that the system had the potential to improve the quality of their work. Significantly, users reacted positively to doing away with paper copy and working entirely on-screen.

I.4.1 Main points

The above case study demonstrates an approach to user interface design that is truly user centred. The Home Office identified the fact that many of their operational requirements could be addressed by usability improvements as opposed to functional extensions. To this end they commissioned a prototyping exercise to demonstrate the benefits to be attained from modern user interfacing technology. These benefits were demonstrated by applying a user-centred approach, including a prototype evaluation.

The techniques of user requirements analysis, dialogue specification and iterative prototyping, as practised during the HOLMES Demonstrator project are all found within STUDIO. The production of a style guide, as found useful by the HOLMES Demonstrator project, is explained within STUDIO. User involvement is also necessary throughout STUDIO. The HOLMES Demonstrator project demonstrated the usability improvements that can be achieved through the application of a user-centred approach to design. STUDIO is a formal and documented approach to user-centred design permitting usability improvements to be achieved by all user interface design projects.

I.5 Structure of this book

The following five chapters describe the five stages of STUDIO in sequence. Chapter 1 describes Stage 1, and so on. This congruity between chapter numbers and stage numbers is the reason for this chapter being numbered I. In this way readers will always know which stage is being described simply by reference to the chapter number. Chapter 1 will show the reader how to plan and justify user interface design activities. Chapter 2 provides the techniques and framework for performing a user requirements analysis. Chapter 3 addresses the design and specification of user interfaces. Usability engineering by prototyping and impact analysis is the subject of Chapter 4. Finally, Chapter 5 briefly provides guidance on delivering and terminating user interface design projects.

Any one of the chapters can largely be read in isolation. For instance, the reader who wishes to learn how to plan and conduct a user interface evaluation should read Chapter 4: 'Usability engineering'.

Each chapter begins with a discussion to argue the case for the activities advocated by the STUDIO stage in question. Each chapter is broken down into separate sections, one for each step in the stage. Summaries of steps and stages are provided at the end of sections and chapters. For the reader who wishes to know more about a particular activity, selective reading lists are provided.

Throughout the following chapters a case study is used as a worked example. This is based on analysis and design work performed at a number of financial institutions.

A set of appendices is also provided. Lists of *deliverables and working documents* (Appendix A) from the various steps and stages of STUDIO, *a quick reference guide* (Appendix B) to the steps and stages, a set of tests that can be applied as a *usability audit* (Appendix C), a list of *standards organisations* (Appendix D), a *glossary*, and *reference list* are provided.

A number of conventions have been adopted throughout STUDIO. These include the following:

- All deliverables are identified as *dnnn* where *d* denotes 'deliverable' and *nnn* is the step that generates the deliverable.
- All working documents are identified in a similar manner as *wnnn*.

1.6 Summary

It is inevitable that a method-based approach to the development of user interfaces for interactive systems will become commonplace. The IT industry cannot continue to develop systems, where upwards of 50 per cent of the system code is for user interfacing purposes, by employing ill-suited practices; a new approach is inevitable. In addition, the buyers and users of IT will not continue to accept systems with poorly designed user interfaces. Businesses have suffered the consequences of poor IT usability and will not continue to do so. Procurers will become increasingly discerning regarding the suppliers they turn to for advice.

STUDIO is an integrated set of techniques. Some of the techniques are well known. Some are unique to STUDIO. It is hoped that readers will find something of interest and import to their work. Above all, it is hoped that this text will both raise awareness of the importance of user interface design and demonstrate that techniques are available for the development of usable systems. Moreover, they can be applied in a structured and manageable manner within the constraints of commercial system development projects.

Further reading

A Guide to Usability. The Open University in Association with the Department of Trade and Industry, 1990. ISBN 0–7492–4344–9.

Baeker, R. and Buxton, W. (eds.) (1987). *Readings in Human–Computer Interaction*, Los Altos, CA: Morgan Kaufman Publishers (a quality collection of papers).

Card, S., Moran, T. and Newell, A. (1983). *The Psychology of Human–Computer Interaction*, Hillsdale, NJ: Lawrence Erlbaum Associates (requires a grounding in psychology if it is to be fully appreciated).

Cox, K. and Walker, D. (1993). *User Interface Design*, Hemel Hempstead: Prentice Hall (an interesting cookbook of user interface activities).

Helander, M. (ed.) (1988). *Handbook of Human–Computer Interaction*, Elsevier, North-Holland (particularly comprehensive collection of papers).

Norman, D. A. (1988). *The Psychology of Everyday Things*, New York: Basic Books (a very readable fun text).

Norman, D. A. and Draper, S.W. (eds.) (1986). *User Centred Systems Design: New perspectives on human–computer interaction*, Hillsdale NJ: Lawrence Erlbaum Associates (good collection of works).

Rouse, W. B. (1991). *Design for Success: A human-centered approach to designing successful products and systems*, Wiley Interscience. (Discusses a structured approach to design. It is not specific to design of user interfaces.)

Shneiderman, B. (1987). *Designing the User Interface*, Ablex Publishing (a general overview of the subject that provides lots of good examples).

Thimbleby, H. (1990) *User Interface Design*, New York: Addison Wesley (will probably become a classic but is overindulgent for readers unfamiliar with the subject area).

1 Project proposing and planning (Stage 1)

A business case for user interface design (UID) may be used to progress ideas for new projects and project activities, or it can be generated to add value to conventional system proposals. As UID activities are still sometimes seen as ancillary or optional activities a business case is often the only way of ensuring their inclusion. Decision makers find it difficult to ignore a well-argued business case.

This, the first stage of STUDIO, addresses the proposal and planning stage of a project, the stage at which a business case needs to be made. The central component of a business case is almost always a cost–benefit analysis. The following section describes how a business case for UID activities might be produced (Mantei and Teorey 1988). Performing a cost–benefit analysis is the first step (Step 101) of the STUDIO method.

Once commitment for UID activities has been gained, the management and quality control practices to be applied to those activities need to be documented. This should form part of the quality plan for a project. The issues that should be addressed in this documentation are discussed under the heading of 'Quality planning' (Step 102).

Project proposing and planning (Stage 1), has two steps (Figure 1.1). These are *cost–benefit analysis* (Step 101) and *quality planning* (Step 102).

STAGE 1: Project Proposal and Planning

```
        101
           Cost-Benefit
           Analysis

                    │
                    ▼  Business Case

        102
           Quality
           Planning

                    │
                    ▼  Quality Plan
```

Deliverables
Business Case (D101)
Quality Plan (D102)

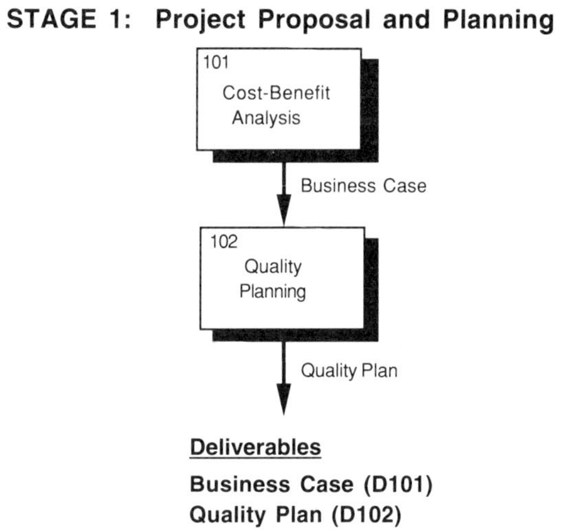

Figure 1.1 *Overview of Stage 1.*

1.1 Cost–benefit analysis (Step 101)

Cost–benefit analysis objectively quantifies the financial costs of performing activities and the tangible benefits to be obtained from those activities.

1.1.1 Benefit procedure

There are three phases to cost–benefit analysis for UID:

- Quantify the benefits to be gained from UID activities and put a value on them.
- Identify the costs of performing those UID activities.
- Analyse the relationship between the costs and quantified benefits.

Benefits

The benefits to be accrued from improved usability are manifold. Improved productivity often results from usability improvements, which in turn can generate increased revenue. Benefits may result from reduced overheads, possibly because of reduced personnel costs. In certain industries risks may be reduced as the opportunity for errors is decreased. Increased usability normally results in reduced training costs.

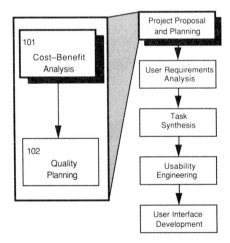

Cost–benefit analysis (Step 101).

The short-term benefits of UID include development cost reductions through the identification and resolution of problems at an early and cost efficient time. These benefits are achieved through the application of techniques advocated in Stages 2, 3 and 4 of STUDIO.

Long-term financial benefits can result. More usable systems can lead to increased sales and revenues. Where users are acting in a sales support role the quicker or more accurately they respond to customers the more likely are increased sales. Users responsible for production, whether it be data entry, decision making or whatever, will be more productive with a usable system. Usable systems are easier to learn. Therefore, usable systems are accompanied by a decrease in training and support costs. Errors resulting from user interaction can be expensive and will possibly require much time to reconcile. Usable systems result in reduced error rates and thus decrease associated costs. Surveys have shown that maintenance costs alone can account for upwards of 60 per cent of the total expenditure on a project. UID activities can reduce such maintenance costs. Usability engineering in particular can identify design inadequacies prior to implementation and can do so cost effectively. Changes cost much less when made while a system is still at the prototype stage. The principle of STUDIO is that user interface design be correct and valid prior to full-scale development.

An often forgotten benefit is user acceptance. UID can make the difference between a system falling into disuse or becoming a vital and indispensable tool.

Costs

The costs of UID activities need to be taken into account. STUDIO proposes many techniques and procedures that can be employed during a development in the pursuit of usability. While it is not suggested that any one project employ all of these techniques, each project does have associated costs which must be identified and made explicit. These costs are related to personnel overheads, materials preparation and, in some instances, capital expenditure.

Cost–benefit relationship

The financial benefit from the application of a method such as STUDIO is the difference between the cash values for a 'usability engineered deliverable' and a 'deliverable as usual'. This difference can rarely be assessed conclusively as no organisation is going to finance two parallel developments to ascertain the comparative costs and benefits. None the less, this is true of all business cases: they cannot be proven in advance but they can be justified. Sound justification for UID work must be provided for decision makers.

1.1.2 **Business case**

Business cases can be made for proposing projects or for planning and resourcing projects. An accepted business case can be used to track a project's cost–benefit status, particularly at major milestones. This permits decisions on the allocation of resources to be reviewed.

The need for cost–benefit analyses normally stems from competition for limited resources. Organisations have to decide how to allocate resources both between and within projects. Such decisions are made easier where the individual costs and projected benefits are to hand.

For IT development projects there are often calls for resources from different disciplines including software designers, programmers, quality assurers, management, and training and support services. In addition, depending on the technologies involved, particular specialisms may also be competing for resources including user interface design, database design, and communications.

For user interface designers to compete effectively, they must provide good business cases. In the preceding chapter it was shown that user interface code production and system maintenance resulting from required changes to user interfaces account for substantial proportions of a project's resources. None the less, at present it is common for only a small proportion of available resources to be allocated for purposes of UID. This is attributable to a lack of understanding on the part of decision makers of the importance of the usability of IT systems. User interface designers must provide business cases that make it difficult for the decision makers to ignore usability as an issue. Decision makers would find it difficult to ignore a coherent business case that argued that UID activities would provide a ten-fold return on investment.

Business cases can be provided at the inception of a project or, indeed, at the time that services are requested, for instance by an invitation to tender.

1.1.3 **Assessment**

Assessment begins by identifying all projected benefits due to improved usability. These may be directly related to the organisation's operation or may accrue from its dealings with customers. Benefits may be tangible in financial terms or intangible.

Intangible benefits are of secondary interest to decision makers. None the less, they should be included in a business case. For instance, while it is hard to place a value on user acceptance of a system, the consequences of rejection can be far reaching. System disuse and misuse can result. The introduction of a new IT system can mean major changes to business operations. Management of change practices can help but experience shows that a user-centred approach, as advocated by STUDIO, also facilitates acceptance.

Determining the value of tangible benefits
Many sources can contribute to the estimation of tangible benefits. These include design, development and maintenance teams. The proposer should establish their

costs, and, where appropriate, establish anticipated costs for training and other support services. Past data, possibly from previous similar projects if available, can be a rich source of financial information. Personnel costs are always a factor. These should be included not simply in terms of salaries but also in terms of overheads.

The value of the benefits should be estimated, preferably per annum.

Example benefit calculations

Usability engineering was performed on a replacement system before installation (Karat 1990, Karat 1991). The user population numbered 22 876 and interacted with the system twelve times per day on average. Usability engineering provided a saving in excess of 4.5 minutes for three main tasks. In excess of 1500 hours of effort were saved with an associated cost saving of over $40 000.

In terms of user productivity, usability engineering provided further savings. Users of the system were expected to complete 1 308 000 tasks per year. Three iterations of usability engineering provided an average saving of 9.6 minutes per task. This would result in a saving of 209 280 hours in the first year with an associated cost, taking account of personnel costs, of nearly $7 000 000.

Training budgets can be the beneficiaries of usability engineering. For a hypothetical situation, a 25 per cent reduction in a two-week training course might result from the usability engineering of a new system. For an organisation having 250 users, a staff turnover rate of 20 per cent and personnel costs of £10 per hour, a saving in the region of £10 000 could be expected. The calculations for this are shown below:

Headcount × turnover (20%)	$250 \times 0.20 = 50$ persons requiring training
Training hours × reduction (25%)	$80 \times 0.25 = 20$ saving in training hours per trainee
Personnel costs per hour	£10
Trainees × reduction in training time × cost per person	$50 \times 20 \times 10 = £10\,000$ cost benefit per year

Service costs are a further area that often obtains benefit indirectly from usability engineering. For instance, a company might make 100 service calls per year to attend to usability problems. Usability engineering might reduce these calls by 75 per cent. If each call costs £150, then a simple calculation shows that an annual saving of £11 250 could be achieved.

A reduction in user errors can also provide appreciable benefits. By way of example, consider a company employing 500 users who each complete 15 tasks per day with an error rate of 0.04. If on average there are 260 working days in the year then the total errors for the year will be approximately 78 000. If personnel costs are estimated to be £25 per hour and it takes 5 minutes to recover from each error, then the following calculations and resulting benefit can be expected:

Errors per year	78 000
Recovery time per error	5/60 hour
Personnel costs	£25 per hour
Benefits	78 000 × 5/60 × 25 = £162 500

Direct project cost reductions, particularly in the area of maintenance, may also be achieved. The following calculation for the cost saving for each change identified at the prototyping rather than the system release stage of a project might be posited:

Cost of change at prototype stage
Hours per change	3
Hourly staff costs	£50
Cost of each change	3 × 50 = £150

Cost of change after system release
Hours per change	24
Hourly staff costs	£50
Cost of each change	24 × 50 = £1 200

If usability engineering resolved ten problems at the prototype stage, which would otherwise have remained until system release, then a saving of £10 500 ((£1 200 × 10) − (£150 × 10)) would accrue.

User interface design costs
To achieve the above benefits requires an investment in activities as proposed by STUDIO. Individual projects may choose not to supply STUDIO in full, but, rather, various combinations of activities. These might include:

User Requirements Analysis
    Evidence collection
    Task analysis

Task Synthesis
    User documentation
    Design specification
    Style guide production

Usability Engineering
    Prototyping
    Impact analysis

Each of the above must be costed to provide an overall expenditure for the UID activities:

	Person months	Cost
User Requirements Analysis	2	£30 000
Task Synthesis	2	£30 000
Usability Engineering	4	£60 000

This fictitious example gives a total cost of £120 000 for the production of a usability engineered prototype with supporting specification and documentation. This has been calculated on the basis of a twenty-day working month at a daily rate of £750. Additional costs for capital expenditure, travel, etc., would need to be added to this total. Where the above activities are replacing other activities such as screen design, then these costs can be traded off. The total cost then has to be assessed against the projected benefits. If this expenditure of £120 000 had an associated projected benefit of £600 000 in the first year, then a strong business case could be made.

The ratio between the projected benefits and expenditure is known as the yield on expenditure. In this example, yield on expenditure is £600 000:£120 000, or 5:1. Where the yield on expenditure does not initially appear to be worthwhile (certainly where yield on expenditure is 1:1 or less), the proposer might seek to identify a level of investment that will have a worthwhile payback. Analysis might reveal a relationship between expenditure and financial benefit that demonstrates how a point is reached, and sometimes overreached, where there are diminishing returns on expenditure. Indeed, there is always a point at which further expenditure is not profitable. Figure 1.2 provides an example of yield against expenditure. Two lines are shown on the graph, one depicting yield per unit expenditure (in this case in multiples of £10 000) against total expenditure, the other depicting cumulative yield against expenditure. It can be seen that a good business case could be made for spending £50 000. A better business case could be made for an expenditure of £40 000. A yield of 4.75 would be achieved with an expenditure of £40 000. Spending £50 000 would give a yield of 3.95. The former provides the better return on investment.

The graph shows that a point is reached where the payback on further investment is of questionable value. In the example this threshold is crossed at the point at which an expenditure of £40 000 is made. A further investment of £10 000 would of itself only provide a further benefit of £7500. Thus there would be no business reason for spending more than £40 000. Indeed, when competing for resources if a yield of greater than 4:1 is required, then there might be a case for only investing £20 000. The purpose of this example is to show that while a cumulative yield might appear to be good, on occasions a better business case can be made for smaller investments.

1.1.4 Decision making

Organisations have various means of determining whether to make an investment. Two of these are explained below. The proposer of a business case should identify the

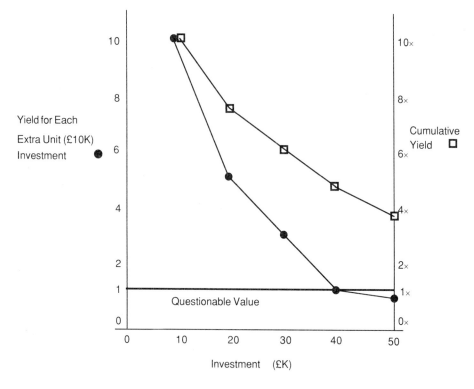

Expenditure	Return on Investment
£10 000	£100 000
£20 000	£150 000
£30 000	£180 000
£40 000	£190 000
£50 000	£197 500

Figure 1.2 *Yield (return on investment).*

recipient's preferred means of evaluating investment decisions and seek to provide a business case in that form.

Payback periods technique

This technique relies upon calculating the amount of time it will take to generate sufficient financial benefits to pay back the initial investment. Organisations may have standard payback periods such that projects providing a positive return on investment in less than this period are selected. Where projects compete for investment, those with the shorter payback periods will be preferred.

If the user interface design investment in a project is £100 000 and the projected financial benefits are £25 000, £30 000, £30 000, £25 000 and £20 000 in the first five years, respectively, then the payback period for the investment is between three and four years.

Interest-based selection technique

A more sophisticated means of calculating return on investment takes account of the changing value of money over time. The equation for calculating the present value of future cash inflows is:

$$P = F_n\left(\frac{1}{1+i}\right)^n$$

where

P = present value
F = future cash inflow in time period n
i = discount rate
PVIF = present value of interest factor is calculated using the following expression:

$\left(\frac{1}{1+i}\right)^n$ Table 1.1 provides a sample set of values for PVIF.

Table 1.1 *Present value of interest factor*

Discount rate Period (years)	12%	13%	14%	15%	16%	17%	18%
1	0.8929	0.8850	0.8772	0.8696	0.8521	0.8547	0.8475
2	0.7972	0.7831	0.7695	0.7561	0.7432	0.7305	0.7182
3	0.7118	0.6931	0.6750	0.6575	0.6407	0.6244	0.6086
4	0.6355	0.6133	0.5921	0.5718	0.5523	0.5337	0.5158
5	0.5674	0.5428	0.5194	0.4972	0.4761	0.4561	0.4371
6	0.5066	0.4803	0.4556	0.4323	0.4104	0.3898	0.3704
7	0.4523	0.4251	0.3996	0.3759	0.3538	0.3332	0.3139
8	0.4039	0.3762	0.3506	0.3269	0.3050	0.2848	0.2660
9	0.3606	0.3329	0.3075	0.2843	0.2630	0.2434	0.2255
10	0.3202	0.2946	0.2697	0.2472	0.2267	0.2080	0.1911

If a project is estimated to generate a one-off cash inflow of £40 000 in the third year and the discount rate to be applied is 16 per cent then the present value of the return on investment is given by:

$$P = 40\,000 \times 0.6407 = £25\,628$$

Projected benefits can be summed over the separate cash inflows for a period of time.

Thus, a project with a life expectancy of three years and expected cash inflows of £50 000, £100 000 and £120 000 in those years, with a discount rate of 14 per cent, has a present value for projected benefits of:

$$P = 50\,000 \times 0.8772 + 100\,000 \times 0.7695 + 120\,000 \times 0.6750 = £201\,810$$

Net present value of a project is calculated as the cost of the project subtracted from the project's cash inflows. If the cost of the project were £220 000, then, given the above calculation for the net present value, it would not be a sound business decision to fund the project.

1.1.5 Example

Throughout this book an example from a financial dealing room will be used to explain how STUDIO is applied and to provide an on-going context.

A major London bank has commissioned a project to design, develop and install a new dealing room. This room is to have 200 positions and provide access to six information vendor services including the bank's own in-house system. The bank has already made the decision that multiple display monitors shall be replaced by single 20″ screens: one per dealer. A consultancy has been given responsibility for the user interface design and provision of all user documentation. A prototyping, including a usability engineering approach to the project, is to be adopted. The contract was awarded on the basis of a good business case, an extract of which follows:

Background data

Cost of employing a dealer	£1000 per day
Cost of recruiting a new dealer	£15 000
Cost of employing backroom staff member	£80 per day
Average training time	3 days
Average number of manual reconciliations resulting from inaccurately recorded deals	200 per day
Deals completed per dealer per day	20
Cost of making a design change at acceptance testing time	£800 each
Average value of each completed deal	£100

Consideration of the bank's terms of reference clearly shows that it has a number of concerns that can be addressed by UID.

The bank's dealers make negative comparisons with the working conditions of friends in similar positions within other banks. Staff turnover, due to natural wastage, has risen from 12 per cent five years ago to 20 per cent. The industry average is 15 per cent. Inaccurately recorded deals cost a lot of money to reconcile and are bad for customer relations. Four full-time 'backroom' staff are employed just for deal reconciliation. Most importantly, the ratio of quotes (providing a price to a client over the phone) to deals completed is approximately 10:1. The bank believes this could be improved to 8:1 if dealers could give quotes more quickly.

Benefits

It is estimated that usability improvements could produce the following benefits (NB an inflation rate of 10 per cent is assumed throughout).

Productivity Conservatively, it is estimated that a 5 per cent improvement in speed of quoting would result in one extra deal being completed per dealer per day. The UID consultants have estimated that the 5 per cent improvement in speed of quoting can be achieved by changes to the presentation of the data upon which quotes are made:

Number of staff	200
Value of each deal	£100
Working days per year	200
Number of extra deals closed each day, per dealer	1

$$\text{Increased revenue in Year 1} = \quad 200 \times 100 \times 200 \times 1 = \text{£4 000 000}$$
$$\text{Year 2} = \quad \text{£4 400 000}$$
$$\text{Year 3} = \quad \text{£4 840 000}$$
$$\text{Year 4} = \quad \text{£5 324 000}$$

Learnability (reduced training costs). It is estimated that with a usable system, staff training time could be reduced from three days to two days. The usability improvements that would streamline training costs are in the area of access to financial pages on the information services. At present, dealers have to memorise multiple character shortcodes to access these pages:

Number of staff	200
Cost of staff being unavailable for work	£1000 per day
Reduction in training time from 3 to 2 days	1 day

$$\text{Saving in Year 1} = \quad 200 \times 1000 \times 1 = \text{£200 000}$$
Year 2 (from Year 2 onwards the
$$\text{savings only apply to new recruits)} = \quad (0.15 \times 200\,000) \times 1.10 = \text{£33 000}$$
$$\text{Year 3} = \quad \text{£36 300}$$
$$\text{Year 4} = \quad \text{£39 930}$$

User satisfaction (reduced staff turnover). By providing a state-of-the-art system it is estimated that staff turnover could be reduced from 20 to 15 per cent per annum. State-of-the-art in the City is 20″ screens to replace multiple 10″ screens:

Number of staff	200
Cost of recruiting	£15 000
Reduction in leavers	0.05 (5%)

Saving in Year 1 =	$200 \times 15\,000 \times 0.05 =$ £150 000
Year 2, adjusted for inflation =	£165 000
Year 3 =	£181 500
Year 4 =	£199 650

Memorability (productivity after holidays). Dealers tend to take few, but long (two weeks), holidays. On returning, their efficiency is impaired through memory lapse. It is expected that the new system will improve this situation to the extent that one extra deal will be closed per holiday. This usability benefit is predicted on the basis that dealers will have no shortcodes to remember and a consistent user interface will replace the multiple interfaces that exist at present:

Number of staff	200
Number of holidays per dealer per year	2
Value of a closed deal	£100
Number of extra deals closed per holiday	1

Extra revenue in Year 1 =	$200 \times 2 \times 100 \times 1 =$ £40 000
Year 2 =	£44 000
Year 3 =	£48 400
Year 4 =	£53 240

Errors (reduction in reconciliation effort). At present, four backroom personnel are employed to perform reconciliations (matching of records to deals). It is estimated that this staffing level could be reduced to two. This is based on the fact that dealers will now be recording deals on-line. By so doing, dealers will be forced to provide deal information in full:

Number of staff	2
Number of working days in year	200
Cost of a backroom staff member per day	£80

Saving in Year 1 =	$2 \times 200 \times 80 =$ £32 000
Year 2 =	£35 200
Year 3 =	£38 720
Year 4 =	£42 592

The five categories of benefits provided above are not an exhaustive list. For instance, the value of reduced remedial system maintenance has not been valued. None the less, the examples do provide a representative sample of the types of savings that can be achieved through UID activities. These categories are more easily remembered through the use of the acronym PLUME, used throughout STUDIO and standing for **P**roductivity, **L**earnability, **U**ser satisfaction, **M**emorability and **E**rrors.

The benefits have been calculated for four years subsequent to the installation of the system. For this particular application this is quite reasonable given that the life expectancy of a dealing room is of the order of four years.

Summing across the benefits gives the following savings by year:

Year 1	£4 620 000
Year 2	£4 677 200
Year 3	£5 144 920
Year 4	£5 659 412

Costs

The costs associated with achieving these benefits through the adoption of STUDIO as the method for UID are given below:

	UID consultant (days)	User time (days)	Prototype developer (days)
User Requirements Analysis			
Preparing the groundwork	10		
Evidence collection	30	20	
Task analysis	20		
Validation	10	20	
Reporting of findings	10		
Task Synthesis			
User support (documentation)	20		
Style guide	10		
Task synthesis	20		
Design specification	20		
Formative evaluation	20	20	
Usability Engineering			
Usability engineering planning	5		
Prepare evaluation materials	20		
Prototype build			40
Design audit	5		
Prototype evaluation	20	40	30
Impact analysis (3 iterations)	10	5	
Update specifications	10		
TOTALS	240	105	70

Estimating the daily rates at £800, £1000 and £400, respectively, for the UID consultant, users (dealers) and prototype developer, the costs of the UID activities in terms of manpower is estimated to be £192 000 + £105 000 + £28 000. In total the manpower costs are £325 000.

To this should be added capital costs and consumables. These are estimated at £30 000 for a prototyping platform and supporting development environment. Use of a room at the bank's offices for the purposes of running the prototype evaluations is estimated at £20 000 for a one-month period. Consumables, travel and incidental expenses will account for a further £25 000.

The total cost for the UID activities is thus £400 000.

Costs associated with Development (Stage 5) are not included. Development would have to take place regardless of any UID input to the project. It is likely that software development and maintenance costs will be reduced as a result of taking a user-centred approach because requirements will be better understood.

Cost–benefit analysis

The bank in question presently applies a discount rate of 15 per cent to its investments. Using this value and the PVIF table the net present value of the UID activities can be calculated thus:

$$(4\ 620\ 000 \times 0.8696) + (4\ 677\ 200 \times 0.7561) + (5\ 144\ 920 \times 0.6575)$$
$$+\ (5\ 659\ 412 \times 0.5718) = £14\ 172\ 819$$

The yield on expenditure for this work is thus 14 172 819 : 400 000, in excess of 35:1. This yield is predicted without recourse to what are arguably the most significant benefits of UID: firstly, the savings of development costs arising because the user interface design is stable and known to be usable prior to development; secondly, the reduced risk associated with implementing the system given that the approach provided by STUDIO ensures that a usable system is developed that will not immediately meet with user dissatisfaction.

1.1.6 Step summary

The above section has provided an introduction to cost–benefit analysis for UID activities. While many assumptions were made throughout the examples, this is a necessary part of any business case and should not dissuade the proposer from seeking to quantify tangible benefits. Also, it should not be forgotten that intangible benefits should also be included in the business case. For instance, it can be very difficult to place a value on a reduced likelihood of user rejection of a system, but it is of crucial importance.

Where a business case is produced, it should be referenced as D101: Business Case. The reference D101 indicates that the document is a *Deliverable (D)* produced during step 101.

1.2 Quality planning (Step 102)

Quality planning is an early activity in the performance of a quality assured project.

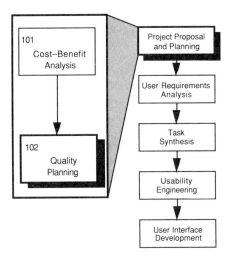

Quality planning (Step 102).

The purposes of quality planning are as follows:

- to provide documentary commitment to a set of practices and procedures that can be agreed by the client;
- to provide documentary commitment to a set of practices such that a third party or body can quality assure the work; such practices might be in accordance with ISO 9001 or BS5750 certification;
- to list standards to be adopted by the project;
- to establish baseline data to be collected during the project with the intent that this data be used for improving the quality assurance practices of subsequent projects.

Quality assurance (QA) for usability is implicit throughout STUDIO. Where STUDIO is adopted, the quality plan can be kept relatively brief by reference to STUDIO. None the less, STUDIO has a number of degrees of freedom and the quality plan needs to state the specific stages and techniques that will be applied. In addition, the quality plan should comment upon any standards to be applied, data collection (for tracking progress and future estimating), and the management and resourcing of iterative prototyping.

Discussion in the following sections is restricted to those aspects of a quality plan that are affected directly by the adoption of STUDIO.

1.2.1 Application of STUDIO

A quality plan may be kept relatively brief through reference to the documented methods to be applied. The plan might simply state that Stages 2 and 3 of SSADM are to be performed. This commits the project to many practices as demanded by those aspects of SSADM. A quality plan can refer to STUDIO in a similar fashion.

Table 1.2 lists the stages and steps of STUDIO with an example list of the techniques that might be applied. Such a table could be included in a quality plan for brevity. This would then serve as a written commitment without needing to duplicate the details of STUDIO in full in the quality plan.

1.2.2 Standards

As mentioned above, standards may be adopted, particularly for quality assurance. Where this is to be the case the choice(s) should be documented in the quality plan. With respect to user interface issues, European directives and forthcoming legislation may compel developers to adopt further standards.

After 31 December 1992, it will be a legal requirement in Europe for software to take account of the principles of software ergonomics. This is a minimum requirement set out in a technical annex to European Directive (90/270/EEC) on the minimum health and safety requirements for work with visual display terminals. Forthcoming standards should help companies to meet these requirements. For instance, sub-committee SC4 (Signals and Controls) of Technical Committee TC159 within ISO is developing an extensive multipart standard ISO 9241: 'Ergonomics requirements for office work with visual display terminals'. The planned contents of this standard are listed below:

Part 1: General introduction
Part 2: Guidance on task requirements
Part 3: Visual display requirements
Part 4: Keyboard requirements
Part 5: Workstation layout and postural requirements
Part 6: Environmental requirements
Part 7: Display requirements with reflections
Part 8: Requirements for displayed colour
Part 9: Requirements for non-keyboard input devices
Part 10: Dialogue principles
Part 11: Usability statements
Part 12: Presentation of information
Part 13: User guidance
Part 14: Menu dialogues
Part 15: Command dialogues
Part 16: Direct manipulation dialogues
Part 17: Form filling dialogues
Part 18: Question and answer dialogues
Part 19: Natural language dialogues

Table 1.2 *Stages and steps of STUDIO*

Stage Step	To be followed in full? Y(es) or N(o)	Techniques
2 User Requirements Analysis		
201 Preparing the groundwork	Y	
202 Evidence collection	Y	Interviews, observation, do-it-yourself
203 Task analysis	Y	THD, KRG, action listing, object listing, TACs, usability analysis
204 Validation	Y	Scenario generation
205 Reporting of findings	Y	URA Report
3 Task Synthesis		
301 Task synthesis	Y	PLUME analysis, allocation of function, outline designs
302 Style guide	Y	Based on CUA from IBM
303 Design specification	Y	Statecharts
304 User support	Y	BSI standard
305 Formative evaluation	Y	Keystroke analysis, INPOA
4 Usability Engineering		
401 Usability engineering planning	Y	PLUME
402 Prototype build	Y	Object-oriented
403 Design audit	Y	Standard STUDIO audit
404 Prepare evaluation materials	Y	
405 Prototype evaluation	Y	Usability laboratory set up on site
406 Impact analysis	Y	Three iterations maximum
407 Update specification	Y	

At the time of writing no part has been released as a full international standard, although drafts of some parts are nearing completion. It can be expected that during the mid-1990s most, or possibly all, parts of the standard will be released.

Many organisations are developing standards relevant to usability. For instance, the Comité Consultatif International Télégraphique et Téléphonique's (CCITT) study group is developing a method for evaluating the usability of telecommunications applications. A list of contact addresses for various standards committees is included in Appendix D.

While compliance with such standards will never guarantee protection from legal consequences, non-compliance may leave a supplier open to litigation.

The quality plan should stipulate any standards with which the design and development work will comply.

User interface design guidelines

On many projects a particular standard is adopted for the purposes of ensuring that the user interface has a consistent 'look and feel'. Commonly followed guidelines include Common User Access (CUA™) from IBM, Open Look™ from Sun and AT & T, and the Apple Desktop Interface™. It is important that any decision to adopt a set of guidelines is documented and any exceptions to following the guidelines, together with reasons, are documented in the quality plan.

1.2.3 Baseline data collection

One of the most difficult and inaccurate procedures on a software development project is resource estimation. While models do exist to help with this activity (e.g. Function Point Analysis, Symons 1991) there is little available at the time of writing that is completely satisfactory for the development of state-of-the-art systems with graphical user interfaces. Thus, most estimation is performed on the basis of the experience of a few individuals who have been party to similar developments. The only means by which suitable models can be developed is data collection, that is, by documenting previous projects rather than relying upon individuals. The question is, what data to collect? STUDIO recommends that data is collected in order that a database can be populated and made available for the purposes of developing models. These models can then be used for estimating future projects.

For the purposes of building user interfaces there are three main categories of data:

- data providing some idea of the 'size' of the interface development;
- data providing some feel for the amount of code and other deliverables produced;
- human resources required by each activity.

When considering graphical user interfaces (GUIs), the first category can be gauged by counts of user interface widgets. The GUI components are typically the number of windows (possibly broken down by type), the number of commands (as found on menus) and the number of graphical data displays. Such data are not specific but are better than none.

The second category is also rather loosely defined. Code for a GUI is increasingly object-oriented. As a result, much of it may have been re-used rather than generated. This distinction is important and should be reflected in the data reported. A system built from base language primitives might require significantly more effort than a larger system that re-uses a great deal of software.

The third category refers to human resource. It is good practice to document the actual man days expended on completing a project. For these data to be useful it should be broken down by activities. These might include user interface design, prototype build, software architecture design, prototype evaluation, analysis, etc.

Individually, these three categories of data provide very little information. Taken together, they can provide heuristics that are helpful in estimating subsequent projects. For instance, it should be feasible to develop a model of the effort required in terms of different activities to develop an interface of a given size. Simplistically, such a model might suggest that every window requires three days of programming. Such models might also be found useful for tracking on-going projects. Of course, the models can be refined as further projects are completed and data is collected.

At the planning stage of a project the developers could estimate the *size* of the interface. Using these models the resources required to accomplish the project could then be estimated for purposes of resourcing and scheduling. The quality plan must state which data are to be collected, how and when.

1.2.4 Documentation

Documentation will be a major deliverable of most projects adopting STUDIO. The quality plan should indicate its likely content.

Design document

Design documentation forms a major point of contact between client and supplier, affording a means of validating a design at an early stage of the development life cycle. Such a document should include material that is amenable to review by the client. This requires that the design be documented in as 'concrete' a manner as possible. Prototyping is the ideal medium for gauging the validity of a design, but even a prototype has to be designed.

Such a design document might include dialogue maps, an interaction lexicon, sample interaction sequences and examples of interface widgets such as icons and buttons. Dialogue map means a linked list of commands (menus) that could be used to validate the expected dialogue routes. An interaction lexicon would include all command names and descriptions of their interpretation.

The design document is likely to undergo many changes as a result of user feedback. It can become difficult to maintain, so procedures must be established for making changes. The document should be subjected to change control procedures. It is also worth recording the reasons for any changes. Eventually, this document will form the basis for the user interface specification to be delivered to programmers. At this stage it will include more abstract specifications such as might be provided in a state transition notation.

Each version of the design document should be reviewed formally and signed off before release to a client.

Forms

Example forms should be included in the quality plan. Examples might include change request and design audit forms.

Termination report

Each project should produce a termination report. This will provide baseline and experiential data that would otherwise be lost. The quality plan should allude to the likely contents of this document. By so doing, documentary commitment to the production of this valuable but expendable document can be obtained.

The termination report from a project is the point at which such data is collated and documented. None the less, the quality plan for a project is the point at which proposed data collection should be stipulated. The collection of data should also be taken into account when planning the project.

Hardware/software listing

All hardware and software purchased for a project should be listed. As these purchases are made, the list should be updated with, at least, version numbers, order numbers and supplier details.

Library

All project documentation and deliverables should be stored in a known place. This library might be held on both *hard* and electronic media. Depending on the sensitivity of the material the location may need to be a secure area. The quality plan should state explicitly where documentation will be stored. A named individual should be appointed as librarian with responsibility for maintaining and distributing documentation.

1.2.5 Management and tracking

Management and tracking issues are no different for a STUDIO project than for any other IT development. None the less, there can be diverse opinions regarding how prototyping activities are to be managed and resourced. The quality plan should stipulate some rules for controlling the resourcing of Stage 4 of STUDIO, for instance by stating how resources will be allocated to prototyping and usability engineering and by stating where control for curtailing usability engineering will reside. Making these issues clear is in the interests of both supplier and client.

The plan should state the sorts of meetings to be held during the project, their frequency, purpose and attendees. It should also stipulate how these meetings will be documented and who will receive minutes.

1.2.6 **Other issues**

Change control

Change control procedures should be established for the project and made explicit in the quality plan. Separate procedures may be required for software and documentation. For example, the procedures for software modification might dictate that all files or modules shall have a header. This header will provide a completion date, a cross-reference to a specification document and an identifier for the programme. In addition, changes should be dated, *signed* and should indicate why the modification was made, possibly with a cross-reference to a change request document or similar. On large projects, change control might usefully be supported by an on-line database that maintains, among other things, a list of cross-references.

Changes to documentation usually take two forms: changes necessitating the release of a new version of a document and changes resulting from pre-release reviews. Where new versions of documents are issued, the document should contain a document control sheet listing all the versions, person(s) responsible for the release, release date and summary of the changes between releases.

Requirements of end-users

Projects adopting STUDIO will necessitate a significant level of commitment from end-users. The quality plan should stipulate the level of this commitment as accurately as possible. Given that clients will be asked to agree to the plan, this is one means of assuring their commitment to the user-centred approach.

Reviews

A detailed project plan should be produced in addition to the quality plan. Nevertheless, it is worth listing the major review points built into the project plan in the quality plan. These may well coincide with the major deliverables and completion of the stages of STUDIO.

Property rights

The quality plan should make clear who shall hold the rights on all purchases made for the project and all deliverables resulting from the project. It should, as far as is possible, state where code or designs are going to be re-used and clarify the legality of the same.

Security procedures

The quality plan should stipulate the access and safety policies to be applied to hardware, software and documentation. For instance, the plan might demand that a copy of all software be held in a fire- and water-proof safe and that this copy is to be no more than one week out of date at any time.

Responsibilities

There should be a clear statement on responsibilities for failure of proprietary hardware and software, for instance should a serious hardware failure occur that would curtail development work for a week then who will bear the associated costs.

Duties

In addition to a person being appointed to the role of librarian to the project, other roles will also be quite clear. Where possible, specific individuals should be named against these roles. These might include the senior user interface designer, the prototyping team leader and project manager.

Staffing

It is worth noting procedures for replacing staff as they are lost to the project. This can avoid contention when a key person departs from the project.

The plan should clearly define the reporting structures to operate during the project. These may be established for both the client and the contractor. In addition, the contact points between client and contractor should be ratified.

1.2.7 Step summary

The quality plan for a project is an extremely important document. It provides an early focus point for agreement between client and contractor. It establishes the working practices for the duration of the project. Commitments made in the quality plan must be realistic, otherwise they will become a stumbling block to progress. On projects where the main method is STUDIO, the quality plan should be referenced as D102: Quality Plan.

1.3 Stage summary

This completes project proposal and planning, the first stage of STUDIO. When performed, this stage can have a major impact on the whole project. Cost–benefit analysis makes the reasons for performing UID activities obvious. Quality planning ensures that best management practices are agreed and adopted.

2 User requirements analysis (Stage 2)

Analysis is the most important and influential stage of any system development. Errors, of whatever kind, occurring at this stage propagate through subsequent stages with associated costs for rectification escalating upwards. Historically, the earliest stages of system development have paid scant attention to requirements pertinent to user interface design. Among the problems arising from this oversight are systems that exhibit poor usability. As a consequence, users have been dissatisfied, work throughput has suffered and training overheads have been higher than expected. This situation is being rectified through user-centred design techniques based on appropriate analysis techniques. User requirements analysis (URA) as introduced below provides a framework and associated techniques for conducting analysis in preparation for user interface design and development.

What is user requirements analysis?

URA is a framework of techniques and notations for the documenting of tasks, actions, requirements, usability criteria and objects. URA provides a clear understanding of user needs upon which user interface design decisions can be based.

URA is not interested in data processing *per se*. The main concern is determining what users require in order that their roles be adequately supported. This will be influenced by the present system, user capabilities, their job profiles, interaction with other parties, etc.

What does user requirements analysis entail?

URA is the first stage of a user interface development, during which the present system, especially the user population and its tasks, are analysed and the requirements for the new system is established. A user interface includes everything that may impact user effectiveness. Thus, documentation, training and the workplace are all user interface considerations.

At the core of URA is an abstraction technique known as task analysis. While this technique comes in many flavours the central concept is always that of *task*:

> A task is defined as a work element with specifiable start and end points that has meaning for the job incumbent(s) and is also goal-directed.

Examples of tasks include the following:

- identifying a particular invoice;
- making a decision to label a document;
- identifying targets on a radar screen;
- deleting a character.

Tasks can be long- or short-term in duration. Their effects can be significant or non-existent. For instance, *decisions* can be made very quickly but may have no discernible effect, while *printing a document* can use a significant amount of resources and have many effects and side-effects.

It is usually necessary to describe tasks as a hierarchy of superordinate and subordinate tasks. The lowest level of the hierarchy is sometimes thought of as a plan for performing the highest-level task. For example, the task of discarding a document might be described by a set of sub-tasks that include choosing a document, checking its identification, and actioning its removal.

Task analysis is applied to those business functions to be supported, or indeed affected, by the new system. Thus the scope for URA will be the intended user population and those who will be affected by the introduction of the new system.

Where functions of the new system do not have an existing counterpart, then it will be the analyst's responsibility to generate task descriptions. These descriptions can be tested later in the context of the entire system during task synthesis (Stage 3) and usability engineering (Stage 4). It is rarely the case that the analyst cannot refer to a system of similar function. A novel multilingual voice messaging system, for instance, could benefit from analysis of voice messaging systems and multilingual information systems.

URA will typically provide a list of tasks in a format that indicates their sequence, dependencies and relative frequencies. It will depict those tasks which could be allocated to the computer and those which could be allocated to the user. A full analysis will include documentation on contextual factors and exceptional circumstances that might arise, and their likely impact, for instance poor decision making at times of crisis and miskeying when operators have dirty, greasy hands. Finally, URA provides a documented account of the objects and actions involved in accomplishing tasks.

Is user requirements analysis another name for systems analysis?

URA is often mistakenly considered as a variant or sub-set of systems analysis, probably because of the superficial similarities. For instance, URA may well begin with interviews, observational exercises and questionnaire production. The source of information for the analyses may also be similar in that the users of any existing system will certainly be canvassed and relevant documentation reviewed.

The major differences between the two sorts of analyses are the objectives of the analyses, the constructs identified and the deliverables from the analyses.

An objective of URA is to establish the bases for enhancing the technical support to enable people to meet targets in the performance of their jobs. It is unusual for systems analysis to concern itself with usability targets.

Systems analysis is generally functionally oriented and data driven. For instance, in SSADM a central concept is that of *entity*, which is defined as '. . . something of significance to the system about which information is to be held and which is capable of being uniquely identified' (Ashworth and Goodland 1990, p. 83). Such a perspective would preclude the identification of a waste bin as an entity because during analysis it would be a major achievement of foresight to attribute significance to a waste bin or to conceive that each instance might involve associated information. Thus, systems analysis would not identify waste bin as an entity and it would be precluded from becoming a user interface artefact as in the manner exemplified by the Apple Desktop Interface. In contrast, URA would identify 'disposal of material into a waste bin' as a task and 'retrieval from a waste bin' as a second task, thus identifying 'waste bin' as a potential metaphor for a user interface element. In a financial control environment the task *process claim* might have import for both a URA and systems analysis, while *assigning a unique number* to a claim may only be of interest for systems analysis. Conversely, a URA might identify that a need exists for *fast paths in interaction* for experienced users.

In addition, function or data driven approaches to analysis fail to capture and model the features of a system in a manner that has meaning to users. One result of this is that users often find it unpalatable, if not impossible, to review and validate the deliverables of a systems analysis satisfactorily. Data flow diagrams and logical data models are often met with resistance by users (Browne *et al.* 1992). As a consequence the progress of a project can be severely impaired or, worse still, users may forgo the opportunity of ensuring that the analysis is correct. The deliverables from a URA are designed to be reviewed by users. It is part of the ethos of user-centred design that users are able to criticise all deliverables.

The task-based descriptions provided by a URA can also be used profitably for organising and indexing documentation. All too often, documentation is organised by system functions as identified by a systems analysis. The documentation thus provided can be difficult for users to search, particularly when they are trying to obtain information in support of a job at hand.

Criticisms of URA

An often cited approach to user interface design is prototyping. While this is a laudable approach and an advance over purely functional approaches to system development, prototyping alone is not a solution. Within STUDIO, prototyping plays an important role but it is acknowledged that the prototypes themselves should be designed on the basis of a URA.

A criticism often levelled at URA is that 'People do not know what they require', the implication being that lobbying the views of users is pointless. There is a degree of truth in this statement but it is of no consequence to URA and only demonstrates a lack of understanding on the part of the protagonist. People perform jobs by conducting tasks in pursuit of goals. People know the jobs they perform. The tasks that constitute these jobs are the subject matter of URA. People can explain where they are satisfied with the technical support provided and where they feel improvements can be made. Thus people, including employers and IT procurers, are in a position to set targets for task performance.

Principles of user requirements analysis

The following principles underlie URA:

- It can only be performed with users or legitimate user representatives.
- The analysis must model the user's tasks that are to be supported by the system.
- It must adhere to any applicable standards and practices documented in the quality plan.
- It must include the establishment of targets referred to as usability criteria.

Scope of user requirements analysis

The scope of URA is most often determined from the terms of reference for a project or, where available, an initial requirements list as might be provided by the client. From these sources the job functions that require analysis can be identified. This is performed during the first step of URA.

On projects using STUDIO in tandem with a data or function driven method such as SSADM, URA should be performed in parallel with systems analysis. For instance, such parallel analyses are required for client/server developments where a data driven approach is required for the analysis and design of a database running on a server. Such an analysis would be completely inadequate with respect to the software providing the user interface. A URA would be required for the latter. The problems and requirements lists generated by these two analyses can be compared subsequently. While it is to be expected that the lists will have many overlaps, it is also to be expected that some requirements will appear on only one list. Comparison must be performed to ensure that the requirements are complete and compatible.

What skills are required for user requirements analysis?

Good analysts demonstrate abilities in the following:

- interpersonal communication;
- maintaining focus;
- listening;
- objectivity;
- adherence to detail;
- acceptance of own limitations;
- achieving rapport;
- knowing when to stop.

Because the analysis is dependent on close user liaison, interpersonal skills are paramount. Good interpersonal skills are essential in order to avoid and surmount the obstacles that can beset analysis. For instance, distrust on the part of users is common especially when the perception exists that the analyst might be in a position to affect job security adversely. Where possible, analysts should attempt to reassure users that their role is that of elicitator providing a medium for users to influence their own futures. In one sense, the analyst's role is to present the needs of the users to the development team.

Good analysts are able to focus themselves and users on the matter at hand; it is all too easy to be distracted.

Analysts must be good listeners. Listening goes beyond knowing when not to speak. Good listeners hear more than is said. Only 40 per cent of person-to-person communication is attributable to the spoken word *per se*. Body language, intonation and common understandings all contribute to communication. Listening is the reception, understanding and use of all of this information for the purposes of further communication.

Good analysis requires that the analyst be as objective as possible. While total objectivity is impossible, given that the sources of information are subjective to begin with, the analyst should not bias the analysis with his or her own pre-conceived beliefs. For instance, the analysis should be unaffected by notions of the target delivery environment.

Analysts should be wary of glossing over detail. What may often appear to be irrelevant can gain significance in the light of further information. Therefore, analysts should pay attention to detail.

All too often, analysts are unwilling to admit their own lack of knowledge. Rather than ask for an introduction to some topic or issue, analysts may prefer to hide their ignorance in the hope that things will become clear later. It is far more effective in the long term to admit one's limitations and seek guidance. Only by so doing can more elaborate analysis take place.

Gaining rapport is probably the greatest skill of any analyst. This is a skill that is very difficult to learn except through practice. None the less, rapport is easier to achieve if the analyst uses the same vocabulary as the user. This at least shows that the analyst is willing to comprehend and converse on an equal level.

Knowing when to stop is another skill of a good analyst which usually comes through experience.

With regard to staffing there is an argument for allocating different individuals to the roles of URA and systems analysis. Because the results of systems analysis may suggest compromises in the user interface design for reasons of computational efficiency or ease of development, it is wise to have different individuals perform the URA in order that they can argue the case for user interface design decisions.

Steps in user requirements analysis
The thrust of URA is to produce a definitive account of task requirements in conjunction with users. This is achieved in STUDIO in five steps: preparation, evidence collection, analysis, validation and reporting of results.

Preparing the groundwork (Step 201)
As with any analysis exercise, the analyst's job begins with preparation. Good preparation will streamline the collection of evidence, facilitate the completeness of

the analysis and ease subsequent analysis. During this step the analyst will scope the analysis in terms of roles to be considered and business functions to be analysed. The analyst will also produce a timetable and plan of activities to be agreed by all parties.

Evidence collection (Step 202)

Within STUDIO, evidence collection is performed using a mix of techniques chosen as appropriate to local circumstance. Typically, the techniques will include at least an amount of interviewing and observation. These analyses will provide sufficient understanding of the problem domain, in terms of user requirements, to permit the validation, documentation and reporting of those requirements to be performed:

> The term 'evidence collection' as opposed to data collection has been adopted in STUDIO. Evidence includes data, confirmations, signs, symptoms and indications. Evidence is a more accurate term than data with respect to the objectives of URA. The use of this term also helps to re-affirm the differences between URA and systems analysis.

Task analysis (Step 203)

Sense must be made of the raw evidence that is collected. This process is referred to as task analysis. The purpose of this step is to document the evidence in a form(s) that is communicable to a third party and can be synthesised into a design.

Validation (Step 204)

During evidence collection and task analysis many anomalies, omissions and points of concern will emerge. Validation is a necessary step towards ensuring that the deliverables from task analysis are as complete and accurate as resources permit. A number of techniques to aid validation are advocated in STUDIO.

Reporting of findings (Step 205)

The results of the task analysis must be packaged in a form that can be reviewed, possibly by a number of parties. The report will be a major deliverable to be used for design at the next stage of the development.

These steps (Figure 2.1) are not performed in a purely serial manner. It is recommended that validation and analysis of findings are performed in conjunction with evidence collection.

The five steps in user requirements analysis are described in detail in subsequent sections.

STAGE 2:   User Requirements Analysis

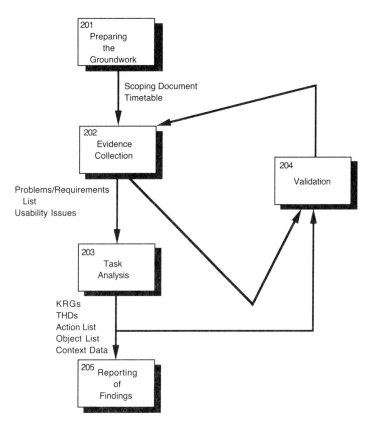

Figure 2.1 *Overview of Stage 2.*

2.1 **Preparing the groundwork (Step 201)**

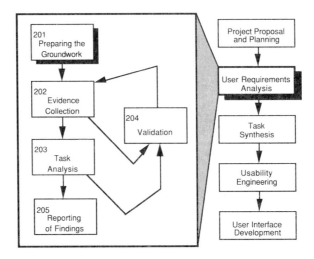

Preparing the groundwork (Step 201).

2.1.1 **Why and what?**

The first principle of any analysis is to understand why you are doing it and what you are aiming to provide. The objective of URA is to collate and document the evidence from which a user interface design can be produced. *Preparing the groundwork* ensures that the analyst understands the scope of the project and that clients understand what will be expected of them in terms of time and resources.

2.1.2 **Planning–gaining an overview**

A lot of effort can be saved by good planning and gaining first-hand exposure to the context of the analysis. This can be achieved in many ways depending on local circumstances.

The user requirements analyst should begin by reading the invitation to tender, and/or terms of reference, and reading or reminding himself or herself of the proposal of work or engagement letter.

The analyst should seek to obtain and read all hard copy material pertaining to the analysis. Such materials may include: organisation charts (including unions), a site plan, user complaints reports, training manuals, lists of names against roles, and client/company procedures.

Material relating to company procedures can be particularly enlightening. It is not uncommon for analysts to be misled due to lack of understanding of why certain practices exist. For instance, users of a large police database have to perform extensive database searches before adding new records to the database. These searches are extremely time-consuming yet rarely provide a reason for not creating the new record. The reasons for this apparent time wastage only become clear when the strict procedures in operation are understood.

The analyst should also obtain, however and from wherever possible: an overview of the pattern of working; answers to questions arising from the invitation to tender, or proposal; staff roles, possibly with staffing numbers and turnover; a contact name for any working groups, i.e. for system problems; and clarification of usability problems such as training overheads, quality of work throughput and user dissatisfaction.

It is a good idea for the analyst to take a guided tour of the workplace, particularly if conducted by the prime client contact. In this way an initial overview can be obtained quickly.

A guided tour should identify physical locations where particular functions are situated. Hopefully, individuals will be identified and a few introductions may take place which will provide access to individuals for your analysis. Your guide may help by explaining to others why you are in attendance. The most useful tours often follow the sequence of the site's main process, for instance, by beginning at purchasing, then goods inwards, through production and finally arriving at dispatch.

A guided tour is recommended as it helps to put everything into perspective. It allows the analyst to create a mental map of what functions are performed and of where and how information or stock flows about a site. If the tour is offered by the prime client contact, then you may in passing gain some insights into his or her motivations. Comments such as 'this is where the real problems are' or 'this area could be dispensed with' can provide useful information.

Following the above familiarisation exercises the analyst should produce the following:

- A scoping document (D201) outlining the roles to be analysed, client's areas of concern and scope of the study.

In addition the analyst should:

- establish the document library and assign librarian responsibilities as outlined in the quality plan.

2.1.3 Arranging access to users

URA can only be conducted with end-users, that is, with those people who perform the jobs that are to be supported by the new system. It is not sufficient to perform task analyses with the system procurers. However, it is not unusual for procurers or client project managers to offer themselves as representatives for analysis purposes. While they are important sources of evidence, they are insufficient by themselves. These persons are unlikely to really understand how the jobs in question are performed, even if they think they do.

*. . . cost estimates were produced in order to validate the design, and to
estimate selling price, profit levels, and so on . . . this information was obtained
from the finance department, as a supplier to research and development.*

*When the research and development group presented the results of their
syndicate, however, not only did this service not appear on the short list, it was
not on the full brainstormed list either. Whilst this information was being
presented, it was noted that one of the members of the finance group was
looking decidedly unwell. At the end of the presentation, he asked why this
feature was not included. He then described the form used to provide the
information in more detail. Suddenly one of the research and development
group said, 'I know what you mean – that form, we don't use it'. 'Why not?'
inquired the man from finance. 'Because we don't understand it', came the
reply. 'How then do you validate designs?' came back the question. 'We use
estimates' was the response. The man from finance then exclaimed, 'I have
worked in this company for over 27 years, this is the first time I have ever sat in
the same room as anyone from R & D before, and I had no idea this was a
problem for them'. Guess what his job had been for those 27 years, and it will be
understood why he had appeared so unwell during the session!'*
Hutchins, 1990, p. 21.

Gaining access to real users can be difficult. To inform senior client contacts that their
knowledge will not suffice and that junior employees can provide what you require
can be tricky. No one wants to be told that their juniors have more to offer than they
do. None the less, the analyst must remember that the goal of the URA is to
understand the jobs to be supported, and as such the analysis can only be conducted
with the intended recipients of the system and not with the buyers. Many tactics may
be used to avoid conflict on this issue. The procurer may be pacified by the argument
that the users will be more accepting of the final design if canvassed from the start.
Alternatively, the analyst can appeal to the client contact's seniority, suggesting that
his or her time is too valuable for such an exercise. It is one of the skills of the analyst
to ensure that the URA is conducted with the most representative set of users. These
users may span a number of distinct roles. Each of the roles affected by, or affecting,
the new system must be analysed.

Having determined the roles to be analysed it is important to choose the users
carefully. Time for analysis is always limited so it must be planned carefully to ensure
that a sufficient cross-section of roles and user experience is addressed. It is normal to
analyse tasks as performed by both the more experienced and less experienced users in
particular roles. In this way, usability problems and how they are dealt with can be
analysed.

It is also possible that time constraints only permit a sub-set of tasks to be analysed.
Given this situation the analyst should plan to analyse what might be termed the
do-wells. Do-wells are the tasks that are of most importance to the business as a whole.
Thus, some administrative or non-problematic tasks may be skimmed over in the
analysis.

The availability of some user groups may also make analysis difficult. *High powered* roles, those that make emergency or continuous calls on persons' time, as might be found in medicine or criminal application domains, cause particular problems. It may be very difficult to reserve time with such users with any confidence that appointments will be upheld. Under such circumstances analysts will need to be flexible, and possibly inventive, in order to gain the attention and time of users.

A further difficulty may concern anonymity or the sensitivity of processes or resources within the domain of analysis. For instance, secret processes within the pharmaceutical industry or patient anonymity in the medical domain may necessitate establishing legal agreements.

A further hurdle to successful analysis is often distrust of your motivations. The user requirements analyst may well be perceived as a sort of work-study engineer; and to some extent this is an accurate description. Users must be assuaged of your motivations. You wish to improve their working environment. Words such as *streamlining* and *efficiency* should be avoided. Ideally, the analyst should create an atmosphere of team work where the users are perceived as the *rulers of their own destiny* and where it is in their interests to be co-operative. Credibility can be gained if you can cite user complaints, high staff turnover, training overheads, etc. as reasons for your presence. The main worries of users are job security and de-skilling.

The analyst should generate the following:

■ a timetable (W201) for interviews/observations, or other evidence collection methods; users involved in these exercises should be informed and their agreement obtained.

2.1.4 Step summary

This step should render the analyst familiar with the background to the project and establish the scope of the analysis. A timetable of events in which the client and end-users are involved should also be documented during this step.

2.2 Evidence collection (Step 202)

This section describes a number of evidence collection techniques and the sort of findings that should be made. While certain techniques are recommended, the analyst will have to use his or her judgement in choosing between the alternatives. These judgements will need to be based on what the analyst believes is practical and will work most effectively in the prevailing circumstances.

The analyst should have gained an overview by reading background material, following a guided tour, and familiarising himself or herself with the invitation to tender and terms of reference, the primary purpose of these undertakings being to gain sufficient understanding to permit work to progress in an informed manner. Once a sufficient level of awareness has been gained the analyst should seek to elicit

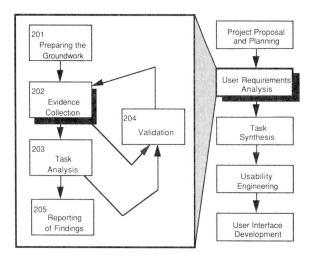

Evidence collection (Step 202).

more in-depth evidence through interviews, observation, questionnaires or other techniques.

The user-centred approach advocated in STUDIO can be highly influential with respect to the management of change. For purposes of acceptance it is desirable to achieve both of the following:

- commitment to the work, from all levels in the organisation;
- sense of ownership and responsibility for the design.

Many techniques exist for alleviating *resistance to change*, but none may be more powerful or straightforward than user involvement. If everyone feels that they are making contributions that are being heeded, then resistance is likely to disappear.

It is the responsibility of the analyst to ensure that users feel committed to the engagement. During evidence collection the analyst can reinforce this spirit of cooperation in pursuit of a common goal.

2.2.1 Review invitation to tender/terms of reference

The analyst should always be aware of the terms of reference. It is good practice to review the terms of reference at regular intervals, including the beginning of the evidence collection step. Only by so doing can a focus on the real issues be maintained. On reading the invitation to tender or terms of reference it is likely that usability issues of concern to the client can be identified. It is good practice at this point to create a document entitled 'Usability issues' (W202), in which notes on the subject can be recorded. Examples of issues would include staff training overheads, absenteeism or errors in processing. Specific figures may be cited such as one in ten invoices have to be re-submitted due to mistakes made during their production. It is increasingly the case that terms of reference establish improvement targets. For instance, clerical assistants should be able to process invoices at the rate of ten an hour with an error rate of less than 2 per cent. It is generally the case that usability targets will be relative rather than absolute, for instance a desire to increase the rate of invoice processing. Such usability targets are extremely important and should not be lost sight of. The 'usability issues' (W202) document should contain fields for noting the source of the issue, a description of the situation, an elaboration on the problems and descriptions of any improvement targets. An example page is shown in Figure 2.2. Most usability issues fall into one of the following categories: productivity, learnability, user satisfaction, memorability and errors. The acronym 'PLUME' is offered as a memory aid for these five categories.

In addition to the usability issues the analyst should begin to generate the 'Problems/requirements list' (D202). It is sensible to start this activity in parallel with generation of the usability issues since the same sources are being reviewed. The problems/requirements list should include fields for noting the job role(s) the requirement effects, how or where the requirement was noted (source), a brief description of the requirement and any possible solutions proposed by either the client or analyst. This list should be appended to as and when further requirements are identified. A few examples of the possible contents of a problems/requirements list are offered in Figure 2.3.

The similarities and differences between the contents of the usability issues and problems/requirements list documents should not concern the analyst unduly.

Many techniques can be employed for the purposes of evidence collection, including interviews, observations, questionnaires, forms analysis, thinking aloud, do-it-yourself, and ergonomics assessment.

Whichever techniques the analyst chooses to employ, the results should be used to update the usability issues and problems/requirements list.

Usability issues may at first seem to be the same as the entries that would appear on a problems/requirements list. Indeed, overlaps may well occur but this is not a cause for concern. Usability issues can arise for a number of reasons, including mismatches between staff abilities and technical support resulting in unnecessary overheads being incurred or business objectives not being met.

Usability issues address practical effectiveness as distinct from pure functionality. The common office telephone provides a simple example. It has approximately seventeen functions, including the ability to transfer calls and a group pick-up facility. These functions would be identified on a problems/requirements list. All well and good but does the interface (packaging) of these functions render them effective in practice? A set of usability issues could also have been generated. These might include the following requirements:

- The phone to be audible from a distance of fifty feet.
- The source of a phone ring to be identifiable to within twenty degrees of arc.
- Calls to be transferable within ten seconds.

USABILITY ISSUES

SOURCE	SITUATION	PROBLEMS	TARGETS
ITT	Absenteeism is running at 10%	Invoicing is late	Understand the reasons for absenteeism
Personnel Records	Staff turnover is 32% per year	Training overheads are high	Reduce training costs
ITT	Clerks produce 10 invoices per hour	Cost of invoicing is reducing margins	Improve productivity to 15 invoices per hour
Consultant's Report	Near-misses are occurring at the rate of 0.5 per day	Air traffic controllers (ATCs) spend 30% of their time looking at the input device as opposed to the radar display	Obviate the need for ATCs to look at input device
Consultant's Report	ATCs cannot deal with the amount of traffic during peak hours	ATCs are asking 3% of aircraft to 'circle'	Advise on ATC throughput
ITT	It takes 4 weeks to train an Indexer	Expensive	Provide a system that only requires two weeks of training
ITT	18% of database records contain errors	Two extra staff are required to deal with queries	Reduce error rate to below 1 in 100 records

Figure 2.2 *Example usability issues.*

- 'Dialling' to be performed with an error rate not exceeding one in ten thousand digits.
- Users to be able to distinguish between an engaged and unobtainable signal with an accuracy of 95 per cent after ten practice trials followed by a gap of two weeks.

Experience shows that the telephone, while having wonderful functionality, still fails to meet reasonable usability objectives. Indeed, because of its lack of usability, very little of its functionality is called upon frequently.

PROBLEMS/REQUIREMENTS LIST

ROLE	SOURCE	DESCRIPTION	PROPOSED SOLUTION
Portfolio Management	ITT	Portfolio management system is isolated from real-time market data	
Foreign Exchange	ITT	Want historical information on a dealer/customer basis	
Foreign Exchange	ITT	Want a facility to help bundle deals together	
General	Client	Make better use of real-time data feeds	

Figure 2.3 *Example requirements list.*

2.2.2 Interviews

Interviews are the most common form of evidence collection. It is best practice to plan for interviews by generating questions in advance. As evidence collection progresses, new questions will arise for purposes of clarification and validation.

Interviewing performed during a URA has the following explicit objectives:

- To elaborate the tasks, including mental tasks, performed by each role.
- To identify usability issues.
- To provide contextual information.

During interviewing it is important that such mental tasks as discrimination, looking, identifying, categorising, planning and recalling are discussed and recorded. Knowledge of such tasks can then be taken into account during design. For example, where users have to discriminate, then the design should facilitate this, possibly through the application of colour or formatting.

The analyst should first contemplate whether the interviewee should prepare for the interview in some way, for instance by having examples of work completed to hand or by having an example job in abeyance. If appropriate, the analyst should inform interviewees in advance of what will be required of them.

There is a straightforward yet important format for the questions posed during an interview. For each task or set of tasks the analyst should begin with 'What'-type questions. These are intended to provide an overview of the tasks that a user performs. Next, the analyst, even if he or she feels that the answer is obvious, should ask 'Why'-type questions. These access the user's understanding of the reasons for performing the tasks. There is an important distinction here between the business objectives for task performance and the task performer's beliefs. For each Why-type question the user should ask as many 'How'-type questions as are necessary to get to the detail of task execution. In summary, an interview should begin with general background discussion to generate rapport. The analyst should then ask What-type questions followed by Why- and related How-type questions for each task.

The analyst can also elicit useful evidence by asking 'Who'- or 'Where'-type questions and by enquiring as to the implications of certain outcomes. Who-type questions might well investigate the recipients of a particular user's work or who the user is dependent on for input. Implication-type questions refer to what might happen if the user's tasks were to be interrupted or modified in some manner. Such questioning identifies the importance of such tasks.

Examples of the sorts of questions an analyst might ask include the following:

> What is your job function?
> What are the products of your job?
> Why is this job important?
> Why is this task performed at this point in the process?
> How do you plan your work?
> How do you check that the task is complete?
> Who is dependent on your work?
> Where do you get the information on which to make that decision?
> If you are taken ill one day what happens?
> If you make a mistake where is the error identified?

The analyst should seek to obtain information on the following:

- training given in preparation for this role;
- use made of available documentation;
- general feelings towards system;
- ways the user plans her(his) work;
- materials (i.e. lists, *aide memoir*) produced to aid task completion;
- possible mistakes during task execution;
- problems encountered from whatever source;
- how errors are resolved;
- frequency of tasks;

- checks made of task accuracy;
- events that can interrupt task completion;
- what denotes the completion of a task;
- information required for task completion.

With regard to users' feelings it may be important to assess user satisfaction critically if this has been identified as an important usability issue. If this is the case, then a rating scale for system attributes should be generated and completed with users.

Further structure can be given to an interview in a number of ways. Questions can be grouped and presented in a sequence aligned with particular task areas or process sequences. One simple, but very helpful, technique for imposing structure is the use of graphical overviews. This would normally provide an overview of some process or job role as understood by the analyst. It does not have to be totally accurate or detailed. Its purpose is to create an agreed framework within which lines of enquiry can be pursued to the mutual agreement of analyst and interviewee. An example of such a graphic, as used during an analysis of the job of a practitioner in the Jackson Structured Development method (Jackson 1982, Cameron 1986), is shown in Figure 2.4. The meaning of graphics used in this way must be self-evident and must not require the interviewee to have any explicit knowledge of a notation.

Interview questions are best documented in the form of a booklet. One booklet per interviewee is the recommendation. The first few questions should always relate to the interviewee's experience. This provides an opportunity to gain rapport while gaining potentially important information about computer skills and training received.

The following heuristics should be applied during the generation of questions:

- The questions should follow a logical sequence.
- Plenty of space should be left between questions to permit the recording of answers.
- All booklets should be uniquely identifiable so that their sources can be traced and they can be stored in the project library.
- Never generate questions having multiple arguments; keep them simple.

Part of the preparation for interviews is choosing the venue. The choice is usually between the workplace or a quiet place. Interviewing persons at their place of work is preferable because interviewees can answer by demonstration if necessary, put their hands on relevant material and, significantly, will not have to rely exclusively on memory. The advantage of conducting interviews away from the workplace is that interruptions are minimised.

A well-prepared interviewer will have:

- informed the interviewee of the purpose of the interview;
- confirmed with the interviewee the time, venue and likely length of the interview;
- prepared a set of structured questions in the form of a uniquely identifiable booklet;
- gained an overview of the interviewee's role, however superficial.

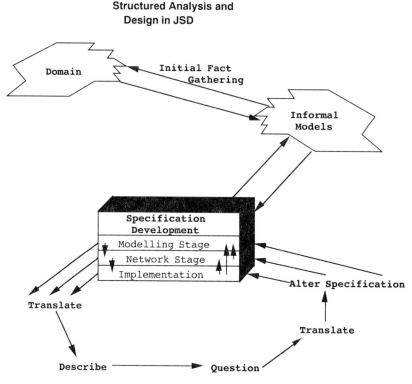

Figure 2.4 *Example graphic as an aid to interviewing.*

Where the analyst feels unable to record and ask questions synchronously, then the use of a tape recorder may be considered. Agreement for this must be obtained from the interviewee. Do not underestimate the overhead associated with transcription from audio media. For instance, a one-hour recording might take four hours to transcribe. Probably the only effective use of a recording is as a definitive record of what was said. All recordings should begin with some identification, such as the time, date and parties involved in the interview.

Interviewing can be performed effectively by pairs of analysts when resources permit. One analyst usually acts as the main questioner and the other as the note taker. Unfortunately, interviewees may feel threatened by multiple interviewers. The analyst will have to make a judgement as to whether one or two interviewers should participate.

The analyst should be aware that descriptions of tasks as identified during interviews are likely to suffer the following shortcomings:

- be somewhat simplistic;
- lack temporal order information;
- only cover the most frequent of task scenarios.

This is not to say that interviewing is not the best way of gaining evidence, only that the analyst must be sceptical and should apply other evidence collection techniques in order to ensure satisfaction with the quality and completeness of the findings.

It is always worthwhile finishing an interview with a recap of what was said and by asking one or two open-ended questions. The recap only needs to review the topics covered and, significantly, re-state what the interview objectives were and whether they were met. You should always complete the interview in a way that leaves the opportunity for a further session open. In the spirit of user-centred design, users should be told that they will be kept informed of developments. The open-ended questions could be of the type 'Is there anything else you think I should know about?' or 'What would you hope this project would achieve?' or 'Is there anything else we should have covered?' Such questions also help to identify task requirements that the analyst may miss because of the inevitable biases inherent in a set of preconceived questions.

2.2.3 Observation

Evidence collection based on observation can be very time-consuming and tiring. Thus preparation for observational work is essential to ensure conservation of effort. The main problem is the difficulty of making observations while recording those observations.

The major means of streamlining the recording process are the use of coding schemes and the use of specially formatted recording sheets. An example of the latter is shown in Figure 2.5. The example is taken from an observational study conducted in the financial trading room of a major bank. The sheet is divided into columns. Entries in a column are left justified but can continue across any columns to their right. The sequence of the record is from top to bottom. The first column is used to record the objective of the subject's activities or the specific task they are undertaking, whichever is the easiest to describe. The next column is used to record all actions performed by the subject. As can be seen, this includes all interactions including those as simple as answering a phone or putting a piece of paper in a tray. Next, any events are recorded, i.e. interruptions to the workflow, occurrences that may be of significance later, and possibly events being awaited by the subject such as the production of a window on a screen. Any verbalisations by the subject are recorded in the next column. It may only be feasible to record the gist of what is said but this can be sufficient to provide important contextual evidence. Information accessed is also recorded. Thus in Figure 2.5 it can be seen that the subject had to obtain foreign exchange rates in order to perform the task *Quote a price*. Timings, at the required level of accuracy, are also recorded and space should be provided to make comments.

As can be seen from the example, during just one minute of observation quite a lot took place and much information had to be recorded. This is why the analyst should attempt to use short-codes where possible.

Such a recording sheet can of course be extended as required. For instance, a column could be added in which changes to the contents of computer screens are recorded.

ENGAGEMENT   _Saltburg Bank_

OBSERVEE _Mr. Coolhand Luke_   **DATE** _13/03/90_

OBJECTIVE/ TASK	ACTIONS	EVENTS	VERBALS	INFO. ACCESSED	TIME	COMMENTS
		Phone rings			7.51	
	Pick up phone					
	Listen					
			'Cable?'			
Quote a price						
	Indicate screen, hits one key					Holds phone in
	Indicate page, types FXFX					crook of shoulder
				Foreign exchange rates		
						Puts index finger on screen at Cable
						Distorted body
			'475'			Means $1.5475
END						
Make a deal						
	Writes 10 @475 on scrap of paper					In parallel
			'Ten at 475'			Sold £10M worth of $ @ $1.5475
	Releases button on handset and throws down receiver					
						Keyboard hit by receiver
	Rips deal ticket off pad					
	Begins filling details on ticket					
			'Is that BZM cable guy in London'			
						Directed at other dealer
			(R) 'London'			
END	Completes deal ticket					
	Places deal ticket in wire basket			7.52	
"	"	"	"	"	"	"
"	"	"	"	"	9.01	"
		Clerk collects tickets from wire basket				

Figure 2.5 _Example observation data collection sheet._

The analyst should be aware that the initial record may be quite messy. It is always worthwhile re-visiting the record as soon as possible after the observation in order to fill-in/fill-out findings that could not be noted at the time. Unobtrusive observations of the sort described above can never unearth mental operations that are taking place, such as decision making, discrimination, categorising, identifying, etc. These tasks can only be inferred during observation. One way of identifying such mental tasks is the use of the thinking-aloud method described in Section 2.2.6. A second way is to work through the transcript with the interviewee and question the user about mental operations performed.

It may be tempting to use a stopwatch for timing highly repetitive tasks. Beware; stopwatches can frighten people and give them the impression that you are a threat. Where it is necessary to obtain accurate timings, then all persons involved, including senior management, should be requested to give their approval.

2.2.4 Questionnaires

When it seems worthwhile to canvass the views of many users and there is no opportunity to do this face-to-face, then evidence collection by questionnaire may be considered. Alternatively, questionnaires may be used in addition to interviews, particularly as a follow-up to interview findings. It is worth bearing in mind that producing quality questionnaires is not a trivial undertaking. All too often questionnaires fail to produce consistent results, or simply fail to be completed. Specialist advice should be sought when time and resources permit. The reasons for this are various but the following guidelines provide some help. It is also important to realise that, normally, only a small percentage of questionnaires are ever returned.

The following guidelines should be applied when generating a questionnaire:

- Avoid using sentences with multiple clauses.
- Use active rather than passive sentences.
- Avoid the use of negatives.
- Use familiar words, but be careful not to use ambiguous words.
- Ask questions about one thing at a time. Avoid the use of boolean expressions.
- Order the questions in a logical sequence, for instance in the temporal order in which the subject matter of the questions would arise.
- Use headings to group related questions.
- Seek alternatives to prose, for instance consider the use of lists.
- Leave sufficient room for answers.
- Use a legible font and use mixed case. This is easier to read than upper case text alone.
- Consider the layout of the questionnaire. Clutter should be avoided as it may make the questionnaire appear daunting.
- Do not ask questions about topics you are unlikely to consider further. Err on the side of brevity.
- Always include an explanation of the objective of the questionnaire. State what the

results will be used for and whether they are to be treated anonymously. Do not forget to state the address to which the completed questionnaire should be returned.

- Be absolutely sure of how the questionnaire results will be analysed.
- Always pilot test the questionnaire.
- Ensure that answers can be recorded easily, for instance through the use of tick boxes.

2.2.5 Forms analysis

Most tasks have some type of form associated with their execution. The design of new systems should, not surprisingly, take account of these forms, not simply to replicate them but to understand their relevance and how they should best be presented, formatted and what functionality should be associated with them. It is often the case that forms have evolved to their present construct for historical rather than for practical reasons, and because of this it is strongly recommended that an exercise in forms analysis is performed as part of evidence collection.

The analyst should identify the forms of interest, including any computer-based forms, and investigate their completion with respect to roles and tasks. The purpose of this exercise is to identify the logical sequence in which they might or should be filled, dependencies between fields, redundant fields and any rules that apply to the completion of fields. The information sought will assist in the design of forms for the new system. For instance, the principle might be applied that the most frequently completed fields appear towards the top of the form. Related fields might be grouped and coded for ease of discrimination. Where dependencies exist between fields it may be possible to prompt for input as the form is completed. Forms analysis can render subsequent design significantly easier.

2.2.6 Thinking aloud

In any iterative design there must be a means of identifying the weak and strong points of a design. One such means is the 'thinking-aloud' method (Ericsson and Simon 1980). Users are asked to provide a detailed running commentary of what they are doing while interacting with the system and its documentation. There is a certain skill in using the method, not least in putting the users at their ease so that they understand that it is not they but the system that is under investigation. Listed below are a number of cautionary notes and guidelines on how to apply the method.

Cautionary notes:

- Users tend to perform better when being observed (Roethliesberger and Dickson 1939). Thus performance data should be treated conservatively.
- The method generates a lot of data, albeit ill-structured. Data is to be treated as evidential rather than quantifiable.
- Data analysis is labour intensive.

■ There will be some inaccuracy in the data as users will retro-fit their commentaries to what they are doing rather than what they wanted to do or expected to happen.

■ Ideally, analysis should be supported by a re-playable record of the session.

■ Subjects must be representative of the end-user population. The method will not work with experienced people trying to second guess the problems that the real users experience.

Application:

■ The method can identify problems that pure observation would not identify. For instance, difficulties with terminology which are mentioned in the commentaries would not be noticed during a conventional observation.

■ The method provides a good source of evidence on mental operations.

■ It is useful as a method for find and fix type investigations. Thus it can be used when testing prototypes as well as during evidence collection.

■ Analysis of the protocol from a thinking aloud session can provide valuable material for verifying findings from other techniques, including interviews.

■ The method is an efficient means of identifying minor difficulties. Often minor problems are simply overlooked or ignored. This is unfortunate because minor difficulties can become a source of irritation for users over time and can lead to compounded problems.

■ The method can be used with small samples of users.

The instructions to users are quite straightforward. Users are asked 'Tell me what you are thinking about as you work.' This instruction can be supplemented with useful categories of thought such as decisions being made, concepts that are found to be confusing and expectations of what will happen next.

The evidence collected during a thinking-aloud session is normally analysed to document episodes where the user has experienced problems. These episodes are listed with a note of their context, which should at least include the task being performed. The episodes as a whole are then related to the system in order to ascertain their effect. This can be performed with subjects if required. The episodes are then grouped as appropriate. Examples of groups would be problems with terminology, cursor control, menu flow, error messages, information access, etc. The frequency of episodes should also be noted. As an analysis technique for understanding problems experienced by users, thinking-aloud is powerful.

2.2.7 Do-it-yourself

This technique is rarely considered although it is usually feasible and is easy to apply. As the name suggests, the analyst personally performs the tasks under supervision. One of the advantages of this approach over those discussed above is that it helps to identify the problems that novices would encounter.

Notes of problems might be made during a session but most evidence will have to be documented retrospectively.

2.2.8 **Video recording**

Where passive analysis is vital, for instance in an operating theatre, then video recording may be adopted as an analysis aid. Video recordings might be discussed with users in retrospect when their full attention can be gained.

Analysis of video recordings can be very time-consuming. Using time-stamped recordings that can be matched with observations conducted in synchrony are helpful for subsequent analysis. Recordings are also useful as a means of obtaining absolute time measures for tasks and as a basis for discussing tasks that the analyst finds difficult to understand. Analysts should be aware of how recordings will be analysed and should plan accordingly.

2.2.9 **Ergonomics assessment**

Where ergonomics is an issue, then an appropriately trained analyst may consider using a light meter, sound meter or measuring tape.

One of the objectives of an ergonomic investigation is to analyse the workplace environment. This includes environmental factors such as lighting and heating but, significantly it also includes anthropometric factors. This latter category is increasingly being recognised as important to the welfare of computer users. Correct posture and viewing distances are essential if visual fatigue, physical stress and repetitive strain injuries are to be avoided. The issues become more complex as the workplace becomes more intricate.

Financial dealers may have upwards of three screens at their disposal, further large screens may be shared by groups of dealers, there may be numerous input devices, auditory communication channels, shared printing facilities, etc. In such complex environments ergonomic factors are extremely important to the well-being of users and the successful execution of duties.

Legislation to be introduced throughout the European Community will make these factors the direct responsibility of employers. Some of the issues regarding computer use are depicted in Figure 2.6

2.2.10 **Step summary**

A number of techniques applicable to evidence collection have been introduced. All these techniques require direct user involvement. Depending on the particular application, different techniques or combinations of techniques will be appropriate. Decisions as to which techniques to apply will have to be made in the light of prevailing conditions.

The raw evidence gathered during this step will be available in the form of interview booklets and observation sheets. The analyst should also have updated the usability issues (W202) and problems/requirements list (D202) documents continuously as relevant evidence has become available. During the next step, task analysis, the raw evidence will be examined.

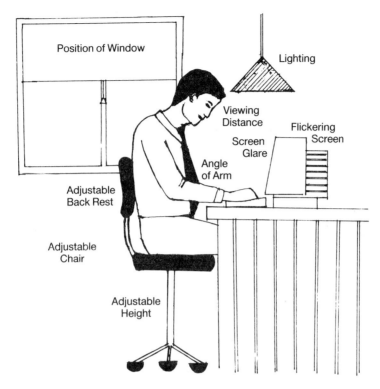

Figure 2.6 *Ergonomic considerations.*

2.3 **Task analysis (Step 203)**

Having collected the raw evidence it must now be sifted, massaged and documented in a manner that can be used for the purposes of user interface design. The principle to be applied is that the evidence should be represented in a form that can be understood by those responsible for task synthesis. It is quite possible that these persons will not have been party to the user requirements analysis.

To these ends this section introduces a number of representations. In addition, guidance is offered on how to move swiftly from the evidence to these representations. Ultimately, the task analysis should provide a sufficiently concise representation of the tasks, and their attributes, the objects and actions involved in task execution, plus usability targets. In addition the task analysis may provide logical task allocation proposals, scoping proposals and symbology/terminology listings.

This section begins by describing the procedures for producing task hierarchy diagrams. These are the main means of representing task execution. Next the concept of Knowledge Representation Grammars (KRG) is introduced which provide an exhaustive list of tasks. From KRG sentences the objects and actions are extracted

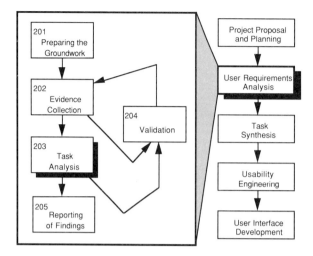

Task analysis (Step 203).

using *generalisation*. These are the main techniques of task analysis as adopted in STUDIO. The deliverables from task analysis and their relationships are shown in Figure 2.7. Additional diagramming techniques are then introduced for representing the allocation of function between human and system and for scoping the user interface functionality. Finally, this section concludes with the important topic of usability. At the end of this stage the relevant usability issues will have been identified and potential usability targets proposed.

2.3.1 Task hierarchy diagramming (THD)

A considerable number of techniques have been proposed for documenting tasks, over two hundred in fact. They range from indented lists to flow-diagram-based techniques. Within STUDIO a form of entity life history has been adopted because this is already familiar to many analysts including those familiar with SSADM.

An entity life history (ELH) is shown in Figure 2.8. This ELH describes the life of an instance of the entity, Customer. An instance of a Customer comes to exist via either the event Booking Request or Customer Application. The small circles in the top right-hand corners of boxes denote selection. Thus either a Booking Request or a Customer Application takes place but not both. During the *life* of the Customer there may be Changes To Customer Details, or an Invoice Issued against that customer or Payment Received from that Customer. Any of these three events may happen many (including zero) times. Iteration such as this is denoted by an asterisk in the top right-hand corner, as shown in the Customer Change box. Sequence of events is denoted by the order in which events appear on an ELH; earlier events appearing to the left of subsequent ones. ELHs capture sequence, selection and iteration in a

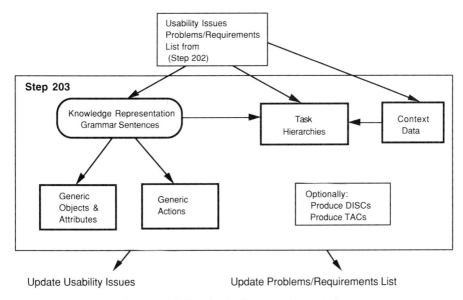

Figure 2.7 *Products from task analysis.*

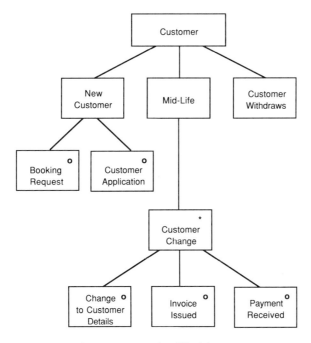

Figure 2.8 *Entity life history.*

succinct manner, hence their appeal as a representation technique. Extensions to this basic notation are introduced and explained in the examples that follow.

Task hierarchy diagramming (THD) is the term used to refer to the particular use made of ELHs within STUDIO. A THD represents a task in terms of sub-tasks/ events that begin and end the task and those sub-tasks that progress the task towards its completion. Where a task is broken down into many levels of sub-task it is permissible to document the detail of any sub-task separately.

THDs provide the following:

- a representation of the normal sequence of tasks/sub-tasks during successful task completion;
- a basis for making user interface design decisions;
- a basis for producing training and documentation materials.

THDs can and should be annotated with comments on tasks/sub-tasks to indicate the following:

- how often the task/sub-task occurs;
- how long they take to complete;
- the errors that might occur;
- how long it takes a user to become proficient in performing the task.

These comments are important for purposes of user interface design, particularly usability engineering (Stage 4).

THDs can also be annotated with contextual data. For instance, a comment might refer to the importance of the task with respect to business objectives. It can also be useful to list any documents, forms, tools, etc., that the user might employ in the performance of the task.

Normally the boxes on a THD are labelled in mixed case but the analyst can choose to limit the detail shown on a particular THD. This is achieved by only showing the box and label representing selected sub-tasks from that particular THD. Sub-tasks treated in this way must be shown in full as separate THDs. Where the analyst chooses not to expand a sub-task in full on a THD then its label should be shown capitalised. This will provide the reader a necessary cue to the fact that more detail on that sub-task can be found elsewhere. If desired the analyst may go one stage further and provide an identifier for the THD on which the sub-task is shown in detail. This identifier should be shown within the bounds of the box for the sub-task. It is vital for the completeness and subsequent use of THDs that all mental tasks/sub-tasks are recorded. These mental tasks are omitted from systems analyses but are basic to the making of user interface design decisions. This is the most striking difference between an ELH and a THD and probably the most difficult aspect for analysts to grasp.

In the example of an observational record introduced in Figure 2.5 and repeated here in Figure 2.9 for clarity, the comment 'Puts Index Finger on screen at Cable' was noted. This comment refers to the fact that the user had to pick out the $/£ exchange rate (Cable) from all the other exchange rates on the screen being read. Such operations of *discrimination* are important for user interface design and should be

ENGAGEMENT   _Saltburg Bank_

OBSERVEE _Mr. Coolhand Luke_   DATE _13/03/90_

OBJECTIVE/ TASK	ACTIONS	EVENTS	VERBALS	INFO. ACCESSED	TIME	COMMENTS
			Phone rings		7.51	
	Pick up phone					
	Listen					
			'Cable?'			
Quote a price						
		Indicate screen, hits one key				Holds phone in crook of shoulder
		Indicate Page, types FXFX				
				Foreign exchange rates		
						Puts index finger on screen at Cable
						Distorted body
			'475'			Means $1.5475
END						
Make a deal						
		Writes 10 @475 on scrap of paper				In parallel
			'Ten at 475'			Sold £10M worth of $ @ $1.5475
	Releases button on handset and throws down receiver					
						Keyboard hit by receiver
	Rips deal ticket off pad					
		Begins filling details on ticket				
			'Is that BZM Cable guy in London?'			Directed at other dealer
			(R) 'London'			
END		Completes deal ticket				
		Places deal ticket in wire basket			7.52	
"	"	"	"	"	"	"
"	"	"	"	"	9.01	"

Clerk collects tickets from wirebasket

Figure 2.9 *Example observation data collection sheet.*

included in the THDs produced at this step in STUDIO. Having identified that a mental task of discrimination is important to successful task completion, the user interface designer can be rendered cognisant of this fact when design begins. The resulting design would hopefully then facilitate discrimination, making it both an easy

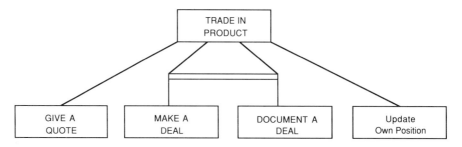

Figure 2.10 *Top-level task breakdown.*

and an unambiguous task. Other common mental operations include monitoring, browsing, navigating, identifying, recognising, choosing, recalling and rationalising. All such mental tasks are important because user interface design is concerned with facilitating such tasks as opposed to simply making them possible.

THDs are an abstract representation of user tasks. They should not include mention of input devices, keying sequences, screen formats or the like as these present means of interaction that are amenable to change with the new design and should not constrain the design.

Figure 2.10 shows a very simple THD as generated from both the observational data in Figure 2.9 and other data as might have been recorded during an interview. The task TRADE IN PRODUCT is shown as having four sub-tasks namely, GIVE A QUOTE, MAKE A DEAL, DOCUMENT A DEAL and Update Own Position. All of these sub-tasks could be further documented as tasks in their own right, in fact three of them are as shown in Figures 2.11 – 2.13, so their labels are all written in upper case. TRADE IN PRODUCT is a sequence of these sub-tasks as read from left to right. MAKE A DEAL and DOCUMENT A DEAL are shown as having an amount of parallelism given that a dealer can be producing documentation while finalising a deal. All task labels are written as *operation* followed by *object*. Thus 'DOCUMENT A DEAL' is correct but 'DEAL DOCUMENTATION' would be incorrect. Parallelism between tasks is shown by the use of a double bar above and spanning the parallel tasks. GIVE A QUOTE is shown as a sub-task of TRADE IN PRODUCT in Figure 2.10 but is elaborated fully in Figure 2.11 as a task in its own right.

Figure 2.11 shows that GIVE A QUOTE is a more complex task than might at first be imagined. The dealer has to 'Identify Existence of Request', then 'Ascertain Content of Request', then 'Identify Information Source', and 'Read Information' before quoting a price. Three of these sub-tasks are further refined on the THD. For instance, 'Identify Information Source' may necessitate the user performing two sub-tasks, namely 'Indicate Screen' and 'Indicate Page Required'. From the example observation data the page would be 'FXFX' for foreign exchange data. Alternatively, the user may not need to do anything if the required page is already in view. This possibility is indicated by the null box.

Figure 2.11 also demonstrates how usability data can be shown on a THD. If a

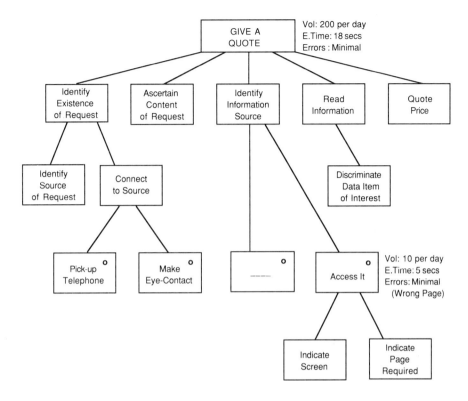

CONTEXT INFORMATION:
   If you are too slow in quoting, then customer will take his/her business elsewhere. More importantly, (s)he may not give you future business either.
   Dealers are grouped physically by specialisation.
   If you make an obviously inaccurate quote the customer wiil simply go away (sniggering).
   Always difficult to know whether a screen has been updated lately

Figure 2.11 *Task hierarchy diagram for 'GIVE A QUOTE'.*

dealer does have to make a page visible (Access It), then this will require approximately 5 seconds to accomplish. This sub-task is likely to occur ten times per day or alternatively, once in every twenty quotes, given that approximately 200 quotes are given per day. This sub-task is rarely performed in error. A simple annotation by the relevant sub-task conveys this information.

Figure 2.12 depicts the THD for 'MAKE A DEAL'. This THD demonstrates the use of the Quit-Resume convention. Where a dealer refuses to deal with a customer because this would exceed his or her limits the dealer will neither 'Re-iterate Deal' or 'Record Deal'. This is represented by placing a uniquely numbered Q by the box from which the Quit occurs and placing an R with the same number at the left of the sub-task at which the task resumes. Figure 2.13 provides a further example for the

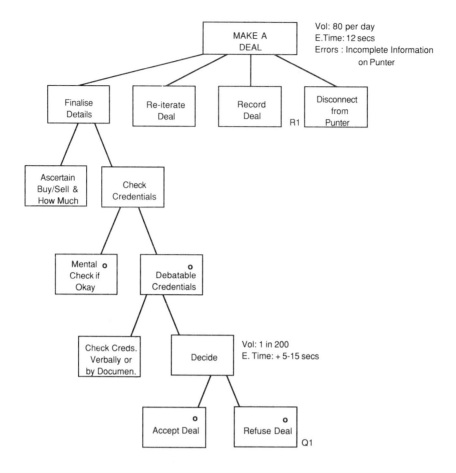

Figure 2.12 *Task hierarchy diagram for 'MAKE A DEAL'.*

task of 'DOCUMENT A DEAL'. THDs provide a representation for task-based data that captures the sequence, selection, iteration, parallelism and consequent behaviour of tasks, sub-tasks and abnormal tasks. By so doing they provide information that will become useful for subsequent user interface design. For instance, the sequencing will help with dialogue structuring and prompting. Parallelism may indicate a requirement for support of multitasking. Selections may indicate menu groupings. Iterations will signify interaction elements where the system should make use of

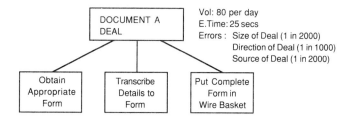

Figure 2.13 *Task hierarchy diagram for 'DOCUMENT A DEAL'.*

contextual information to facilitate usability. Abnormal sub-tasks may indicate dialogue points where dialogue termination sequences are required.

THDs provide anchor points for noting usability data. For instance, we have seen how 'sub-tasks' contribute to the normal elapsed time of a task. Where these sub-tasks are frequent the designer might seek to facilitate interaction, possibly by using contextual information or predictive techniques. This information from THDs is used subsequently in the task synthesis stage of STUDIO.

2.3.2 Context

The value to a user interface designer of contextual data gathered during user requirements analysis should not be underestimated. Usually, contextual data are collected during any analysis but are then lost during further analysis and design activities. This may occur because contextual data by their very nature are diverse and difficult to document in a concise manner. Contextual data can only be documented in the form of English or, at best, structured English. Within STUDIO, contextual data are recorded directly on THDs.

Table 2.1 offers some categories of contextual data. These provide headings as catalysts to help the analyst identify and document relevant contextual data. Short examples taken from the financial dealing room domain are provided under the category headings.

It can be appreciated from Table 2.1 that contextual data have the potential to be very useful. Contextual data may be the only source of input for avoiding some existing problems. For instance, the maintenance problem is easily resolved once the problem has been identified. The terminology and symbology that is often taken for

Table 2.1 *Example categories of contextual data*

Categories		Dealing room examples
Users		
	Roles	CABLE dealer
	Working groups	GILTS, Foreign Exchange, exotics
	Knowledge/background	No mathematics to 'A' level
Workstation		
	Seating	Cushion on chair
	Glare	DIY visor attached to CRT
	Keyboards	Three, one for each screen
	Room layout	By work group
Physical		
	Viewing distance	100 cm for personal screens 3–15 m for broadcast screens
	Potential damage	Telephone handsets against CRTs Pens on CRTs causing scratches
	Eye contact	Dealers need to see beyond their desks to other dealers
	Telephones	Need two hands free while using telephones
Maintenance		
	Replacement of keyboard	Requires dealer to vacate desk because connection is difficult to reach
	Moving to a new position	Very inconvenient because each desk is configured personally
Sequencing		
	Incomplete tasks	No running record of deals made so difficult to assess that the present position is up to date
	Retrievable tasks	Even after a deal ticket is completed the possibility remains, for up to one hour, of amending the ticket.

Categories		Dealing room examples
Infrequent events		
	Daily	Team meeting @ 08.00
	Weekly	Generate newsletter for clients
	Monthly	Team briefing after work
Communication		
	Shared understanding	i.e. 'CABLE 475' means $/£ exchange rate of X.Y475 whatever the likely values of X and Y are at the time
Problems		
	With methods	Sceptical of charting
	Speed	Cannot quote quickly enough
	Information/forgetting	Cannot remember customer details when filling deal ticket
	Errors	Mis-read FXFX screen when looking for $/DM rate
	Repetitiveness	Procedure for obtaining hardcopy of deals completed is tedious
	Training	No training required but unsure that getting best out of system
Tools		
	WP facilities	Poor for table production
	Calculators	Use my own, bank one does not store equations
Other aids		
	Whiteboards	Expected price ranges/movements
	Notepad	Deal details
	Clocks	Times around the world
	Calendars	Number of banking days between two dates

Categories		Dealing room examples
	Keyboards overlays	What the function keys do
	Aides memoir	Post-it note for meetings
	Graphs	Charting purposes
	Addresses	Offices of different banks
	Personal data sheet	For daily records
	Guide book	Deal limits
Short codes		
	FXFX	Foreign Exchange page on Reuters
	CABLE	$/£ Exchange Rate
Frequency of information use		
	FXFX page	250 per day
	CABLE price	200 per day
Terminology/ symbology		
	M	Million
	Y	Yen
	Lining	Dealing outside agreed limits
If-then rules		
		If too slow in quoting, then customer will get a quote from elsewhere and is less likely to offer you business on a future occasion
		If not a regular client, then have to check whether he is *lining*
Other problems		
		Uncertainty about whether screens are up to date

granted might well be incorporated in a user interface design. Problems that users have identified can be attended to. Inadequacies of available peripheral tools can be addressed. Contexts themselves can be established. Of course, the list in Table 2.1 is specific to financial dealing rooms but the categories of contextual data collected can be amended to suit local circumstances. Contextual data should also be recorded on the THDs by the tasks to which they most obviously apply.

2.3.3 Knowledge representation grammar (KRG)

User requirements analysis data are also represented by KRG sentences. KRG sentences are most easily extracted from interview responses and are a quick means of recording operations, including mental operations performed by the users. KRG sentences serve the following two main purposes:

- as a check on the completeness of the THDs;
- as a means of extracting the generic actions and objects involved in task performance.

KRG sentences do not capture the sequencing of tasks.

The form of a KRG sentence (S) is one of action (A) followed by one or more object (O) phrases.

$$S := A, O$$

The following provides a transcript from an interview with a dealer. The interview covered how a dealer performs the task of 'TRADE IN PRODUCT'.

What I have to do is find out what the punter wants and who he is. For instance, he might be interested in buying dollars. Once I know what he wants I can give him a quote. To do this I check the exchange rates as listed on Telerate or Reuters. I know the pages off by heart so if I can't see what I want I type in the page number. I'll choose between Telerate and Reuters depending on which is most dependable; up to date. Depending on the punter and how valuable his custom is, I will quote one or two pips either side of the price either giving him a good deal or a mediocre one. My quote may also depend on my position. If I'm trying to stay long in dollars then I'll give him a poor quote and so on.

If he bites then he will tell me how much he wants, that is how many millions of pounds worth. I re-iterate the deal and that's that. I then have to fill-in a deal ticket and update my own position. Oh yeah, sometimes I might not know the punter too well and I might have to check his limits with us.

Transcript of interview.

The KRG sentences that would be extracted from this transcript are as follows:

A. Find-out/Requirement/(from) Punter.
B. Give/Quote/(to) Punter
C. Check/Exchange Rates/(using) Telerate/(using) Reuters
D. Recall/Pages
E. Type-in/Page Number
F. Select/Price/(from) Page
G. Calculate/Quote/(using) Price ± 1 or 2 pips/(using) Customer Knowledge/(using) Own Position
H. Present/Quote/(to) Customer
I. Ascertain/Size of Deal/(from) Punter
J. Re-iterate/Deal/(using) Size of Deal/(using) Quote/(using) Product
K. Fill-in/Deal Ticket
L. Update/Own Position
M. Check/Punter Limits
N. Decide/(on) Service

The KRG sentences are simple and can be read easily. The terms in brackets such as 'using', 'from'. and 'to', are for readability. It is clear from the sentences that some sub-tasks of TRADE IN PRODUCT have been omitted from the THDs. Once the THDs have been edited to remove synonyms and duplications they will be compared with the THDs for completeness and compatibility of terminology.

Optimisation

Optimisation is necessary because the first draft of the sentences always includes many synonyms and duplications. For instance, sentences B and H are really saying the same thing. Their existence and differences are simply a result of the interviewee saying the same thing in different ways. The above also provides an example of synonymous action and object naming. 'Give' and 'Present' are synonyms for one action. During optimisation the analyst can choose to use either of these labels or identify a completely new label. 'Punter' and 'Customer' refer to the same object. Again, one of these or a new term could be chosen. Indeed, the analyst could choose to change the term 'Quote', particularly given its possible misinterpretation as an action rather than an object. In this example sentences B and H are combined to form the sentence:

Announce/Quote/(to) Customer

Each instance of 'Punter' in the sentences should now be replaced with 'Customer'. All instances of 'Give' and 'Present' that refer to a verbal communication of information should also be replaced by Announce throughout the sentences. While this process of optimisation is being performed the analyst builds up lists of generic objects and actions. Thus Customer and Announce would be added to these lists.

A.   Ascertain/Product/(from) Customer
B.   Announce/Quote/(to) Customer
C.   Access/Service
D.   Recall/Page Number
E.   Type-in/Page Number
F.   Discriminate/Price/(from) Page
G.   (Mentally) Calculate/Quote/(using) Price + 1 or 2 pips/(using) Customer
      Knowledge/(using) Own Position
H.   Present/Quote/(to)Customer
I.   Ascertain/Size of Deal/(from) Customer
J.   Announce/Deal/(using) Size of Deal/(using) Quote/(using) Product
K.   Fill-in/Deal Ticket/(using) Size of Deal/(using) Quote/(using)
      Product/(using) Customer Identification
L.   Update/Own Position/(using) Size of Deal/(using) Product
M. Check/Customer Limits/(using) Limits Book
N.   Decide/(on)Service.

Each KRG sentence represents a single operation that can be considered as happening at an instant in time. It may be necessary for the analyst to re-check his or her understanding with a user when generating the sentences. For instance, in sentence K the new object 'Customer Identification' has been added. This could have occurred as a result of further questioning of the user or by reflecting on the results of a forms analysis (Section 2.2.5).

Once the analyst is satisfied with the sentences, that is, no further optimisation or generalisations are sensible, the THDs and KRG sentences are cross-checked. By generating the sentences and THDs independently, omissions and anomalies can be rectified and terminology used in the two representations can be consolidated.

Cross-checking

It is recommended that all KRG sentences are uniquely labelled as above with letters of the alphabet. These labels are then used to mark the leaf nodes on the THD to which they correspond. Those leaf nodes unmarked at the end of this exercise indicate KRG sentences that must be generated. Similarly for KRG sentences that have no corresponding leaf nodes; here additions should be made to the THDs. The terminology developed during optimisation of the KRG sentences should be adopted throughout the THDs.

The changes to the THDs generated for the dealing room example can be seen in Figures 2.14 – 2.17. Changes in terminology and 'new' nodes are labelled in italics on the updated THDs. The full set of KRG sentences following the cross-checking exercise is shown below:

A.   Ascertain/Product/(from) Customer
B.   Announce/Quote/(to) Customer
C.   Access/Service
D.   Recall/Page Number

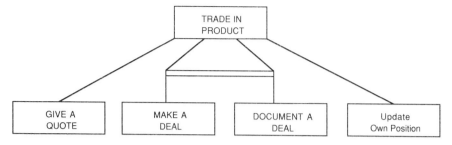

Figure 2.14 *Top-level task breakdown.*

E. Type-in/Page Number
F. Discriminate/Price/(from) Page
G. (Mentally) Calculate/Quote/(using) Price ± 1 or 2 pips/(using) Customer Knowledge/(using) Own Position
H. Present/Quote/(to) Customer
I. Ascertain/Size of Deal/(from) Customer
J. Announce/Deal/(using) Size of Deal/(using) Quote/(using) Product
K. Fill-in/Deal Ticket/(using) Size of Deal/(using) Quote/(using) Product/(using) Customer Identification
L. Update/Own Position/(using) Size of Deal/(using) Product
M. Check/Customer Limits/(using) Limits Book
N. Decide/(on) Service
P. Identify/Source/(of) Request
Q. Pick-up/Telephone
R. Make/Eye-contact
S. Indicate/Screen
T. (Mentally) Check/Credentials
U. Accept/Deal
V. Refuse/Deal
W. Record/Deal/(on) Scrap of Paper
X. Disconnect/(from) Customer
Y. Obtain/Deal Ticket
Z. Place/Deal Ticket/(in) Wire Basket

A quick review of the THDs of Figures 2.14–2.17 identifies a number of issues that, even at this stage, are recognisable as being of particular importance to usability:

- Making a deal and documenting a deal are necessarily parallel activities.
- Details of a deal are recorded twice by dealers.
- Quotes must be given quickly and prices are not always easy to read.
- In order to access a price it is sometimes necessary for dealers to make three decisions, namely which screen, which service and which page. This seems unnecessarily abstract given that the dealer knows the item of data required. A redeeming factor here is that this scenario is relatively infrequent.

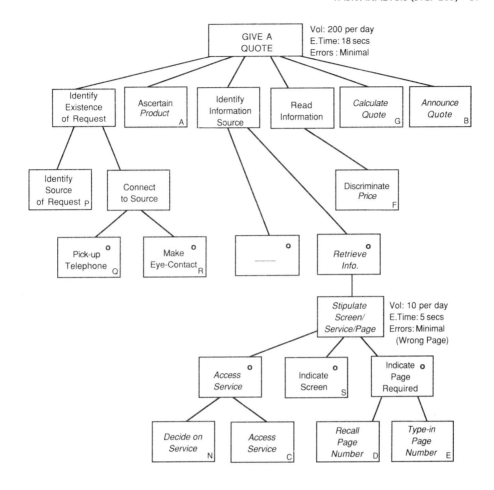

Figure 2.15 *Task hierarchy diagram for 'GIVE A QUOTE'.*

CONTEXT INFORMATION:
   If you are too slow in quoting, then the customer will take his/her business elsewhere. More importantly, he may not give you future business either.
   Dealers are grouped physically by specialisation.
   If you make an obviously inaccurate quote the customer will simply go away (sniggering).
   Always difficult to know whether a screen has been updated lately.

- Dealers have to calculate quotes quickly on the basis of a number of heuristics and data items. The latter are not always to hand.
- Dealing places many ergonomic requirements on the display of data and the layout of dealing rooms.
- A simple aid would be to indicate the interval since screens were updated.

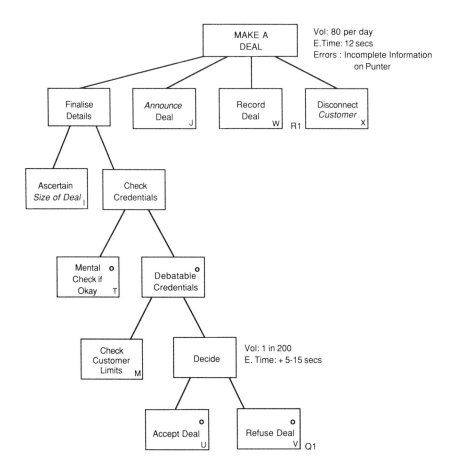

CONTEXT INFORMATION
 If not regular client then may have to check 'if lining'
 Record Deal is usually done on a scrap of paper.

DOCUMENTS/FORMS
 Scrap of paper for deal.

Figure 2.16 *Task hierarchy diagram for 'MAKE A DEAL'.*

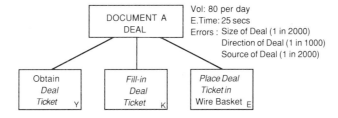

Figure 2.17 *Task hierarchy diagram for 'DOCUMENT A DEAL'.*

This is a far from exhaustive list of issues requiring attention during user interface design. Indeed, this list has been generated on the basis of just one interview and observational record and only addresses one major task.

As issues are identified they should be appended to the problems/requirements list (D202) and usability issues list (W202).

2.3.4 Action lists

An action list is simply an exhaustive catalogue of the actions appearing in the KRG sentences. An action is any operation, physical or mental, performed by the user. Actions are not unique to tasks. For instance, a dealer might have to *read* many different prices and graphs and news reports. The reason for creating an action list is so that generalisations can be made. For instance, all terminations, ends, finishes and conclusions can be treated similarly when user interfacing decisions are made. The action list should be generated and maintained as the THDs and KRG sentences are developed.

The entries on this list are annotated with the objects on which the actions have effect and a short description of the action where this is thought helpful. Volumes, timings, error rates may also be included. Table 2.2 provides an example action list which includes a column for volumes. Each volume has been further qualified by the object to which it refers. For instance, the action 'Announce' has two volumes associated with it: one for announcing quotes and one for announcing deals. The action list for the example would include those shown in Table 2.2.

Table 2.2 *Example action list with volumes*

Actions	Objects	Description	Volumes (per day)
Accept	Deal	Continue transaction on basis of information available	75–80 × Deal
Announce	Quote, Deal	Provide new or further information	200 × Quote 80 × Deal
Ascertain	Product, Size of Deal	Acquire information verbally	200 × Quote 80 × Size of Deal
Calculate	Quote	Perform mental calculation, possibly with aid of pen and paper.	200 × Quote
Check	Customer Limits Credentials	Validate piece of implicit information	80 × Credentials 2 × Customer Limits
Decide	Service	Choose among a finite set of options	<10 × Service
Disconnect	Customer	Terminate a verbal discourse	190 × Customer
Discriminate	Price	Discern a required item from many possibles	>200 × Price
Fill-in	Deal Ticket	Provide a number of pieces of data on a pro-forma	80 × Deal Ticket
Indicate	Screen	Invoke a choice	>10 × Screen
Make	Eye Contact	Attain some behavioural outcome	10 × Eye-Contact
Obtain	Deal Ticket	Procure an instance of some physical object	80 × Deal Ticket
Pick-up	Telephone	Physically lift an object	200 × Telephone
Place	Deal Ticket	Physically put some object in a meaningful location	80 × Deal Ticket
Recall	Page Number	Retrieve an item of data from memory	<10 × Page Number
Record	Deal	Make a physical note of some information	80 × Deal
Refuse	Deal	Decline to perform some task	<1 × Deal per week
Type-in	Page Number	Provide some alphanumeric input to a system	10 × Page Number
Update	Own Position	Modify an existing piece of information	80 × Own Position

The above example suggests that each action only effects a few objects but it only takes account of one task. As more tasks are analysed it would be found that the same actions take place in different tasks but on different objects. For instance, we might find that Update also affects the objects *Client data*, and *Profit/Loss account*.

2.3.5 Object lists

An object is any item, either physical or symbolic, of import in task performance. An object list should be generated and maintained as the THDs and KRG sentences are produced. Each object plays a part in one or more tasks. As such, each object will be affected by one or more of the entries on the action list. In due course these objects may become menu items, task qualifiers, or items about which data are held.

The object list should include attributes and a description of the object where necessary. Object attributes are loosely defined as elements of the object that are meaningful in their own right, are required to qualify an instance of the object or are a source/sink for the object.

Objects are identified from the KRG sentences. They are the items on which actions perform. The attributes of the objects are the qualifying parts of the sentences. Table 2.3 provides an object list based on the case study.

Table 2.3 *Example object list*

Objects	Object attributes	Description	Volumes
Customer	None	Someone wishing to make a financial transaction. Could be a bank employee	40 regular per dealer
Customer Limits	Limits Book	The size of transactions permitted with a given customer	
Deal	Size of Deal, Quote, Product, Scrap of Paper	A financial transaction	80 created per day
Deal Ticket	Size of Deal, Quote, Product, Customer Identification, Wire Basket	The form on which the details of a deal are noted	80 created per day
Eye Contact	None	Visual contact between two people. Important for ergonomic considerations	10 per day

Objects	Object attributes	Description	Volumes
Own Position	Size of Deal, Product	A dealer's current standing in the various products traded	1 continually updated
Page Number	None	A unique identifier for a piece of information from one of the information vendors (i.e. Reuters, Telerate).	150 per service
Price	None	The present, widely quoted, cost of a product	Thousands
Product	Customer	A customer is interested in a particular commodity at a given time. Given the variety of commodities (gilts, equities, etc.), they are collectively referred to as products	Thousands. Only a small set are dealt with by any one dealer
Quote	Customer, Price ±1 or 2 pips, Customer Knowledge, Own Position	A verbal contract between dealer and customer	200 created per day
Screen	None	An information source	3 or 4 per dealer
Service	None	Information from a particular vendor	Two plus an in-house system
Size of Deal	Customer	Usually the number of millions of pounds that the customer wishes to transact	
Telephone	None		Two per dealer

2.3.6 **Task Allocation Charts (TACs)**

Task allocation charting (Ip *et al.* 1990a, b) considers the allocation of tasks between user and technology. In so doing it addresses business process design. TAC permits task allocation and process design decisions to be made early in the system life cycle.

TACs represent the allocation of tasks between computer and user roles. Each task is shown as a rectangle labelled with the name of the task. Task sequence is indicated by arrows linking task boxes. A similar notation to that used for entity life histories is used to indicate sequence, selection and iteration. Entities external to the system are shown as labelled ellipses.

Example TACs are shown in Figure 2.18. The case study is again used to provide an example. Updating one's trading position is usually performed by completing a deal ticket which is placed in a wire basket from where it is collected by a clerk. From there the tickets are transferred to the back office where the individual deals are recorded. A computer system then updates all the individual positions. The dealers can then access their own positions via a computer screen at their work positions. The tasks and roles involved in this process are shown in TAC1 Option 1 in Figure 2.18. The problem with this process is that there is a built-in time delay of between 15 and 90 minutes before the effects of any one deal appear on the system. Option 2 shows an alternative scenario based on dealers entering their own deals on-line. In this scenario individual positions are never more than a minute out of date.

TACs can be used to:

■ determine the boundary of the computer system;
■ explore job design options;
■ communicate design options to users.

In practice TACs can be understood with a minimum of effort. Thus they can facilitate communication and collaborative decision making with clients. Given this, they offer the opportunity to incorporate the users' views and requirements early in the development life cycle.

TACs are a powerful visual aid to representing the impact of alternative options on job allocation. They can be applied early in a project for the purposes of scoping and as an aid to managing change.

2.3.7 **DIchotomy Scoping Charts (DISCs)**

DIchotomy Scoping Charts (DISCs) are a visual aid to scoping the user interface. An example DISC is shown in Figure 2.19. The innermost circle of a DISC encloses those tasks that must have system support. The larger circle encloses all tasks that it is felt should be automated. Tasks above the horizontal line are those which must be performed as part of the user's role. Those below the horizontal dividing line are not necessary for job accomplishment but it is believed that they would be of value if they were undertaken. Tasks to the right of the vertical dividing line are considered straightforward to the extent that they are not difficult to comprehend and specify

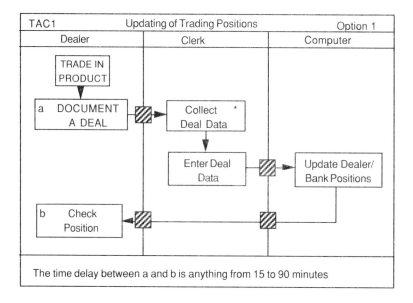

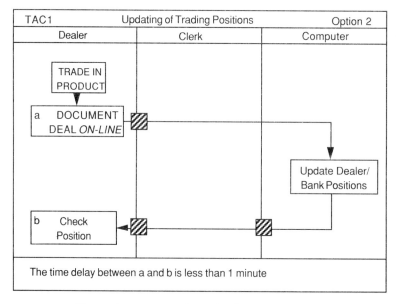

Figure 2.18 *Example task allocation charts.*

in-depth and are thus relatively risk-free. This is not to say that they are easily and cheaply automatable. Tasks to the left of the vertical are deemed to require further investigation if a full understanding (costing) is to be gained. Quite often, decision making tasks and planning tasks are shown to the left of the vertical divide. Tasks placed outside the circles are not expected to be automated.

The value of DISCs is twofold. Firstly, their production helps to focus the analyst on what the final system could support. As such they are an exercise in considering business system options. The results of a DISC analysis should be used to update the on-going requirements list. Given that DISC analysis will determine that some tasks are outside the bounds of the final system, this should be noted on the requirements list. All task support, even that defined as being outside the project, should remain on the requirements list. Each requirement can then be labelled as being mandatory, highly desirable, desirable or not required. Their second value is as a communication aid. DISCs can be explained to users and purchasers who can then appreciate and comment on the value of providing support for individual tasks.

Figure 2.19 has been filled with tasks taken from the dealing room example. The letters represent the tasks as listed in the KRG sentences, i.e. 'C' represents 'Access/Service'. The positioning of the tasks on the DISC are proposals. The remit of users and clients would be to determine the value of supporting individual tasks and the suppliers' responsibility would be to provide costings for this support.

In the 'proposed DISC', tasks C,F,S,D and E are deemed to be essential. In fact, these tasks are already supported by the present system. They basically refer to the access and presentation of data from on-line financial services such as Reuters.

It is proposed that tasks M,Y,K and Z could be supported by the system and that this would be relatively risk-free. Supporting K,Y and Z would require the equivalent of Deal Ticket completion to be performed on-line, thus obviating the need for a clerk to collect hardcopies of the deal tickets. This is congruent with option 2 of the task allocation charts shown in Figure 2.18. Where both TACs and DISCs are employed to present options to clients they act as useful counterpoints. Supporting M would require that Customer Limits be stored on-line. This might be worthwhile, particularly where those limits are modified regularly. This is a case where user/client involvement in deciding the level of automation would be vital.

Tasks L and W have been placed on the *risky side*, to the left of the vertical, because knowing how to update an individual dealer's position and how to record a deal on-line as it is being struck are open to conjecture. It might be possible to use a graphics tablet to capture deals as they are made, or a mouse-based point and click system might be feasible if the set of selections is limited sufficiently. On the basis of the analyst's present knowledge he has placed W and L in the large circle, indicating his belief that these tasks will be automated.

Task G, Calculation of Quotes has been placed outside the circles on the basis that this would be moving into the realms of automatic trading, which is beyond the scope of this project.

Tasks P,T and Q are not proposed as candidates for automation because of their physical, perceptual and cognitive nature.

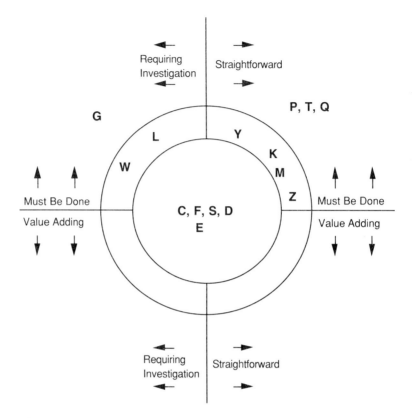

OFF-Line Tasks:-

A, B, I, J, N, R, U, V, X

G:- Might be automated if 'dealer position' and
Customer Knowledge were stored
and Product and Customer were input.

D, E:- Would alter if dealers were promoted
with page identifiers.

Figure 2.19 *DIchotomy Scoping Chart (DISC).*

As stated above, the positioning of tasks on a DISC is at the discretion of the analyst but it should be mediated through discussions with the client. Expected project costs, timescales and cost–benefit analyses will all moderate the analyst's proposals. Once a DISC has been generated the users/purchasers can be lobbied for their views. It is quite possible that they would modify the scope of the system dramatically. For instance, they might decide that K,L,W,Y and Z are not to be within the scope of the system, but Q (Pick-up Telephone) should be. Indeed, dealers might realise that handsets pose sufficient problems to warrant the introduction of headsets as worn by professional telephonists.

As can be seen, the present DISC shows no tasks below the horizontal dividing line. This is because in the case study we have not diversified into which new tasks might become a part of the system beyond those performed presently. For instance, background fact finding might identify the fact that automatic charting and chart analysis are feasible aims that would be of benefit. The provision of group financial positions in addition to individual or institution positions might be desirable. Composite paging allowing the tailoring of screens could also be attractive.

2.3.8 Problems/requirements list

Problems/requirements will have been listed in D202 (problems/requirements list) as evidence collection and analysis have progressed. None the less, it is worthwhile reviewing the raw evidence specifically for the purposes of identifying requirements. Even the smallest of problems may be indicative of requirements.

Reviewing the example observational record would identify the following requirements:

- need to have both hands free when talking to customers;
- better readability of prices;
- a source of addresses for clients.

Reviewing the THDs would identify the following:

- a means of quickly recording the details of a deal in a way that is 'undo-able' but could contribute to a definitive record;
- minimum of visual obstructions between dealers;
- accessing prices should not require memorising page numbers.

Reviewing the context tables would identify the following requirements:

- screen glare must be minimised;
- rationalise keyboard requirements;
- dealer workplace should be designed with maintenance in mind;
- need a macro facility for the production of hardcopy;
- a function for calculating the number of banking days between two dates would be useful;
- some clear indication of how long since a screen was updated, as opposed to the actual time it was updated.

Some of the above, for example 'a macro facility for the production of hardcopy', may contribute to functional requirements in addition to purely user interfacing artifacts. The user requirements analysis is a valid source of functional requirements and as such there is little reason for omitting these requirements.

Newly identified requirements should be appended to the problems/requirements list (D202). This should cross-reference to the source of the requirement and also to its status. By status is meant the client's consideration of the requirement. Status indicators might include mandatory, highly desirable, desirable and not required.

2.3.9 Usability

During Step 202 a list of usability issues will have been generated. These issues can now be re-addressed in the light of the task analysis. Indeed, new issues may have arisen as a result of the analysis and these should be appended to the usability issues document. At this step the issues should be translated into targets and criteria. The context data attached to the THDs provide some baseline usability measures for the current system, but the interview transcripts and observational findings from Step 202 should be reviewed for further data. Where it is known that data is required but has not beeen obtained, then users and other sources must be canvassed for this data.

The five categories of usability that are most often considered are Productivity, Learnability, User satisfaction, Memorability and Errors (PLUME). Data pertinent to productivity and errors should certainly have been collected through observational analysis. Special effort may be required to collect data on the other three categories. Any formal/informal training given, documentation read, and advice sought will provide data relevant to learnability. Memorability of the present system may be a little difficult to assess, but the analyst might consider arranging observational sessions with individuals returning from vacation or others who have recently changed roles. The volume of user complaints can be used as an indicator of user satisfaction, but rating scales should be considered where this issue is of particular importance to the client.

It should not be forgotten that different categories of usability will be more or less important depending on the type of system under consideration. Indeed, categories over and above the main five may be most pertinent on occasions. In the financial dealing room case study, speed of task performance would, without doubt, be the most important issue but a further usability category might be data relevance. For instance, a cable dealer may have little or no interest in foreign exchange rates except those that involve the dollar or the pound. A non-specialist foreign exchange dealer would find all major exchange rates of interest. Thus to increase the relevance of data, special provision could be made for cable dealers. By so doing, the usability of the system would be enhanced as measured by a data relevancy metric.

It is important to bear in mind that the categories of usability will contribute to business objectives. For instance, the fictitious bank in the case study might have a business objective of improving the quality of its service. The bank might also aim to offer a quote on any foreign exchange transaction, however exotic. Customer requests are likely to be re-routed at least once. Quality of service might thus be judged by how often a customer request is re-routed. The usability of any call transfer mechanism would therefore be central to quality of service. For a transfer mechanism to be usable, the operator (dealer) must have adequate information to hand, i.e. who deals in Portuguese escudos? Usability here would be judged on both speed of task performance and data availability/relevance.

Examples of usability issues with accompanying data and targets are provided in Table 2.4, which also provides a reference to the source of the issue and includes baseline data on the present situation with regard to the issue and the impact of the problem from a business perspective. The target column gives as accurate an assessment as possible of a reasonable and desirable measure for the usability of a new system with regard to each issue. Some of these targets may have been set by the client or proposed by the analyst. These targets could be classified as criteria under circumstances where the client has determined that they be a part of a binding contract. For instance, the failure rate quoted for keyboards is a mandatory requirement and as such the target of < 1 failure per month is a usability criteria.

Table 2.4 *Usability issues*

Issue	Source	Baseline/ qualifier	Problem (business)	Target	Comments
Errors (in documenting deals)	ITT	2 in 1000 Experienced dealer, foreign exchange	Loss of custom, expensive	1 in 10 000	Determine location of errors
Speed (of quoting)	ITT	Mean = 30 secs Mode = 25 secs Experienced dealer, foreign exchange	Missing business (belief)	Mean = 25 secs Mode = 20 secs	Desirable
Learnability	Interviews 6,12	Takes a trainee 10 days before he doesn't have to refer to Crib cards	Too slow, losing business	Trainee up to speed in one day and not at the cost of business	Could require a self-teach system. Mandatory
Durability (of keyboards)	Interview 17	1 keyboard per week fails	Expensive, including on-site maintenance engineer	<1 keyboard failure per month	Mandatory

Issue	Source	Baseline/ qualifier	Problem (business)	Target	Comments
Durability (of monitors)	Maintenance log	Life expectancy of monitors is 8 months, due to scratching	Costs £250 000 p.a.	Life expectancy of 18 months	Annual saving of £150 000. Mandatory
Disuse of services	Interviews 18,23	Cost of service is >£40M p.a. Sold on a per page basis	Volume of trade cannot withstand this expenditure	Reduce costs of services by 10%	Find a means to reduce number of pages accessed by >10%. Highly desirable
User dissatis-faction	Dealing room manager	Complaints that other banks provide dealers with better systems	Staff unsettled	Provide state-of-the-art system	Would require A3 size screens
Poor information	ITT	Bank position is at least one hour out of date	Occasional over exposure	Reduce time lag to less than 5 minutes	Likely to require on-line deal capture

2.3.10 Step summary

At the end of Step 203 the analyst should have an optimised list of KRG sentences and THDs. These will have been cross-checked by the analyst who will have assured himself or herself that they are complete.

Task analysis (Step 203) provides a perspective on the requirements of a planned interactive system development that would not be provided by a traditional system analysis. The THDs provide a representation of tasks that will be indispensable for the design of interactive dialogues. In addition, the THDs provide a basis for the production of training and documentation materials that would otherwise be ill-founded. The action and object lists will provide a basis for naming and grouping commands and their parameters. TACs can be used to investigate possible job implications at an early and cost effective stage of a project. DISCs can be used to refine the scope of the developments. Taken in conjunction with the usability data, developments can be prioritised on the basis of costs and benefits.

The various products of task analysis should be documented. These will include the following:

W203a: task hierarchy diagrams (THDs);
W203b: knowledge representation grammar sentences (KRGs);
W203c: action list;
W203d: object list;
W203e: context data.

In addition, the analysis may have generated the following:

W203f: dichotomy scoping charts (DISCs);
W203g: task allocation charts.

Task analysis will probably have resulted in additions being made to the following:

W202: usability issues;
D202: problems/requirements list.

2.4 **Validation (Step 204)**

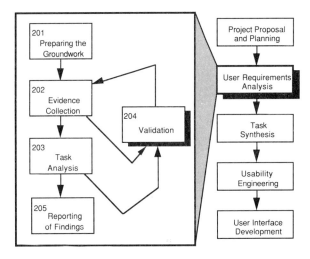

Validation (Step 204).

Validation is an integral part of user requirements analysis. Validation ensures that the deliverables from user requirements analysis, especially the task analyses as understood by the analyst, are both accurate and complete. This section discusses the validation that should take place during user requirements analysis.

Validation should not be thought of as a step that happens following evidence collection (Step 202) and task analysis (Step 203). Validation is an on-going process during these steps.

2.4.1 Validation techniques

During evidence collection the analyst will be continuously confirming present understanding. This requires skill on the part of the analyst. For instance, during interviewing it is not sufficient to ask the same questions repeatedly; this would only elicit the same or similar responses repeatedly. The analyst should re-frame questions in order that the interviewee can generalise or exemplify in new ways. Confirmation of understanding can also be facilitated by the use of scenarios. This requires the analyst to create and describe realistic circumstances and then invite interviewees to explain the actions they would take.

Question re-framing and scenario generation are validation strategies that are often taken for granted by experienced analysts. For the less experienced they are powerful techniques that need to be learned and practised. By so doing, analysts can build up repertoires with which they feel comfortable.

Validation can also be performed during observational analyses. The skill of the analyst will help him or her to decide when to interject in order to confirm or falsify understanding. When a lull exists in an observee's work the analyst might probe the reasoning behind actions taken, decisions made and mental tasks performed.

As evidence collection progresses the analyst should seek to identify areas where misinterpretation may have occurred or where understanding is sketchy. While anomalies will need to be clarified, the analyst needs to bundle questions together rather than continuously interrupt users. If sessions with users have been completed in an open manner, then it should be non-problematic to arrange further meetings for purposes of validation and clarification. It is often worth generating diagrams that depict your understanding and walking users through the diagrams, asking outstanding questions en route. In this way the user has an opportunity to identify your misunderstandings. In addition, the use of an alternative medium, such as graphics, to compliment the spoken word often aids communication.

During task analysis (Step 203) the representation techniques employed provide ways to identify inconsistencies and anomalies. For instance, the THDs and KRG sentences provide counterpoints, as do TACs and DISCs. It is not recommended that THDs or KRG sentences be presented to users for criticism. Users are often reticient to spend time in understanding notations that analysts are employing to facilitate their own understanding. TACs and DISCs should be discussed with clients. TACs do not need to be understood in depth for users/clients to comment upon them. Indeed, the analyst can step users through them with little or no explanation of the notation.

Wherever possible, and certainly at points where the analyst feels that representations (THDs, KRG sentences, TACs, DISCs) are complete and accurate, peer reviews should be sought. In this way an independent critique of the findings can be performed prior to making presentations to the client. Peer reviews can have a shorter turnaround time than client presentations. Thus they can foreshorten the validation process by rectifying many inaccuracies quickly.

It is vital that walkthroughs are arranged and agreements are obtained. Analysis should not proceed to Stage 3 until both the analyst and client are happy with the scope of the work performed and with the initial findings and conclusions reached. Walkthroughs should be conducted with a suitable audience and set of materials. The audience must include both users and clients with executive powers. The walk-throughs should overview the work performed and concentrate on the crucial aspects of tasks and the usability problems encountered. They should also cover the agreements reached regarding task allocation and usability targets.

2.4.2 Step summary

Validation is an on-going process throughout user requirements analysis. It is all too easy for analysts working to difficult deadlines to assume that their understanding is complete and accurate. Because the deliverables from analysis are crucial to design, and to the ultimate success of a project, it is important that the analysis is not concluded until analysis findings are validated. A number of techniques are offered to help with this process. Each of these techniques requires users to act as reviewers of the analyst's work. As a result analysts must be prepared to modify their understanding and their documentation.

2.5 Reporting of findings (Step 205)

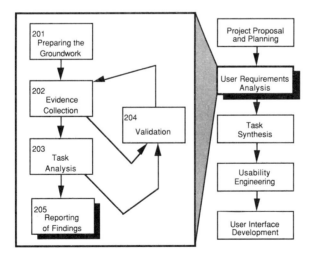

Reporting of findings (Step 205).

The culmination of Stage 2 is the documentation of the user requirements analysis findings. This documentation will be the main input to the next stage and as such must be self-explanatory and unambiguous.

2.5.1 Documentation

The major document is the user requirements analysis report (W205). This brings together all the deliverables from the user requirements analysis. Prior to producing this report, all working papers should have been updated in accordance with all decisions resulting from such exercises as walkthroughs. All material should include cross-references to sources.

The report should include all the major products from this stage. This document is for the use of those responsible for Stage 2 of the development, as distinct from the client directly. All the raw evidence should be indexed, collated and presented as an appendix to the user requirements analysis report. The reason for holding the raw evidence is that the task analysis findings may still refer to the raw evidence and the report should support the traceability of inferences and conclusions. The report should be self-explanatory and should stand alone. A suggested contents list for this report is given below:

1. scope of the analysis;
2. task hierarchy diagrams;
3. context tables;
4. KRG sentences;
5. problems/requirements list;
6. object list;
7. action list;
8. usability issues/criteria;
9. appendix, raw evidence.

A second report must be produced for the client (D205). This deliverable is a direct sub-set of the complete report comprising the following sections:

1. scope of the analysis;
2. task hierarchy diagrams;
3. problems/requirements list;
4. usability issues/criteria;
(5. DISCs and TACs).

The intention is not one of withholding information from clients but, rather, one of not overloading clients with irrelevant, (from their perspective) information.

2.5.2 Step summary

Many days of effort may have been expended on user requirements analysis. To ensure that this effort is worth while, the findings must be fully documented.

2.6 Stage summary

User requirements analysis as described in this chapter incorporates many techniques and notations for analysing and documenting user requirements. These requirements are substantially different from those associated with systems analysis as they major on usability requirements. They are documented such that user interface design can be undertaken in a well-informed manner.

Further reading

Diaper, D. (ed.) (1989). *Task Analysis for Human–Computer Interaction*. Chichester: Ellis Horwood (a mixed collection of papers that provides a good introduction to task analysis).

3   Task synthesis (Stage 3)

In user requirements analysis, evidence was collected regarding the user interfacing and usability requirements of the intended users of the system. This provided a user-oriented perspective on requirements by documenting the tasks that need to be supported at the user interface. In Stage 3, task synthesis, the evidence and requirements are transformed into a user interface design for the intended system. This design will provide a well-reasoned starting point for the evaluation that will take place in Stage 4.

Task synthesis provides a user interface design that is documented using example screen layouts and rules of interface syntax and style. This design is then specified in a notation based on state transition diagrams and subsequently evaluated. During this stage all user documentation is designed and a style guide for the interface is documented. These deliverables are produced by applying best practice together with techniques and notations.

There are five steps in Stage 3. *Task synthesis* (Step 301) is the transformation of the deliverables from Stage 2 into a design for the interactive aspects of the system. This transformation is facilitated by a number of heuristics based on best practice. *Style guide* (Step 302) discusses the design options available, such as window management, and provides guidance on how a particular style can be determined. The design is specified using a notation based on state transition networks during *Design specification* (Step 303). *User support* (Step 304) addresses the requirements for documentation to accompany the system. This can take many forms including hardcopy manuals, on-line help/tutorials and training. The specifications for both the user interface and the documentation are then submitted to *Formative evaluation* (Step 305) prior to the development of a prototype in Stage 4. In this way the specifications themselves can be evaluated and rectified more cost effectively than could inadequacies identified following development.

The relationship between these steps are portrayed in Figure 3.1.

STAGE 3: Task Synthesis

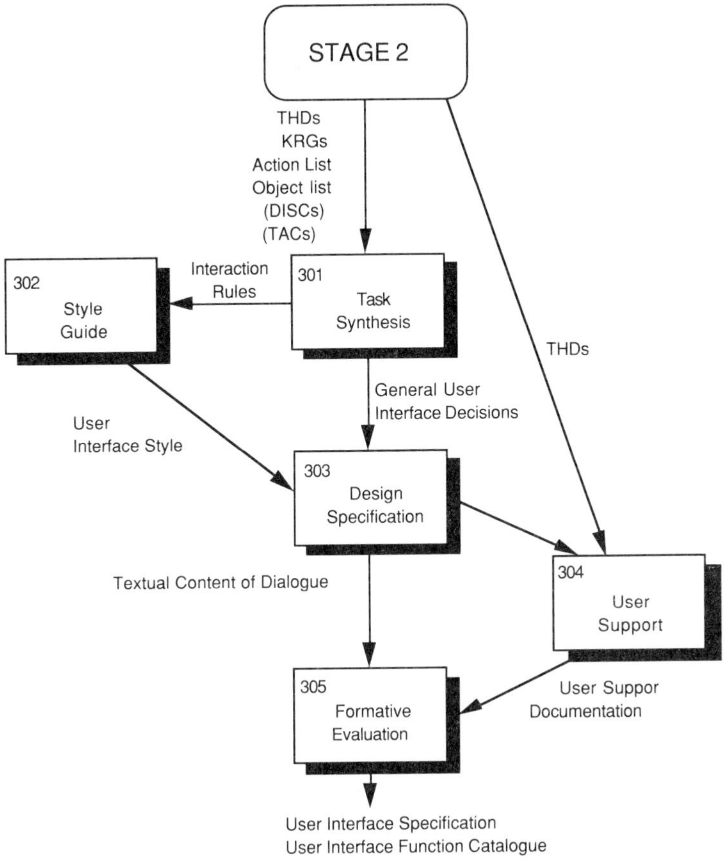

Deliverables

General UI Decisions (D301)
User Interface Style (D302)
Textual Content of the Dialogue (D303)
User Support Documentation (D304)
UI Specification (D305a)
UI Function Catalogue (D305b)

Working Papers

User Requirements Documentation (W304a)
Timetable (W304b)
User Support: Logical Design (W304c)

Figure 3.1 *Overview of Stage 3.*

3.1 Task synthesis (Step 301)

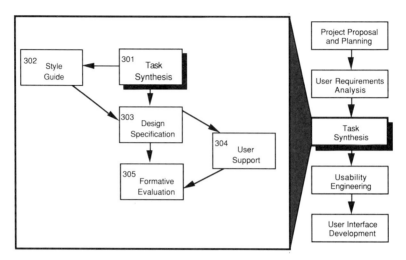

Task synthesis (Step 301).

The objective of this step is to convert the analysis findings into a user interface design. By taking the task hierarchy diagrams, knowledge representation grammar sentences, dichotomy scoping charts, task allocation charts and context information, the basic structure of the design can be produced. In Step 303, 'Design specification', this basic structure will be specified using a suitable notation.

Within task synthesis the designer will:

- determine and document dialogue sequences;
- produce some example screen layouts for validation purposes;
- determine the interface syntax;
- make decisions regarding the style of the interface.

The above are achieved by following a sequence of processes. Firstly, the designer must generate outline designs for the tasks deemed most crucial for the success of the system. A PLUME analysis is performed on these tasks in order for the designer to be reminded of the usability targets that need to be satisfied. Design is then undertaken by first deciding how the dialogue should be partitioned between screen areas or windows. A number of heuristics are provided to help the designer with this exercise. The design is further developed by recourse to the task hierarchy diagrams. The outline designs generated are then assessed in terms of their likely usability and practicality. If they are found to be unsuitable or inadequate, then new designs are generated until satisfactory designs, in terms of usability and task support, are determined. Many design alternatives may need to be generated before the designer can feel assured of the suitability of any one set of designs.

These outline designs provide a basis for drawing general conclusions regarding the entire user interface design. These conclusions include user interface syntax rules, command language, formats for windows, relationships between windows, interface behaviour under exceptional circumstances and user interface style implications. All these implications are documented. The design is then completed for all tasks.

The process of task synthesis is explained below by reference to the dealing room example.

3.1.1 Generate alternative outline designs

Task synthesis is one of the most difficult steps in user interface design. Designers must gain an appreciation for the complete set of user requirements and must remain objective and not make decisions on the basis of what they feel they would want but, rather, on what the user would benefit from. The first few decisions made in the design process can be the most critical. Design suffers from a primacy effect whereby early decisions are resistant to change. Thus it is advisable for designers not to rush into decisions but, rather, to keep an open mind for as long as possible.

Identify crucial tasks
The beginnings of a design should focus on those aspects which are most crucial. Thus the most frequently performed tasks or the most business-critical tasks should be considered first. If suitable designs can be provided for these, then it becomes easier to make subsequent decisions that fit into a basic framework and are consistent.

The most frequently performed tasks are identified from the contextual information contained within the task hierarchy diagrams. The relative importance of tasks may be assessed, if necessary, by asking users. A pair matching exercise can be used if users find it difficult to assess relative importance. Pair matching requires the designer to ask users, for pairs of tasks, which task is most important (possibly in terms of personal effectiveness or business objectives). The designer should take account of the task allocation decisions that have been made as documented on the DIchotomy Scoping Charts (DISCs), otherwise important tasks might be missed.

Design cannot be proceduralised to the extent that you put in the ingredients, turn the handle and out comes a perfect specification. Therefore, very little time should be spent on the initial designs. Ideas should be pushed as far as possible until they are found to be inadequate. Where changes can be made to the design which solve the inadequacy, all well and good. Where any changes to the design are still going to be found wanting it is worth *going back to the drawing board*, so to speak.

Initial design ideas will have to be validated with the client and systems people for practicality. This is another reason for not spending too much time on refining a design in the first instance. For example, the design might require a 20″ screen for it to be practical in terms of readability. If, for other reasons, this is an impractical technical option, then the design will have to be re-engineered.

The following advice should be applied during task synthesis:

■ Scope the initial design in terms of the most crucial (in business terms), or frequent, tasks.

■ Do not spend very long on generating initial design ideas. It is important that they are *correct* eventually, but in the early stages the best way of ensuring this is to investigate alternatives and keep an open mind, rather than focus quickly on an outline design and make it *work*.

■ Check initial thoughts with the design team and client for their practicality.

■ Keep the design simple to begin with.

Having scoped the work in terms of the most crucial tasks, initial design can commence. The objective at this point is to produce something that can be assessed, however crudely, for practicality and required usability. As stated above, decisions made at this point can set a precedent for everything that follows and should be taken with care and in the light of available understanding. Pre-conceived ideas should not play a role in determining the way forward.

Perform PLUME analysis

A PLUME analysis sets usability targets for selected tasks. Such an analysis should be applied to the crucial tasks listed above in order to identify important considerations before starting the design. In this way the usability objectives can be kept in mind. A PLUME analysis as applied to the dealing room scenario, specifically the task GIVE A QUOTE, might be something like the following:

> Productivity: the design must allow dealers to give a quote quickly; in fact in less than 18 seconds. The institution as a whole aims to give dealers more up-to-date information which should enhance their trading margins.

> Learnability: dealers are not accustomed to using a mouse. Experience shows that professional users become fluent with a mouse in a matter of minutes.

> User satisfaction: the design should be comparable to new installations at other dealing rooms such that favourable comparisons can be made.

> Memorability: dealers are full-time system users. Mnemonics abound in this environment. If a *point and click* rather than a *remember and type style* of dialogue is produced, then improvements in memorability and use of functionality can be expected.

> Errors: these must be kept to a minimum. The designer should be careful not to make data input so easy that dealers do not check their work. Redundancy could be built in as a way of checking the accuracy but dealers do tend to be impatient and may be unwilling to supply more data than is strictly necessary.

A PLUME analysis lays a groundwork of targets and guiding lights that might otherwise be overlooked during the design.

Investigate logical division of screen real-estate

The most salient aspect of any user interface design is ultimately the division of the screen into reserved areas. This is often referred to as the question of *screen real-estate* because space is often a premium given the amount of data that the user may require to see at any one moment. People have likened this usability issue to trying to read *The Financial Times* through a keyhole.

It may seem that such presentational matters should not be the starting piont for a design. This misses the point that the separation into logical screen areas is based on user requirements. Superficial aspects of screen management and layout are not being considered yet. At this point the driving forces for the design are the task requirements for input and output from the computer system. The task hierarchy diagrams have captured the required sequencing of operations performed by the user and their requirements for information.

For most developments the designer will be expecting to provide a windowed interface and should thus begin by fleshing out what information should be in distinct windows and which windows might be open at the same time. The designer should not leap to the immediate conclusion that a windowed interface should be provided without first considering whether a character-based, form-filling or question–answer style dialogue would be sufficient. It is best to begin with as simple a set of interface widgets as possible and then build on these until the need and benefit of more complicated widgets, such as windows, accelerators, etc., can be established.

Where (sub)tasks have intrinsic parallelism, then it is likely that benefit can be gained from a windowed interface. Where both the supply and retrieval of information are entwined, then windows can often help to clarify the logical divisions.

In the dealing room example, traders have to both document their deals and make those deals on the basis of both recently acquired information and stored data in a highly dependent fashion. This is why dealers record deals on scraps of paper as they go along. This parallelism suggests that dealers could benefit from a windowed interface. In fact, to all intents and purposes most dealers already have a windowed interface, in that they have access to different information displayed on up to four screens. Of course, this is not windowing in the true sense because the operation of each screen is completely independent.

Application of the following heuristics help the designer to select data groups as candidates for implementation as windows:

- Given a task, what group of data items would constitute the set of inputs for the purpose of executing that task? Such a set would be a candidate to be grouped and implemented as a window.
- Identify each point in the task at which the user's knowledge of the task increases such that the user could supply some new data item to the system. On receiving these data would it be feasible for the system to display some task-related data items or perform some useful function and display the results? If so, then this generated data set is a candidate for implementation as a window.
- Identify each point in the dialogue at which the user has to make a decision. The information required by the user for a decision to be made is a candidate for implementation as a window.
- Input data and system output can be placed in separate windows, although default values might be offered in an input data window.

■ Textual messages such as Help, errors, and warnings should be given separate windows.

By way of example these heuristics will be applied to the task of GIVE A QUOTE.

Applying the first heuristic to the task hierarchy diagrams in Figures 3.2 and 3.3 identifies that the dealer inputs a number of pieces of data to the existing computer system. The dealer can, on occasion supply a screen, service and page identifier, and also record details of the deal on a scrap of paper. These notes are later transcribed to a deal ticket for transfer to a clerk. Documenting of deals is to be performed on-line in the new system (as shown as DISCs). By examining the results (D204a) of the forms analysis on a deal ticket we would find that dealers provide the following data:

> screen, service and page identifiers, customer identifier, product quote, buy/ sell, time, size of deal and signature.

The analyst should now remove from the list all those data items that are system imposed rather than related to the task specifically. These data items are screen, service and page identifiers. These are only on the list as a consequence of the present system's implementation. The rest of the items on the list constitute a possible data set for a window:

> screen, service and page identifiers, customer identifier, product, quote, buy/sell, time, size of deal and signature.

Applying the second heuristic identifies the following sub-tasks as rendering the dealer better informed:

> Identify source of Request > Customer
> Ascertain Product > Product
> Read Information > Price
> Ascertain Size of Deal > Size of Deal

For each of Customer, Product, Price and Size of Deal can the system supply any useful information or perform a function and present results?

For Customer the system might identify trading limits and previous deals.

For a Product the system can provide Prices from different data vendors (i.e. Reuters and Telerate), possibly showing historical trends.

Given the Price, the system could offer alternative Quotes on the Product.

Size of Deal can be used for very little. None the less, this and all the above inferences can and should be verified with dealers.

Applying the third heuristic identifies two points in the task at which decisions are necessary. Namely, Calculate a Quote and Accept Deal/Refuse Deal.

> Calculate Quote > Quote
> Accept Deal/Refuse Deal

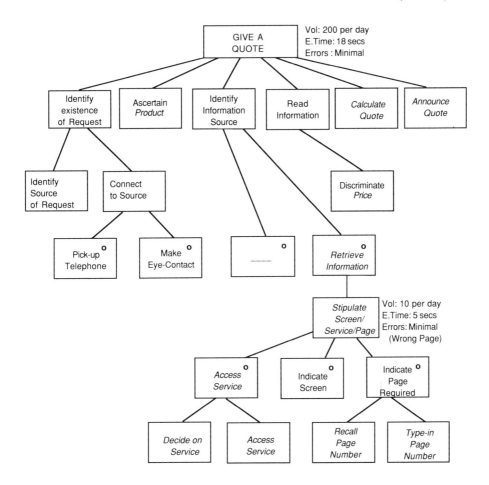

CONTEXT INFORMATION:
   If you are too slow in quoting, then the customer will take his or her business elsewhere. More importantly, (s)he may not give you future business either.
   Dealers are physically grouped by specification.
   If you make an obviously inaccurate quote the customer will simply go away (sniggering).
   Always difficult to know whether a screen has been updated lately

Figure 3.2 *Task hierarchy diagram for 'GIVE A QUOTE'.*

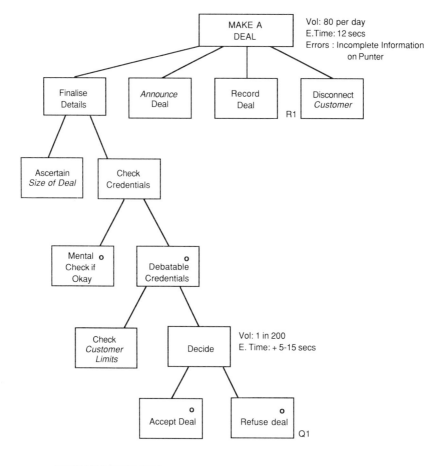

Figure 3.3 *Task hierarchy diagram for 'MAKE A DEAL'.*

By cross-checking with the knowledge representation grammar sentences the designer can identify the information required to make these decisions. For Quote, the dealer needs data on Price, Customer and his Own Position. These are a candidate set of data items for a window.

For Accept Deal and Refuse Deal the determining factor is the Customer's Limits. This alone could be displayed as a window.

Taken together we now have candidate windows for the following:

- input of the deal (heuristic: a) DEAL RECORD,
- display of customer details (heuristic: b) CUSTOMER DETAILS,
- display of product details (heuristic: b) PRODUCT DETAILS,
- display possible quotes (heuristic b) POSSIBLE QUOTES,
- display of price (for a product), Customer details, and Own Position (heuristic: c) QUOTE FACTORS,
- display Customer Limits (heuristic c) CUSTOMER LIMITS.

For ease of explanation the candidate windows have been labelled as shown in upper case. The above list includes some data duplication across windows. For instance, the QUOTE FACTORS window is an amalgam of data from other candidate windows. This might be legitimate and useful but duplication of data across windows should be questioned.

Generate outline designs

The designer's experience plays a major role at this point. Because the analysis and design activities thus far have created an abstract view of the required system, albeit based on the existing system, and the technical limitations of the old system are not considered as constraining the new design, a radically new system can result. The experience of the designer and the user-centred approach taken thus far steer the design towards a task supportive conclusion rather than a data and function oriented conclusion.

The analyst should now 'walk' through the task hierarchy diagrams for the crucial tasks, (i.e. GIVE A QUOTE) to determine when the candidate windows might be displayed. In the dealing room example the designer might take the stance that the dealer will simply input Customer, Product and a request for his Own Position into the system as and when required. An alternative is for the dealer to begin inputting the deal specifically as the task progresses. This latter scenario is better aligned with the dealer's objective of completing a deal and the agreed requirement that dealing take place on-line. Thus the first window (DEAL RECORD) could be a version of the original deal ticket (Figure 3.4) with fields for Customer, Product, Quote, Size of Deal, Buy/Sell, Date, Time, and Signature. At this point considerations of how the dealer will provide input to the system are ignored.

On input of a Customer identifier, we have established that a number of details about the customer could be displayed automatically by the system in a window (CUSTOMER DETAILS).

Next the dealer becomes aware of the Product concerned in the deal. The system can use this information to provide Prices and possibly other information on the Product in a window (PRODUCT DETAILS). (This would replace all the sub-tasks required by the present system for accessing information pages, from particular services on particular screens.) The dealer can then read the Price(s) for the Product before Calculating a Quote. It is known, from the knowledge representation grammar sentences, that to Calculate a Quote the dealer requires access to data on his Own

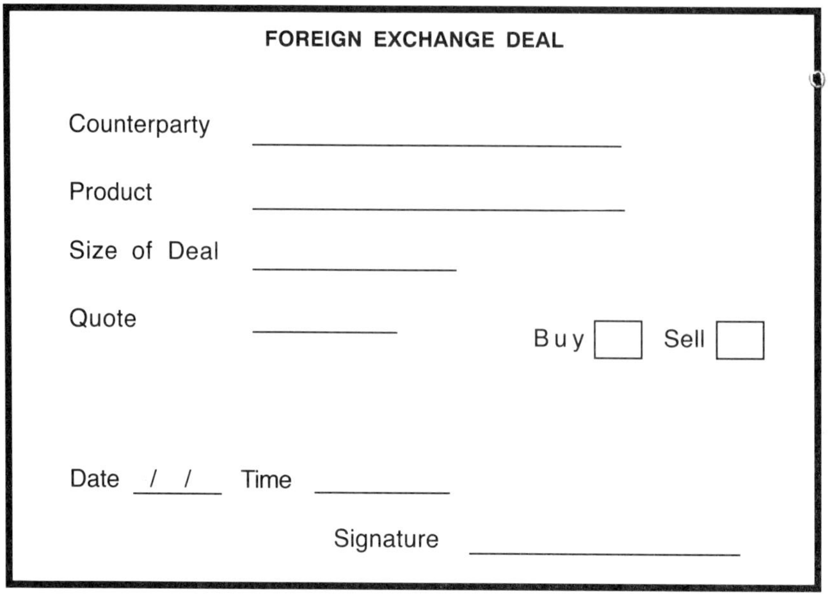

```
┌─────────────────────────────────────────────────────────┐
│               FOREIGN EXCHANGE DEAL                      │
│                                                          │
│     Counterparty      _____        │
│                                                          │
│     Product           _____        │
│                                                          │
│     Size of Deal      _____                     │
│                                                          │
│     Quote             _____                         │
│                                       Buy [   ]  Sell [   ]│
│                                                          │
│                                                          │
│     Date  /  /   Time  _____                        │
│                                                          │
│                  Signature   _____        │
│                                                          │
└─────────────────────────────────────────────────────────┘
```

Figure 3.4 *Deal ticket format.*

Position, as well as Customer data and the Product's present Price. The latter two pieces of data have already been displayed but a 'trigger' is needed to show the dealer's Own Position. Given that Own Position does not change throughout TRADING A PRODUCT it could be displayed any time from the beginning of the task prior to Calculating a Quote. The suggestion is to display it at the beginning of the task unless other factors, such as lack of screen space, precludes this.

The idea of displaying possible quotes (give a Price) in a window (POSSIBLE QUOTES) was also posited. This could be useful anytime before Calculate Quote and after the Product Price has been determined. A design might consider amalgamating this with the PRODUCT DETAILS window. In the present example the designer chooses not to include such a window. An alternative window (QUOTE FACTORS) to help with Calculate Quote was suggested. Given that all factors contributing to a Quote are already displayed, there seems little point in displaying it again. Should further good reasons for collating this data into a single window be found, then this decision might be reversed.

Finally, the Size of Deal is given to the dealer. It was determined that Customer details (Limits) contribute to the tasks of Accept Deal and Refuse Deal. Again this information should already be on-screen in the CUSTOMER DETAILS window so there seems little point in re-presenting it. Later, the designer might consider ways of drawing the dealer's attention to customers who are *lining* (dealing beyond their agreed limits). The system could do this on the basis of the Size of Deal and Customer Limits.

The above procedure has succeeded in generating a possible design requiring four windows, namely, CUSTOMER DETAILS, PRODUCT DETAILS, DEAL RECORD and OWN POSITION. This design has been based on task allocation, required system functionality (DISCs) and usability targets as produced in Stage 2. It has also mapped out how and when these windows will appear. This dialogue is depicted in Figures 3.5–3.8.

A design produced without recourse to the findings of user requirements analysis would almost certainly generate something completely different. In all likelihood one of the windows would be a replica of the FXFX screen (Figure 3.9) which holds a lot of redundant data.

3.1.2 Assess alternative designs

Assess suitability of outline design with regard to usability
The task hierarchy diagrams and accompanying contextual information provide evidence as to how quickly the dealer would have to GIVE A QUOTE and MAKE A DEAL, remembering that, at present, deals are recorded on scraps of paper. An

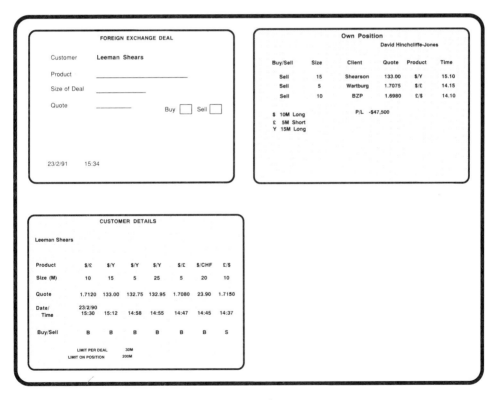

Figure 3.5 *Example Screen A.*

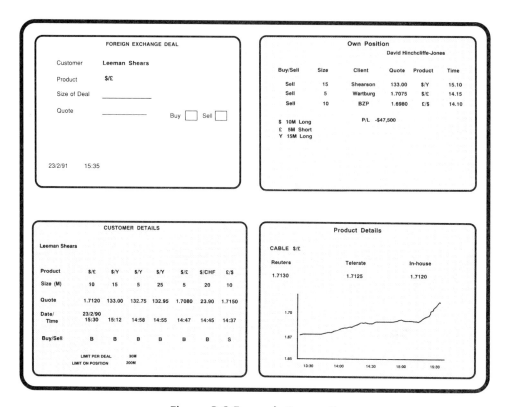

Figure 3.6 *Example Screen B.*

on-line version of this task would have to be as quick if not quicker in operation. In total, quoting a deal and making a deal normally takes about 30 seconds to complete up to the point that it is recorded formally. This time span should not increase with the introduction of the new system and, in fact, the usability issues document (W202) has stipulated a target of 25 seconds. The designer would need to assure himself or herself that this target is not unreasonable given the design. Thus the time required to note the Customer, Product, and Size of Deal, and to communicate with the customer and access the required information and calculate a quote should take five seconds less than it does with the present system. This raises the question of where this saving is going to be made. Possibilities include: data entry/recording should be quicker; information accessing and discrimination should be quicker; or calculating should be quicker. Working through the task hierarchy diagrams, the designer may decide that the dealer, given appropriate *point and click* facilities could record the identity of the Customer and the Product as the Customer's request is being communicated. It is not unreasonable to expect that a point and click interface could be used rapidly and synchronously while talking on the telephone. For a portion of deals the dealer will not have to stipulate screens, services or pages, thus a saving in time should be

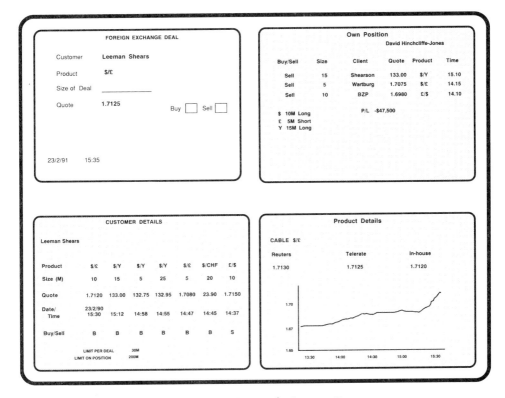

Figure 3.7 *Example Screen C.*

forthcoming. By reducing data redundancy, discrimination time should be decreased. All usability factors should be assessed as far as is possible before the design progresses any further. In this way major usability limitations can be addressed early on.

Assess the practicality of the design

Little effort should have been expended by the designer up to this point in generating what is a very superficial design. Stopping at this stage and reviewing the practicality of this design inevitably identifies issues that require further investigation. For instance, on the deal ticket there is a field for the dealer's signature. This is not easily captured electronically, although it is feasible using a bitpad. A second example is the collation of data from different vendors in the PRODUCT DETAILS window. This is desirable in order to increase the information content (reduce the redundant information). None the less, it may require some quite sophisticated software that takes video signals and then filters out or filters in only those items of data that are required. Practical difficulties such as these show how consideration of what is required at the user interface can create requirements for what might be thought to be interface-independent aspects of the system. Thus close liaison between system

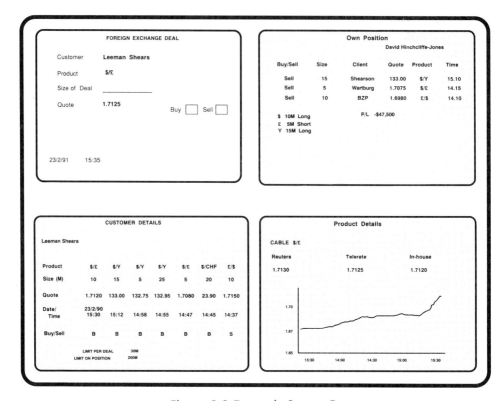

Figure 3.8 *Example Screen D.*

analysts/software designers and user interface designers is crucial during task synthesis.

Solutions may exist for these practical problems. For instance, signatures might be captured by using a bitpad, or by using locally produced hardcopy of a deal ticket. Alternatively, a sort of personal identification scheme might have to be introduced. A composite paging facility could be introduced for the problem of collating vendor data.

Where the design is impractical, the designer will have to make amendments. Depending on the extent of the inadequacies the designer could have to backtrack as far as the generation of outline designs.

Re-apply PLUME analysis

The design should now be re-submitted to a PLUME analysis. This will identify design inadequacies in terms of usability:

> Productivity: business productivity cannot be altered directly, although if dealing is quicker, then a higher percentage of requests should culminate in deals. The productivity of dealers in terms of providing faster quotes should be improved by 5 seconds. More up-to-date information will certainly be made available.

1533	CCY	PAGE	NAME *	REUTER	SPOT RATES *	PREV	HI*EURO*LO	FXFX
1532	DEM	CIEF	CITIBANK	FFT	1.8765/75	60/70	1.8855	1.8755
1532	GBP	CIBC	CAN IMPL	TOP	1.7135/45	35/45	1.7158	1.7065
1532	CHF	RBCM	ROYAL BK	TOR	1.5710/20	15/25	1.5790	1.5705
1533	JPY	CINY	CITIBANK	N.Y	132.90/00	85/95	133.35	132.85
1532	FRF	CINY	CITIBANK	N.Y	6.3655/85	40/90	6.3980	6.3600
1532	NLG	WMCE	NATWEST	LDN	2.1185/95	75/85	2.1275	2.1165
1532	ITL	WMCG	NATWEST	LDN	1392.50/3.50	00/00	1397.75	1392
1533	XEU	MGTX	MORGAN	N.Y	1.1087/92	86/92	1.1085	1.1040

US BUS INVENT +0.7

XAU	RNBG	432.60/433,10 * ED3	8.62/8.75 * FED	PREB * GOVA SEP
XAG	RNBG	6.80/6.82 * ED6	8.93/9.06 * 8.12-	8.12 * A 8414

T-BOND FROM LFDA

Figure 3.9 *Example FXFX screen.*

Learnability: the user might have to learn to use a mouse/bitpad and windows. This should not be a problem. The design has a good mapping between task objects and design objects.

User satisfaction: the design is state-of-the-art, utilising modern input devices and large display screens. With appropriate dealing room design, the whole workplace should look very professional and should contribute to user satisfaction.

Memorability: given that most of the interaction is to be prompted, this should not be an issue.

Errors: because dealers are usually choosing, rather than generating, data, errors should be reduced. None the less, care should be taken in designing the syntactic elements of the interface to ensure that the speed of interaction does not lead to errors.

Any shortcomings of the design with respect to usability should be documented for later discussion with developers and client. Where it is thought that re-design could ameliorate these difficulties, then the designer may consider unwinding the design, possibly to the point of generating new outline designs.

Document new functional requirements

New functional requirements, as identified in preceding sections, should be documented. These can then be presented to the system designers and software developers for consideration given all cost and usability implications.

An example of a new functional requirement, taken from the dealing room example, would be a facility for composite paging to support the PRODUCT DETAILS window. This new facility would permit data to be retrieved from different information sources and then to be displayed in a single window.

3.1.3 Draw general conclusions

At this point the designer needs to be satisfied that the outline design is both practical and likely to meet the usability targets. The design should not progress further until such reassurances have been obtained. Where the designer is not confident that the usability criteria can be met, then the client should be informed and requested to relax the usability criteria.

A distinction can be made between the syntactic and semantic elements of a design. Syntax is the device-dependent knowledge required of a user. Examples of syntax are the application of menus and the accessing of windows. Look and feel guidelines address some of the syntactic issues of an interface, laying down rules to be followed in order to attain a consistent design. Because syntax can be relatively arbitrary, engendering a design with a consistent syntax can be helpful, especially for the novice user who has to learn a system's syntax by rote and practice. In general, the syntax of a design should be as follows:

- describable by as few rules as possible; ideally the syntax should become second nature to the user;
- as objective as possible;
- based on consistent patterns.

The earlier steps of STUDIO have collated evidence that can now be used to render the syntax of a design less arbitrary than the simple application of a look and feel standard. The user requirements analysis has provided an abstract view of the sequence of operations for each task. The terminology of the workplace has also been captured as part of requirements analysis and will be used to label actions and objects in the design. Additionally, the various design options are assessed for suitability, including syntax.

Semantics can be subdivided into *computer semantics* and *task semantics*.

Computer semantics are often based on hardware, software and performance considerations. File storage structures and database relationships are examples of computer semantics. Such semantics should not be imposed on the user. Where such structures and relationships are an essential part of the interface, for purposes of organisation and navigation, then their manifestation should be based on what comes naturally to the user.

Task semantics are the user's understandings of tasks, the relationships between tasks, and the constraints on the accomplishment of tasks. These understandings have been captured during the user requirements analysis and have been the basis for the production of outline designs thus far.

The following procedures seek to help the designer to refine and stipulate the syntax and semantics of the interface.

Derive the command language

The designer should review the action list generated in the user requirements analysis and determine which of the actions will need to exist as operations at the user interface. Such a review, as applied to the case study, is shown in Table 3.1.

Table 3.1 *Action list re-visited*

Action–object pair	Requirement
ACCEPT Deal	Specific to DEAL RECORD window
ANNOUNCE Quote/Deal	Off–line
ASCERTAIN Product/Size of Deal/Customer	Off-line
CALCULATE Quote	Off-line. Supported by system; result is input to the system
CHECK Customer Limits/Credentials	Off-line. Supported by system, affects continuation of task
DECIDE Service	Redundant (at least for this task)
DISCONNECT Customer	Off-line
DISCRIMINATE Price	Off-line. Supported by system, efforts made to make this easy and error-free
FILL-IN Deal Ticket	Dedicated Input Window. Performed by providing data values
INDICATE Screen	Redundant
MAKE Eye contact	Off-line
OBTAIN Deal Ticket	Indicates start of task
PICK-UP Telephone	Off-line
PLACE Deal Ticket	Represents end of task cf. ACCEPT Deal
RECALL Page Number	Redundant
RECORD Deal	cf. FILL-IN Deal Ticket
REFUSE Deal	Extraordinary end of task. Converse of ACCEPT Deal
TYPE-IN Page number	Redundant
UPDATE Own Position	System Function

It can be seen from the table that many actions remain off-line. These are mainly concerned with using the telephone system, which is not a part of the designer's remit but was included in the user requirements analysis because it does impact task completion. Also, a number of actions have become redundant, although when all tasks are taken together these actions may need to exist. None the less, within the context of TRADE IN PRODUCT there is no requirement for actions relating to the specification of access paths to data values.

Action analysis as performed above should always identify actions for starting and finishing the task. The action OBTAIN Deal Ticket can be used as the trigger for indicating the start of TRADE IN PRODUCT. The designer may choose to modify the label for this action but, basically, the point at which an equivalent to the old deal ticket appears on-screen (cf. Figure 3.5) is the time at which the task begins. This action, or its equivalent, would be a candidate as a global menu option because a user may wish to begin this task at any moment during interaction. Similarly, there should always be an action that signifies the end of the task. In this case there are three such actions. ACCEPT Deal and PLACE Deal Ticket both signify that the Deal is to terminate. These two actions will be treated synonymously in the new system. An extraordinary termination action also exists called REFUSE Deal. This is the converse of ACCEPT Deal and the design should take account of this congruence. These are all the actions that need to be implemented as system operations. UPDATE Own Position is to be performed by the system on the basis of the deals progressed to completion.

The design needs to include a means for the user to ACCEPT Deal and REFUSE Deal, each of which are specific to the DEAL RECORD window and terminate the task. Rather than use the label REFUSE Deal, the designer might choose the label CANCEL Deal as this is more congruent with ACCEPT Deal. The analysis has shown that the command language for TRADE IN PRODUCT requires just these three operations.

Determine the interface syntax

The designer should now develop a syntax to support the command language. The syntax should be kept as simple as possible, simplicity being judged by how many rules are required in order to explain the syntax.

Among the issues for which rules may have to be produced are the following:

- access to menus;
- picking from menus;
- input of data (validation and prompting);
- error/warning provision;
- listener window indication;
- scrolling.

Access to menus

Actions that are obviously attached to a window should be specific to that window. For instance, CANCEL Deal (neé REFUSE Deal) and ACCEPT Deal are specific to the DEAL RECORD window. Global menus may be provided for actions that have window-independent meaning. For instance, a command for indicating the start of TRADE IN PRODUCT (cf. OBTAIN Deal Ticket) is required. This might be offered as an option on a global menu such as a menu bar. Examples of global operations are often those with file management, access to applications and general functions such as 'screen refresh'. Thus example syntax rules might be as follows:

- *Actions that are task-independent or invoke tasks will be accessed via a menu bar.*
- *Actions specific to a window will be accessed via push buttons (labelled mouse-sensitive screen areas that mimic buttons) permanently displayed towards the bottom of that window.*

Picking from menus

Picking from menus will depend to some extent on the type of menu structure and also on any prevailing requirements. For instance, fastpath access to operations listed on menus may be a requirement. Under such circumstances the designer will have to provide function key or double key (i.e. Control, Shift, Alt) access to operations. The designer also needs to consider the way in which menu operation is going to give feedback to the user. For instance, will the menu option become highlighted as the cursor hangs over it or only when a mouse button is depressed? If the user hovers over an option for a length of time will a Help message explaining that operation appear? Example rules might be as follows:

- *Each menu option can be accessed without displaying the menu by depressing the control key and the first letter of the option simultaneously.*
- *As the mouse cursor is over a menu option, that option will be shown in reverse video.*
- *If the mouse cursor hangs over an option for two seconds, then an explanation of that option will appear at the top of the menu.*

Data input

The designer should determine how much data and in what combinations it is to be accepted before the system processes it. For instance, will the user be required to provide values for all the data entry fields in a window or will each data field be analysed and responded to as it is entered? The normal design is for the latter, but sometimes the dependencies between individual data items mean that the system cannot do anything useful until multiple data items are entered. Another question is to what extent the user will be prompted for input. Where there is a finite set of data values, then the user might be offered the option of picking from a menu. Such prompting might only include the most likely data items with the user having to type in less frequently used data values. Syntax rules for data input might include the following:

- *Data values will be validated individually as they are entered.*
- *Where there are less than ten data values for an input field the user will be given a list of those values from which a choice can be made.*

■ *Where ten or less data values account for 90 or more per cent of the data values input, then the user will be prompted to choose a data value but keyboard input will also be accepted.*

Errors and warnings

Errors and warnings should be designed out as far as possible. None the less, exceptions and errors will occur. The designer must decide how best to deal with these, for instance whether errors and exceptions are to appear close to the position of the original fault or in a predefined area of the screen; how the message will be made distinctive in order to gain the user's attention; it is often helpful to use auditory feedback in addition to displaying a message. Will errors and warnings be further coded in some way to indicate their significance? These design questions can only be answered knowledgeably in the light of the user requirements analysis, particularly through consideration of the contextual evidence. Example rules might include the following:

■ *All error messages will be presented in error boxes as close as possible to the physical location of the error's commission.*
■ *Warnings will be presented in boxes that have to be acknowledged by a mouse click before they will disappear.*
■ *All errors and warnings will be presented in a physical location that does not obscure the data value in question.*
■ *Users should be able to recall lost error/warning messages.*

Listener window

The listener window is the window that is presently accepting input from the keyboard. The listener window should always be distinct from other windows in some manner. There are many ways in which this can be achieved. The border of the window can be modified, possibly by thickening; the mouse cursor can change while within the listener's borders; the title bar of the window can change in some way, etc. These methods can be used individually or in combination. The designer should also stipulate the way in which the user controls the choice of listener. Common methods are simply by the location of the mouse cursor or by clicking the mouse while the cursor is within the borders of a window. The designer might also wish to consider restricting the mouse cursor's movement to within the borders of a particular window until a certain operation(s) is invoked. Possible rules include the following:

■ *The listener window will be distinguished by having a double thickness border.*
■ *The choice of listener window will be under user control and determined by the location of the mouse cursor.*
■ *The mouse cursor will change to an arrow when in the listener window.*

For many applications it is required that the contents of a window be scrollable, that is, the contents of the window will move with respect to the borders of the window. Many scroll options exist. Scrolling can take place on the vertical, horizontal or both axes. Scrolling can be in one direction only. Scrolling can be invoked by moving a slider or by clicking at a point on a slider bar. It can be smooth or stochastic, possibly causing movement on a page-by-page basis. Scroll bars can be implemented that give an indication of the relative length of the window's contents. Thus there are many ways in which scrolling can be implemented. It may be necessary to specify separate syntax rules for different windows depending on their contents.

Further syntax rules may need to be generated for such actions as the following:

- selection of objects;
- operation of icons;
- use of cut and paste;
- access to help;
- use of colour, etc.

Syntax rules are not to be considered as inviolate. Their primary purpose is to provide consistency across the interface so that users can generalise and transfer their understanding. None the less, where good arguments based on usability improvements can be provided for violating a rule, then doing so is legitimate.

Determine the layout of each window

At this stage of the design each of the windows is open to some design decisions as regards its layout. For instance, questions can be asked of the sequence of input fields in an input window. The ordering of columns can be questioned for ease of comparison between data figures. The designer should assure himself or herself that the presentation of data best facilitates the user's likely use of those data. For instance, rather than tabular data, a graphical representation may be more suitable, especially where trends are important. A good example of this comes from the use of analogue and digital displays as speedometers in cars. At one time, manufacturers provided digital displays only to find that users did not like them. The reason for this appeared to be that users could not gain an appreciation of acceleration.

With regard to the preliminary design as shown in Figure 3.8, the designer might consider the input window first. It is normal for input fields to be displayed in the sequence of likely data entry from left to right across the window and from top to bottom down the window. In the design as it stands, Size of Deal, which is the last field to be entered, appears above Quote. The designer would probably choose to reverse the order of these. By way of further example, the CUSTOMER DETAILS window shows the most recent transactions to the left of the window. Given that sequence is usually from left to right, the designer might consider re-ordering the data in this window. Also the Buy/Sell row is only a binary field. This row could be removed if colour were used to differentiate between buy and sell. Comparing the CUSTOMER DETAILS window and Own Position windows shows that in one window the data is ordered by column and in the other by row. The designer would probably seek to be consistent in this respect, especially given that some of the fields are shared, i.e. Quote and Product.

Generally, the layout of a window's contents should support ease of discrimination and reading. Logical groupings, as perceived by the user, should be achieved and the sequence of data input and data display should be rendered consistent with general practice. By following these guidelines it will be possible to provide automatic movement between fields and minimise the amount of cursor movement required of users.

The designer should consider the justification of labels to ease legibility, employ means to help users to quickly ascertain the item of data they require, and use highlighting where appropriate. The process of considering how layout can be improved can render a design more usable. All too often, it is the case that once a design is produced it remains unchanged for evermore because this exercise is never undertaken.

By way of example some of the design changes discussed above have been made to the initial case study design and are shown in Figure 3.10.

Consider the layout between windows

It is also important to determine the layout of windows relative to each other. The designer should aim to reduce the overhead of window management placed on users,

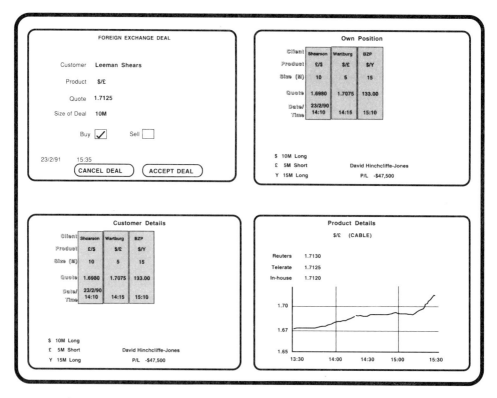

Figure 3.10 *Example screen following window layout re-design.*

while ensuring that the readability of window contents are not degraded. Ideally, users should be able to access all the information they require at the time they require it without having to perform window management, which can include opening, closing and resizing windows. It is often forgotten that these operations are overheads for the users that do not contribute directly to task completion. The designer can undertake a number of exercises to derive rules for window layout and appearance; for instance, on a task-by-task basis the designer can determine the windows that should be presented at the beginning of a task, on the basis of the events at which further windows will appear and where, and the events that will terminate the task along with the effect on the windows. Figure 3.11 shows a format for depicting window opening and closing as applied to the case study. It is also worthwhile, time permitting, to generate example windows, similar to those depicted in Figure 3.10, and conduct a walkthrough with users. Users find it easy to comment on such a realistic example and can help determine window management rules. Window management rules might include the following:

- *Within the context of TRADE IN PRODUCT, when the task begins, the DEAL RECORD and OWN POSITION windows should both be displayed.*
- *The windows, DEAL RECORD, OWN POSITION, CUSTOMER DETAILS and PRODUCT DETAILS should not overlap.*

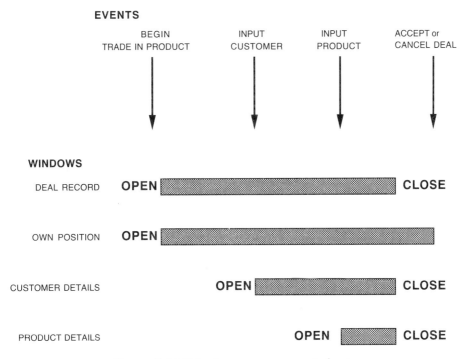

Figure 3.11 *Window management chart.*

Consider exceptional circumstances

The designer should also consider all potential exceptions to the expected dialogue. These circumstances will range from the user clicking outside windows to attempts to invoke illegal operations. As stated previously, such exceptions should be designed out where possible. For instance, the mouse cursor may not be allowed to stray outside the bounds of a window and unavailable operations could be disabled. Only by considering the worst and most absurd scenarios can exceptional interaction sequences be identified. What the designer can be assured of is that if something can happen, then at some time a user will make it happen. By considering exceptions the designer may generate further rules of interaction, such as the following:

- *Mouse clicks outside the bounds of any window will only be acknowledge by a beep from the system.*
- *Menu options that are unavailable will be greyed out.*

Style implications

The rules generated thus far will contribute to the production of the style guide discussed in Section 3.2. The priority of these rules when contested by existing standards will have to be judged by the designer on the basis of respective merits, for instance, the designer may have generated a rule which states that each window will have visible pushbuttons to show all operations that can be invoked on that window. An existing standard might stipulate that all operations be invoked from a menu bar displayed at the tops of windows. The designer will have to judge the relative merits of these rules in the context of the whole design and make a judgement. The reasons behind such judgements should be recorded in the style guide document. Only by recording the reasons can there by any confidence that the decision will not subsequently be overruled.

Considering all tasks

In all the examples discussed thus far only the crucial tasks have been considered. Of course, the design has to support all interactive tasks as previously agreed with the client. STUDIO recommends that the most crucial tasks be considered first so that the general framework and rules for the design can be fleshed out. Having performed this successfully to the extent that the usability and practicality of the design have been assessed as far as is possible, the designer should then produce designs for the remaining tasks by following the same procedures and applying the rules derived for the crucial tasks.

Having completed the design for all tasks the designer should then produce a dialogue map. This depicts the navigation routes through the dialogue. Thus a dialogue map shows all the operations available at the interface and the sequencing between them. Access to operations is shown on the dialogue map as menus, pushbuttons, icons, etc., just as they will be presented at the interface. An example dialogue map is shown in Figure 3.12. Dialogue maps are an aid to assessing the complexity of the dialogue and the designer should use them as an aid to simplifying

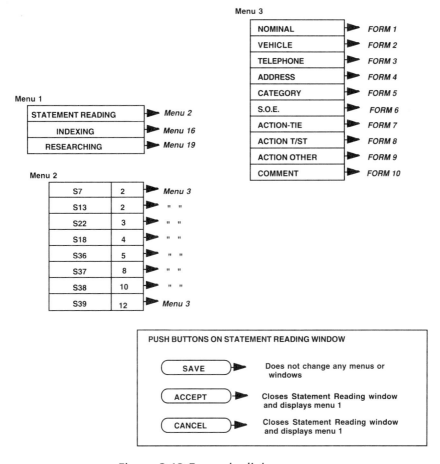

Figure 3.12 *Example dialogue map.*

the dialogue wherever possible. For instance, the designer should use the map to assess how many operations the user will have to undertake in order to begin each task. If the sequence is long, more than four operations, or the task needs to be particularly accessible, then the designer should consider modifications to the design.

3.1.4 Step summary

In performing task synthesis the designer should have performed the following:

Generated alternative outline designs:
- identified crucial tasks;
- performed a PLUME analysis;

- investigated the division of input and output by reserved screen areas (windows);
- generated outline designs(s).

Assessed alternative designs:
- assessed the suitability of outline designs with regard to usability, generating new designs if necessary;
- assessed the practicality of designs with regard to technical and business objectives, generating new designs if necessary;
- performed a PLUME analysis in the light of the prevailing design and drawn attention to any usability targets that are unlikely to be met;
- documented new functional requirements arising from the design and assessed their technical feasibility and cost implications; documented any technical or cost cul-de-sacs and started again if necessary.

Drawn general conclusions:
- derived the command language;
- determined the interface syntax;
- considered the layout of each window;
- considered layout between windows;
- considered exceptional circumstances;
- documented style implications;
- considered all tasks.

Task synthesis is probably the most difficult and demanding step for the designer. Experience of design work will certainly help the designer to use the deliverables of user requirements analysis to the benefit of usability. During this step many opportunities exist for the generation of example screens similar to the one shown in Figure 3.10. The designer is encouraged to produce such layouts and discuss them with users. This has the benefit of both obtaining valuable user feedback at a formative stage and also of keeping users informed of developments. By so doing, the user's commitment to the work can be maintained.

Deliverables from this step should be collated into a single document, 'General user interface decisions' (D301). The contents of this document should include dialogue maps, example screen layouts, syntax rules, window management rules, individual window layouts, new functional requirements and command language description. In addition, this step will have provided input to the style guide.

At this juncture, the main framework of the user interface design has been determined. The syntax and semantics of the interface have been determined and many of the presentational issues have been addressed. All of this has been accomplished in the context of the user requirements analysis including the usability targets. Users have been kept aware of developments and their comments have been sought.

3.2 **Style guide (Step 302)**

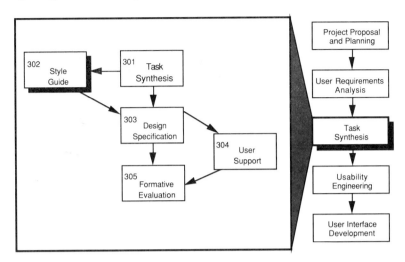

Style guide (Step 302).

This section provides a framework for the production of a style guide. This framework includes a set of principles for user interface design and a list of the user interface issues for which rules should be established in a style guide. An outline for the possible structure of a style guide is suggested.

The purpose of a style guide is to establish an unequivocal set of user interface standards to be applied on graphical user interface (GUI) developments. All user interfaces conforming to a style guide are both self-consistent and mutually consistent. Consistency at the user interface manifests itself in many ways. In essence, consistency means that the presentational, behavioural, syntactic, semantic and literal aspects of the interface can be described by rules that are applicable generally. The fewer the rules the more consistent an interface.

Consistency is a desirable objective for many reasons. End-users can transfer their experience from previous applications more quickly to a consistent interface and thus can become productive quickly. In addition, consistency enhances productivity, reduces error rates and contributes positively to user acceptance of and satisfaction with systems.

Moving between consistent computer applications is as simple as driving different cars. Because the controls are in the same places and they function in the same manner, the skills learned on one car are equally applicable to another.

Adoption of a style guide limits the scope for design decisions, thus reducing the number of arbitrary decisions. This is not to say that design is de-skilled but, rather, that designers will be able to spend more time meeting their main objective of producing designs that support user tasks.

Having a style guide allows development to be streamlined through the creation of common libraries of code that are fully tested and can be re-used.

Quality assurance and the management of developments is enhanced by the adoption of a style guide as it provides a basis for accountability and acceptance testing.

Consistency across applications also permits the streamlining of training courses. Interaction with consistent interfaces is based on a finite set of skills which can be learned once and then generalised across applications.

3.2.1 Background

Early attempts to provide standards for user interfacing took the form of sets of recommendations. Examples included the following:

- Input fields should not require leading zeros.
- Error messages should be presented as soon after the commission of the error as possible.
- Error messages should only be presented once the user reaches a natural breakpoint in a dialogue.
- Users should always be in control of interactive dialogues.
- Novice users should be provided with a system-led dialogue.

The main argument against such recommendations is their apparent, yet misleading, level of generality. Given certain user characteristics, application properties or operating environments, they may be found wanting. In the examples offered above, conflicts can be noted. Regardless of these problems some authorities have devoted considerable effort to generating tomes full of such recommendations. While they can be 'thought-provoking' and can lead designers to ask searching questions, their limitations need to be realised and heeded.

Recommendations have, on occasion, been integrated with Computer Aided Software Engineering (CASE) tool technology in order that conformance be guaranteed. Certain development tools constrain designs to conform to standard sets of recommendations.

Were a standards approach to the complete car design process to be adopted, then it might ensure that all automobiles have four wheels, that the steering column is to the right-hand side and that there are pedals for controlling fuel supply, braking and de-clutching. Unfortunately, such guidelines can say nothing about such things as the dependencies between different controls, what control options should be available and when, and what the criteria for usability of a particular car might be. The standards would find it difficult to account for the differences between a car required for off the road travel as opposed to formula one racing. For example, what would standards be able to state regarding the appropriate action/response correspondence between accelerator pedal movement and fuel injection. Many design decisions are dependent on the tasks that the machine is to be used for, the environment in which the machine will be used and the capabilities of the expected users. As a consequence, only the most superficial of design requirements can be captured in simple, generally applicable rules. These rules can only address the rudiments of the surface structure of a device.

The advent of graphical user interfaces (GUIs) and capabilities such as Undo/Redo, context sensitivity, tailorability and a multitude of windowing styles has increased the user interface design space dramatically. Paradoxically, this has led to more opportunity for bad design. In response to this, attempts have been made to constrain the design space of GUIs through the employment of recommendations in the form of style guides. Examples include, OSF/MOTIF^{tm} from the Open Software Foundation (1990), CUA^{tm} from IBM (1991), XUI Style Guide from Digital Equipment Corporation (X Window System^{tm}, 1988), and Open Look^{tm} from AT&T and Sun (1989). These guides are often referred to as '*look and feels*'. This reflects the fact that they only address the surface structure of the user interface, i.e. its look and feel. These interface styles offer nothing to the designer in terms of stipulating the organisation of the interface, the sequencing in a dialogue, the navigation requirements of the user, suitable data formats, or the naming of application-specific commands. This is not surprising; the guides are designed to be generally applicable across all applications developed under a particular operating system regardless of specific requirements. To this end they succeed admirably.

Style guides can be designed with different ranges of applicability in mind. Organisations are beginning to prepare their own in-house style guides, the perceived benefits being that employees will more easily transfer their skills between different applications, conforming to a single style, and training can be streamlined. This approach has limitations that should not be overreached. Different applications pose different sets of requirements for which different styles or variants on a style are most appropriate.

IT procurers may establish guidelines to be applied when purchasing, for instance, by insisting that all products conform to a look and feel, or that development tools must facilitate conformance, or, indeed, that contracts must be fulfilled in accordance with a style.

A further and more refined approach to ensuring consistency within a development is to establish guidelines to be applied during a particular development. On this level it is possible to take account of user, task and local requirements to a greater degree than is permitted by the more generalist approaches. This approach does not preclude adherence to existing style guides whether they be at corporate or project level. Before a designer generates a style guide he or she must establish the scope of the style guide and convey this scope to the client in advance. The style guide itself should also stipulate its applicability clearly, whether this be purely to a single development or to all developments using a particular development platform.

3.2.2 **Further benefits of standardisation**

Style guides can also be produced in order to realise benefits beyond usability. It is often considered that a style guide will enforce good practice on the part of designers and programmers. Given that style guides provide a framework for development, they should enhance designs not just at the user interface level but also at the program specification and coding levels. Indeed, guides should permit the coding of user interface widgets in a manner that facilitates the re-use of code. For instance, if all windows are to operate in a similar and known fashion, then code can be generated specifically for those aspects of a window that are unchanging. Code can then be re-used throughout that application and possibly in subsequent developments.

Guides may also help in the planning and management of teamed developments. The basic widgets of an interface can be developed and tested early in a project and can then be made available to all team members. A style guide helps by establishing the range of widgets that will be required, thus reducing uncertainty with respect to the scope of the interface.

3.2.3 **Caveats**

It must be borne in mind that style guides do not guarantee usability, far from it. They only provide a basic framework that constrains a development. All the navigation, sequencing, use of context, content of all messages (i.e. errors, warnings, help, prompts) and presentation of data remain outside the possible coverage of a style guide and as such must be designed on the basis of a user requirements analysis.

An often asked question is 'How much better are windowed interfaces?' (Temple *et al.* 1990.) This question begs some sort of quantification as though it were possible to say that a windowed interface is 'ten times quicker to use', or similar. The question is flawed (Whiteside *et al.* 1985). The quality of any user interface, whether it conforms to a particular style or not can only be judged on the basis of the use to which it is put. For instance, many repetitive data entry tasks may benefit from a character-based, form-filling style of interface rather than a windowed one because the overhead of users performing window management functions is simply not warranted.

Style guides are by necessity dynamic documents. Circumstances will be identified during developments where a guideline is not applicable and should be disregarded.

3.2.4 **Examples from standards/guidelines**

As stated above, style guides can exist on many different levels and for many different purposes. Three lists of guidelines taken from quite different sources are given below. Shneiderman (1987) suggests the following eight guidelines or golden rules for user interface design:

- Strive for consistency.
- Support internal locus of control (users should feel they are in control of the dialogue).

- Offer simple error handling.
- Enable frequent users to use short cuts.
- Offer informative feedback.
- Design dialogues to yield closure (group actions on the basis of tasks).
- Permit easy reversal of actions.
- Reduce short-term memory load.

The Open Network Architecture User Interface Style Guide from British Telecom suggests the following ten principles:

- Ensure consistency and conformity.
- Provide immediate feedback.
- Allow the user to observe and control the system.
- Use the user's model.
- Introduce through experience.
- Design the system to be user-centred.
- Log activities.
- Avoid the unexpected.
- Validate entered data where possible.
- Provide help information.

The following make up a sub-set of the principles proffered by Apple Inc.:

- Effective applications are both consistent within themselves and consistent with one another.
- Keep the user informed. Provide immediate feedback.
- The user, not the computer, initiates and controls all actions.
- Users make mistakes, forgive them.
- Use concrete metaphors and make them plain, so that users have a set of expectations to apply to computer environments.
- Communicate with the user in concise and simple terms.
- Users should be able to control the superficial appearance of their computer workplaces.
- With few exceptions, a given action on the user's part should always have the same result, irrespective of past activities.
- Always provide a way out.

While these principles are sympathetic to the plight of users, they offer little help to designers. At best they raise questions, and possibly awareness; at worst they simply raise more questions and considerations than they answer. What does it mean to strive for consistency? How does a designer know when consistency has been achieved? What is the meaning of informative? What is the binding feature that can be used to generate logical groups of actions?

A further type of guideline stipulates the desirable attributes of the interface. These guidelines make statements about how the user interface should appear physically, and operate on the basis of assumptions about what is good for the ubiquitous user.

- There should be no significant difference between what the user sees on the screen and what eventually gets printed (cf. WYSIWYG – What You See Is What You Get).
- Most things – menu items, icons, buttons, and so forth – should be highlighted by reversing the white background with the coloured or black bits when selected.
- Since the focus of attention is on the content region of the window, colour should be used only in that area.
- Sound should never be the only indication that something has happened; there should always be a visible indication on the screen.

3.2.5 User interface principles

STUDIO distinguishes principles from standards. STUDIO acknowledges that it is useful to have principles as decision aids. It also acknowledges that it can be helpful to have a standard as an opening position, even if it is rejected in the light of prevailing evidence from user requirements analysis.

STUDIO offers a set of principles which should be borne in mind during a user interface design exercise. These principles must always be balanced against the present needs of users and the all important usability targets. STUDIO also offers advice in the form of user interface options, their attributes and utility.

It is most important to remember that the STUDIO method, particularly the user-centred procedures for analysis and evaluation, are the most powerful means of rendering a design usable. The following section describes the set of user interface principles advocated by STUDIO.

Principles

Principles are objectives to be achieved where possible. The following offers some principles and then qualifies their value, generality, relationship to usability criteria and how the STUDIO method helps to apply the principle.

Always strive for usability. All other principles are subservient to this principle. In the light of evidence, any, or even all, other principles can be compromised if improved usability will result. The procedures embodied by STUDIO focus on enhancing usability.

Strive for consistency. As stated previously the perceived benefits of consistency are in terms of skills transfer and reduced training overheads. (Unfortunately consistency is not a straightforward concept.) Consistency is achieved when the same rules of interaction apply, without exception, throughout an interface. For example, within a consistent interface users who know how to operate one menu can apply this knowledge successfully to the operation of all menus. A difficulty exists in trying to quantify consistency. One might say that one interface is more consistent than another because there are fewer rules of interaction. This would be an oversimplification given that applications vary in their intrinsic complexity. None the less, designers can apply the principle that they should strive for consistency by applying the same rules unfailingly, simplifying rules that appear overly complex and, where possible, combining similar rules.

Consistency in design is facilitated within STUDIO through the use of specialised notations and the submission of these specifications to formative evaluations (Step 305).

Group actions logically. The important term in this principle is *logically*. In many structured system development methods the logical grouping of actions/operations is on the basis of such functional considerations as optimised data groups. Here the term 'logical' relates to the user's perception of the system and its function. The binding force for the grouping of actions is a task.

The task hierarchy diagrams and action list, with associated attributes, provide the necessary information to group actions logically.

A term often used to explain why logical groupings are important is *closure*, which is the point at which a task is considered finished. At such points the user gains a feeling of accomplishment. All cognitive resources tied to that task can be freed and used for a new task.

Reduce both short-term and working memory requirements. Users often encounter problems resulting from the poor sequencing of information and the inaccessibility of information at the time it is required. This is to be avoided as it forces users to adopt strategies such as note taking and memorisation that are both taxing, error prone and interfere adversely with interaction. Usually, the need for such strategies is avoidable.

This principle draws the designer's attention to the information needs of users and facilitates them to minimise the load placed on users' short term and working memory.

All actions should be reversible. Whenever the user invokes an operation that will change the state of the system or, indeed, the state of an object held by the system, the operation should be reversible. Application of this principle helps to reduce the anxiety often felt by users when experiencing a system for the first time. By so doing, users are encouraged to be more adventurous and discover the full functionality of a system in the knowledge that they can return the application to a known state. Reversibility can take many forms, which vary in sophistication. Examples include cancel keys, the need for commit before actioning, and Undo/Redo functions.

Designers can only be encouraged to provide such facilities. Their importance may be highlighted during analysis but ultimately these facilities are dispensable. Their value will have to be balanced against the costs of limited system use and error-prone interaction.

Errors should be designed out. Some style guides make a big play of how errors should be dealt with. While sympathy for users' mishaps is important, from a designer's perspective the most important point is that errors should be designed out.

This is a far stronger principle than the alternative retrospective approach. If users cannot make errors, then there will be no need for remedial action.

Task analysis helps to avoid errors by making the likely occasions for their commission apparent. Of course, not all errors can be avoided. The designer has no control over the numeric values that a user enters into a system. None the less, an understanding of what is feasible and likely can help immensely in preventing and trapping errors.

Provide information not data. The crux of applying this principle is understanding what is *informative*. Information content is dependent on what users know already, what they need to know, what they can infer and how much redundant data is supplied with the informative data. To a stockbroker the financial pages of a tabloid newspaper are probably not very informative as they do not give him or her all the information required. To tabloid readers these pages may be quite informative if they only own shares in recently privatised companies. The tabloid readers are saved from having to search reams of irrelevant data in order to find the prices of their stock. Information is distinct from data. Data only becomes information once it is used.

During user requirements analysis the different roles of users are taken into account. In this way their differing information needs can be considered and, where feasible, catered for in user interface design.

Use the terminology of the user. Every industry, service or administrative function has its own vocabulary. Whatever the political or historical reasons, this vocabulary is accepted and understood. Attempts should be made to utilise this vocabulary in the design of a new system. There is no good reason for altering an accepted vocabulary, but there are many reasons why one should not. Confusion will arise and communication problems will result if a system utilises an analogous yet distinct terminology from that which pervades the working environment. The same principle applies equally well to symbology. For instance, engineers have many symbols for valves with which they and their peers are accustomed. Modifications to these symbols can only lead to re-learning problems.

STUDIO helps with the documentation of terminology and symbology in two ways. Firstly, the knowledge representation grammar sentences retain the prevailing terminology. Secondly, collection of contextual data including terminology and symbology is encouraged.

Provide feedback at all times. Users should be kept informed of the status and progress of a dialogue at all times. They should never be left guessing as to whether the system is busy processing or awaiting user input. Where a large amount of processing is taking place the system should attempt to indicate how long it is likely to be busy. Adherence to this principle helps users to plan and schedule their immediate tasks and reduce the frustration that is often caused by uncertainty.

Modes should be avoided, operations should have the same effect wherever they

are invoked. Moded systems appear schizophrenic. Depending on the present mode, the system will *behave* differently and will expect the user to behave differently. Users do learn *fixed action patterns* and then apply them without recourse to system mode. This often results in the user having normally acceptable input rejected or misinterpreted by the system.

Support contexts. Contexts are different from modes in that they are based on data or tasks. The principle is that a context provides information which can be used by the system in order to facilitate interaction. Ideally, a context is a state of shared understanding between system and user. The use of contexts is not uncommon. For instance, in generating this document I do not have to continually re-affirm the identity of the document. Attempts should be made to help the user to establish contexts and then work within them. Imagine the stock controller preparing his monthly report. The context for this may be all the stock movement data for the last month. Would it not be helpful for this user if a filter could be instantiated for a finite period of time such that the controller did not have to keep stipulating the data needed each time a data enquiry was invoked?

In summary, the principles advocated by STUDIO are as follows:

- Always strive for usability.
- Strive for consistency.
- Group actions logically.
- Reduce both short-term and working memory requirements.
- All actions should be reversible.
- Errors should be designed out.
- Provide information not data.
- Use the terminology of the user.
- Provide feedback at all times.
- Modes should be avoided; operations should have the same effect wherever they are invoked.
- Support contexts.

The reasons for ignoring some of the other principles provided as examples on preceding pages are discussed below.

A number of principles are implicit in the STUDIO method:

- Design the system to be user-centred (implicit in STUDIO).
- Log activities (to be covered in Stage 4).
- Introduce through experience (relates to prototyping, Stage 4).

Some of the example principles do not have sufficient generality:

- Provide short cuts for frequent users.
- Communicate with the user in concise and simple terms.
- Users should be able to control the superficial appearance of their computer workplace.

Some principles are really guidelines that refer to user interface attributes:

- Always provide a way out.
- Provide help information.
- Validate entered data where possible.

User interface options

The following section discusses some of the options available in the employment of user interface features. These options will be discussed in terms of merit and applicability with relation to usability. Features include widgets such as menus and windows, functions such as Undo/Redo, and aesthetics such as formats and colour.

Features do not *sell* systems, but employed correctly, features can provide benefits, particularly in terms of usability. Benefits do sell systems, both to procurers and users. It should not be forgotten that features are just attributes of a system. It is important that features are bundled appropriately to provide a uniform system. Features cannot be judged individually; the sum of the parts is not always equal to the whole. One of the great attractions of prototyping (Stage 4) is that it provides an early and first opportunity to evaluate the sum of a system's features.

Colour. The appeal and usability of a system can be enhanced by the appropriate application of colour, which should be used with caution as it can have adverse effects. In general, colour is useful for drawing distinctions between items and as an aid to classifying, gaining attention and indicating context. Colour can be used in association with other cues to reinforce distinctions and offer users alternative strategies for organising their own understanding.

Modern workstations offer enormous palettes of colour that invite overuse of this powerful visual cue. Due to the physical characteristics of the visual system it is advisable to avoid the colour combinations listed in Table 3.2.

Table 3.2 *Colour combinations to be avoided*

Foreground colour	Background colours to avoid
Red	Blue, orange, magenta
Orange	Red, blue, yellow, white
Yellow	Orange, white, cyan, magenta
Green	Cyan
Cyan	Blue, green
Blue	Red, magenta
Magenta	Yellow, red, blue, orange, cyan
Black	Brown, blue
White	Yellow, cyan

Stereotyped meanings for colours existing either in society (i.e red for stop), or in the working environment (i.e. yellow for radiation) should be taken into account when employing colour.

Windows. Many designers gloss over the many variations of windowing technique that exist. This may be due to the imposition of a particular look and feel as a standard, thus limiting window functioning in advance of design. Alternatively, designers may not appreciate the benefits of some windowing techniques over others and, even if they did, would not have the necessary understanding of user requirements to make an informed choice. In this section the various types of windows are described briefly along with the bases for choices.

While most window-based systems have at least the components depicted in Figure 3.13, there are more window formats than one might at first imagine. The most salient choice is between overlapping (Figure 3.14) and tiled (Figure 3.15) windows. The original version of Microsoft Windows[tm] and the Cedar[tm] window system (Teitelman 1984) both required that windows be tiled. Some window managers that support overlapping can still be configured to determine the placement of windows. Overlapping windows may be implemented so that parts of windows are off-screen. In a tiled interface the windows appear side by side and never overlap. Typically, the system is responsible for sizing/resizing and placement of windows so that they can all be seen, although they may not be readable. Normally, when overlapping windows are employed it is the responsibility of the user to move, size and close windows in order

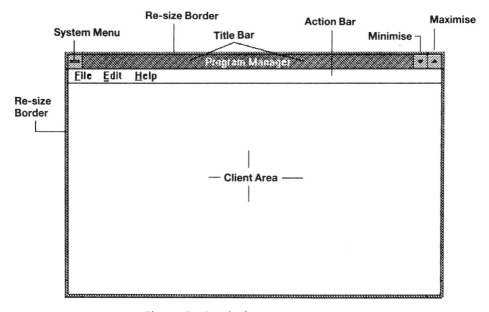

Figure 3.13 *Window components.*

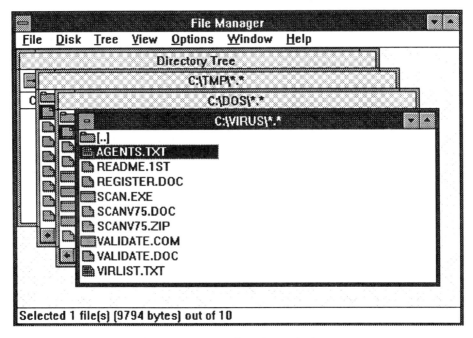

Figure 3.14 *Overlapping windows.*

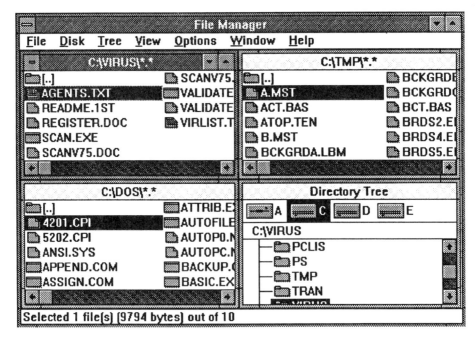

Figure 3.15 *Tiled windows.*

·order to obtain a configuration with which they are satisfied. The main concern for the designer is twofold. Firstly, what is the overhead of expecting users to perform window management in terms of time, interruption, and productivity. Secondly, what are the users' requirements for seeing information from different windows simultaneously and will that information be legible.

There are also various ways in which the interface can denote the active window, or *listener*, at any time. This window is the one to which any keyboard input will be directed. The listener can be denoted in a number of different ways. The border of the listener may be made distinctive, the cursor in the listener may be unique or it may simply be that the listener is in the foreground. The choice of listener denotation is dependent on the choice of windowing format and on how clear the distinction needs to be.

Normally, the additional input device for working with windows is a mouse. A mouse can have one to three buttons and can be implemented with or without the need for multiclicking to denote certain operations. The need for multiclicking is often accepted without question, but caution should be shown. Some users find the manual dexterity required for double clicking problematic. Others may find multi-clicking difficult in their particular working environment, for instance if they are standing up. When multiclicking is used, modes are often introduced unwittingly such that a double click has different implications in different screen areas.

Title lines and borders can be configured variously. Title lines can be used to provide information, particularly regarding context, such as the document, application or file being accessed.

Some window systems permit the use of icons. Again, there are many options. Icons are often used to represent windows that can be opened, for instance a window on to an application. The presentation of icons is variable. An icon might just be a shrunken version of a window's title line, or a truly symbolic representation, or indeed a combination of symbols and text. The most suitable representation is dependent on many factors including the size of the set of items that it is desirable to iconise. If there are many, then text may have to be included in the icons to make them distinct. In at least one system (Sapphire[tm], Myers 1984), icons are used to provide status information such as process progress indication and error occurrence. Icons may or may not be movable and sizable. Icons may indicate whether they can be invoked by using shading.

Most windows are rectangular but some systems such as NeWS[tm] (Sun Microsystems 1986) do permit other shapes such as ellipses.

Reserved areas may be established in windows for such things as the display of error messages, status information and prompts. An area may be reserved for icons that are window-specific.

Window operations are numerous. They include sizing, moving, opening, closing, panning and scrolling. There are various ways of supporting such operations, from having reserved areas on a window to having pop-up menus listing the operations. The choice should be made on the basis of familiarity, consistency with existing applications, frequency of operation and consistency with other interface features.

The design choice can be complex, based on what is possible given a chosen development platform, the nature of the tasks to be supported and user familiarity with windowed interfaces.

The cursor can also be designed so that its visual appearance changes depending on where it is situated on a screen or what its operation will be. For instance, the cursor might change as it moves across different reserved areas. Alternatively, the cursor might change after the invocation of a particular operation but before the object of the operation is chosen, so that after a delete the cursor looks like a hatchet, or after a zoom it looks like a magnifying glass. The value of this feedback to users would be to prevent them from deleting an object that they would otherwise have expected to be enlarged (zoomed). Such choices have to be made in the knowledge of the likelihood of choosing the wrong operation, the cost of mistakes and the cost of implementation, that is, human factors not standards should determine the design.

There are an enormous number of design choices when considering the implementation of menus in a windowed environment. Menus can be on-screen continuously or only on request. Menus can be configured to be window-specific or generally applicable. They can be implemented as pull-downs from a single menu bar applicable to all windows or from menu bars attached to individual windows. On a menu, items may be grouped by function, listed alphabetically, listed by frequency of use, etc. Menu items may be denoted by text or icon or by a combination of both. Each item may be invoked by mouse click on one part or any part of that row of the menu. The unavailability of a menu item may be denoted by its absence from the menu or by shading/colouring.

Figures 3.16 and 3.17 provide an overview of the various windowing options available under the headings presentational and operational choices respectively.

Hopefully, the above provides some appreciation of the design space available with regard to the window features of a graphical user interface. To reinforce the point, consider an application where the user is always working with a document which he or she wishes to be in view at all times and which for good reasons should never be obscured. In addition, the user may wish to perform many other tasks such as word processing and database updates, but all related to the document. How might a windowed interface for such a user be designed? Alternatively, consider the user whose task execution shows enormous amounts of parallelism and interdependencies. What features should be provided for this user? The point is that an enormous amount of flexibility is often available to the designer of a windowed interface. The designer must simplify the options available by documenting, within a style guide, how windows can and cannot be employed to support user tasks.

Tailoring. There is a growing lobby among user interface designers to provide users with the means to tailor their interfaces (Browne *et al.* 1990). The proposal is that users be permitted to change some of the presentational or operational attributes of systems. Examples would be that users be able to change colours for, say, the background, or that they should be able to change the names of commands. One of the advantages of this approach is that developers are saved the trouble of making

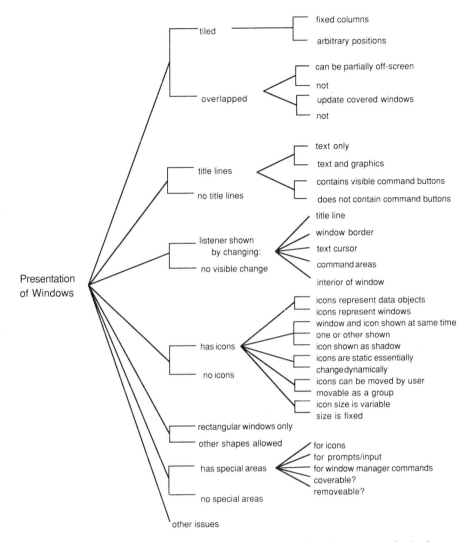

Figure 3.16 *Options available for the presentational aspects of windows.*

definitive design decisions and, in theory, users should be able to help match their system to their own preferences. The disadvantages include the overhead of implementing tailorability, the possibility that users will make bad decisions, consistency across interfaces may be compromised thus hindering the transfer of expertise between users and the fact that users often simply do not bother to avail themselves of tailoring features. A case may be made for tailorability where distinct differences between user requirements is identified but where each requirement cannot be satisfied in advance, possibly because machines are shared or users are not going to identify themselves to the machine.

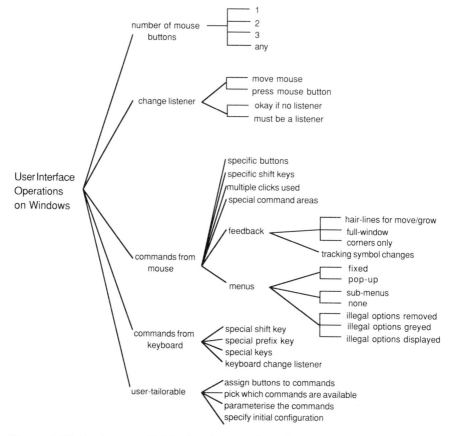

Figure 3.17 *Options available for the user interface operations of windows.*

Undo/redo. The ability to *unwind* previous operations can be a powerful user interface feature. If users can work in the knowledge that anything they do is recoverable, this can be a boon to user acceptance. Users often learn a small part of a system and never venture beyond the bounds of this knowledge in the fear that they will make a catastrophical mistake. Having an Undo capability should reduce this fear. A Redo is the reversal of an Undo. Thus even if something is undone by mistake the error can be rectified. Undo/Redo capabilities can be implemented to various degrees of sophistication. The simplest is to permit users to undo the last operation they invoked but nothing more historical than that. In theory, Undo can be implemented infinitely provided that the Undos are invoked in the reverse sequence to the original operations. If the sequence changes, then there can be no guarantee of returning to an exact replica of a previous state. The choice of how sophisticated an Undo mechanism is warranted really depends on the type of tasks being performed and the difficulty of reversing mistaken operations through regeneration. In many applications users spend a lot of time checking the accuracy of previous work before committing themselves. If this checking procedure is vitally important in itself, then it may be counterproductive to provide an Undo capability that detracts from the checking process. Alternatively, an application might encourage 'playing', as in scenario generation and many decision-making tasks. Under such applications an Undo capability might be just what is required to facilitate adventurous and lateral thinking.

Response time. In years past a great deal of store was placed on the response time of systems. This was probably due to the inordinately slow response times experienced. With the increased processing power of modern technology, response time targets are far less difficult to meet. In fact, system response time is only a small fraction of the time usually required to prepare input for processing. There is far more benefit to be gained from providing users with productive user interfaces. As a result, IT clients are tending to stipulate increasingly refined targets for user input.

Where long delays are anticipated, features such as tick lines, counting down clocks or messages can be used to keep the user informed of progress. The most frustrating aspect of system response delays, from a user's point of view, is not the delay *per se* but, rather, the variability of delays. When users can anticipate the length of a delay with some certainty, then they are far more accepting and may perform other tasks in the interim. Feedback contributes to a user's feeling of being in control. Where possible, variability in delays should be minimised and users should be given continuous feedback on the progress of any lengthy processing.

If at all possible, delays should be commensurate with the perceived complexity of a task. In respect of this, designers may consider part-processing tasks as they are being performed.

Menus. Some of the issues relating to menus were discussed under windows, others remain. Menus are normally used for either choosing between commands or for accessing information. Menus for commands should not be longer than eight items in length. Menu hierarchies should never be more than three levels deep. This restriction is not easily enforced for dynamic menus listing items of information. Menus have the distinct advantage over typing commands that they are less error-prone. Menus present operations to users, particularly infrequent users, that might otherwise remain unknown. Menus place very little load on users' memory for commands or syntax. Minimal typing skills are required and users learn to operate menus very quickly.

Menus can work in many ways. These include pop-up menus that usually appear at the position of the mouse cursor. Pull-down menus are displayed when the cursor rests over an item on a menu bar (Figure 3.18). Walking menus provide a further level of structuring. They operate by having sub-menus appear when the cursor rests over a menu item. In this way users can make a quite specific command choice with just one mouse button press. The choice of menu structure and presentation should be based on the structure of the actions that users will wish to perform. As mentioned under

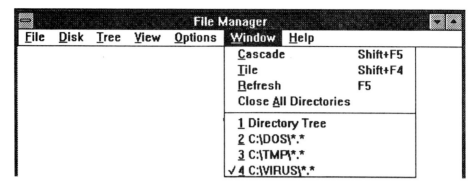

Figure 3.18 *Example pull-down menu.*

windows, menus can also be associated specifically with a window, possibly with each window having its own menu bar.

Where an application becomes very large, there may be so many commands that users can no longer find what they require. In such situations it will be necessary to provide further means of structuring the commands.

Some authorities demand that menus are not the sole means of interacting with a system. The suggestion is often that short-cut methods such as *control characters* or abbreviated command names be permissible alternatives to menu choices. For instance, using the menu depicted in Figure 3.18, if the user pressed 'F5' the screen would be refreshed.

In all developments, rules should be developed for the method:

- by which a menu option is selected;
- for executing a selected option;
- for obtaining help about each menu option (could be that a Help box is automatically presented should a user hover over an option for more than a fixed length of time);
- for returning directly to the top level of any menu hierarchy.

Menu design and the implementation of short cuts can have a significant impact on the speed of interaction (productivity). Designs need to be based on consideration of the logical (as perceived by users) groupings of commands such that users find commands where they might expect to find them.

Mouse. Many types of input device are available today. These include tracker balls, mice, touch-sensitive screen overlays and light pens. Each of these has merits depending on the application under consideration, but the mouse is by far the most frequently used. The simple mouse might be expected to be so straightforward that no design issues, or even choices, actually exist. This is not the case. There are two main forms of mouse, mechanical and optical. Each has merits and drawbacks. Optical mice require a pad which can take up valuable desk space, particularly in cluttered working environments. Mechanical mice can suffer failure in dirty environments. Both types of mouse require relatively flat surfaces. Mice can have one, two or three buttons. Single-button mice may appear the simplest but this depends somewhat on other interface considerations. If the user is to be required to make multiclicks, then a multibutton approach might be more usable.

The position and velocity of the mouse movement can be made to correspond to the position and velocity of the cursor in different ways. The correspondence can often be adjusted in magnitude so that finer physical movements of the mouse are not required. This correspondence might also be made to depend on the particular activity that the user is undertaking. For instance, cursor movement over a menu might be rendered stochastic.

Other software controls over the cursor position might also be considered, for instance that the cursor not be permitted to move outside the listener window, or that the cursor be placed in a specific position relative to the boundaries of any newly opened window. Decisions on such undertakings can only be based on their value with respect to usability, possibly for purposes of speeding up interaction.

It should be remembered that mice are not always the most suitable of input devices and on occasions alternatives may be sought. Mice are totally inadequate for free-hand drawing. For such tasks the designer might consider a light pen. Joysticks have appeal for tracking tasks, and bitpads are another alternative.

Errors. As stated previously, the best method of dealing with errors is to design so that they do not occur. Obviously, this is rarely fully achievable.

Mechanisms should be established for the following:

- informing the user of errors, presenting error messages;
- determining the timing of error diagnosis;
- formatting error messages in terms of diagnosis, remedy and further help.

The main choice for the presentation of error messages is between whether messages should be presented in a consistent part of the screen or at a point close to the commission of the error. Error diagnosis can be made soon after the error's commission or at a natural break point in a dialogue such as the completion of a form. The choice should be based on the likely frequency of errors and the relative frequency of form-filling tasks and continuous activities.

Users are frequently reluctant to read error messages. Often all they consciously notice is the fact that an error has occurred. The accompanying message often remains unread. For this reason it is often worth making messages distinctive so that the relative significance of an error is denoted using a distinctive highlighting cue such as colour or typeface.

Forms. On-screen form design should be influenced by any persistent hardcopy forms and task structures. Large forms may need to be divided over numerous windows. Field partitioning should be on the basis of task-related fields and/or the most frequently completed fields. Related fields should be ordered consistently with

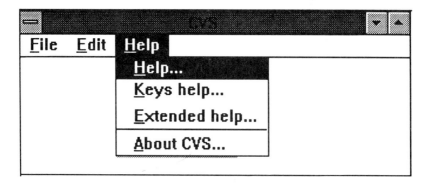

Figure 3.19 *Access to Help.*

the likely order of field completion. The designer should also consider how to take account of completion of related fields. For instance, completion of a field may determine the input value of another field, should the system automatically complete this field or expect the user to complete it as a validation check. On occasions, data input will offer an opportunity to prompt users with finite lists of valid input for other fields.

Help. There is almost always a good case for providing some degree of on-line help. An example access method to Help as provided by a pull-down menu is shown in Figure 3.19. Many of the rules established for the production of hardcopy documentation should also be applied to on-line Help. Indeed, electronic and hardcopy documentation should be consistent in terms of content. Help should be structured by some means other than command name. Users want to get something done and it is often their lack of knowledge of commands that prevents them from progressing. If their access to a Help system is by command name, then they are likely to be stymied. It is more sensible to organise help by task names or attributes as would be identified in the task hierarchy diagrams.

If the user population is variable in terms of experience, then there may be a case for providing Help at various levels of complexity. In this way novices can be aided in getting started and experts can be presented with more advanced system features that may improve their productivity.

Scrolling. Scrolling can be supported in many ways. The most common is the use of a scroll bar, possibly with accelerators. Figure 3.20 identifies the most common components of a scroll bar. Even scroll bars can be implemented in many different ways, for instance the position of a window relative to the underlying image can be signified by a greyed area on the scroll bar. This feature can be enhanced further if the size of the greyed area reflects the present percentage of the image in view. This can be particularly helpful when lengthy documents are being browsed. Consideration may also be given to combining a paging as well as a smooth scrolling feature where the underlying object (document) has an inherent structure such as page length. Scroll bars may also permit users to skip to known parts of an image such as the head and tail.

3.2.6 **Style guide structure**

Style guides can be one of the largest documentary deliverables from a user interface design project. As such they must adhere to the documentation standards established for the project as stipulated in the quality plan.

The designer must first determine the structure of the document. What follows is an example structure for such a document. All style guides should begin with an introduction that at least states the purpose and scope of the document. The introduction should also argue the case for consistency so that the reader is convinced of the value of such a document. The introduction may also discuss its relationship to international guidelines.

The second chapter should elaborate on the principles of user interface design. In this way the reader will hopefully be reminded that design is not simply the application of the rules provided within the style guide.

Next, it is usual to provide rules for each of the components of the user interface. These include windows, menus, and forms, as discussed previously. It is not sufficient to state just the style rules; they must also be argued if the reader is to be convinced. The chapter on user interface components is often rather long and may be better divided into multiple chapters.

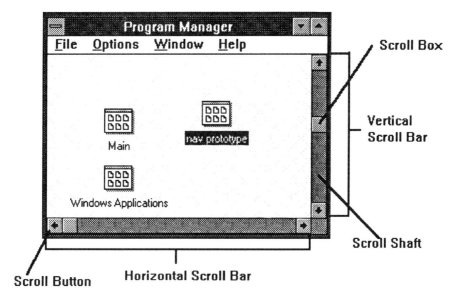

Figure 3.20 *Components of a scroll bar.*

On-line Help is best dealt with as a separate chapter. Depending on the development platform chosen by the project it may be necessary to stipulate many rules specific to the provision of Help. This chapter should at least provide rules for the writing of Help and how these Help texts are to be accessed by the user.

At least one chapter should be devoted to interface processes. These are behavioural aspects of the interface including the timing of validation, the signalling of error situations, provision of feedback, defaulting behaviour, response times and the use of modal dialogues.

A chapter should be included that provides worked examples of interface designs that conform to the style guide. Readers often find this a useful starting point for appreciating a style.

Projects and corporations employ particular symbology and terminology that is specific to their business. A chapter of the style guide should document this terminology in terms of how it will be apparent at the user interface. Thus lists of icons and literals, together with their accepted meanings, should be documented.

It is good practice also to include a chapter describing how common functions must be supported. Such a chapter should stipulate, for instance, how dialogues for the creation, deletion, and amending of data will be supported.

A further chapter may be included, as deemed necessary, covering the method to be used for user interface design. At least one appendix should also be provided that includes a checklist to be used when checking a user interface for conformance with the style guide.

As with all large documents the style guide should include a list of contents, a list of figures, a management summary and an index. The format of the document should utilise plenty of graphics to supplement textual descriptions of style rules. The rules themselves should be highlighted within the text of the document to facilitate quick reference.

3.2.7 Style guide generation

The content of a style guide is based on a number of sources. These include the styles implicit in existing applications to which users of the new system will be exposed, relevant international style guidelines given the chosen development platform, and the types of tasks that users will be expected to perform with the new system. Each of these sources must be reviewed before writing the style guide's content.

As the content of the document is produced, the style rules should be discussed with users. This may require the production of mock-ups that can be viewed by users in order to convey the implications of the style rules. For instance, rules for distinguishing editable from non-editable fields on a form may be embodied by a screen and presented to users for their consideration.

Before the document is finalised it must be submitted to a review by a selected sample of users or their representatives and developers. It is important that developers take part in this review because they may identify style conventions that are not supported by the chosen development environment.

On the basis of the review, the style guide should be updated accordingly and published as a project deliverable. Because this document is intended as a standard for continuous use throughout the development, it should be bound and well presented. The style guide should also be submitted to version control as stipulated in the quality plan.

3.2.8 Step summary

During this step the designer will have established user interface style rules. These will include rules for the behaviour and appearance of user interface components. The style guide is expected to become a standard to be followed throughout development. As such it should be published to a high standard. The 'User interface style' should be delivered as document D302.

3.3 Design specification (Step 303)

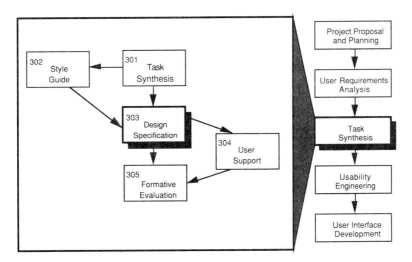

Design specification (Step 303).

It might be thought that to produce a specification for the user interface design after already having put significant effort into documenting how the interface will look and behave is a step backwards. STUDIO considers the production of a specification as important because it provides the following:

- an aid to assuring the consistency of the design;
- further means of assessing the quality of the design;
- a useful aid to communicating design requirements to implementors, which in turn helps them to plan, estimate and organise effort;

- a cost-effective means of validating a design;
- an aid to simplifying the design.

It should be noted that the idea of using a specification notation as an aid to communication with users or clients is not considered a justifiable reason for having a specification. Experience has shown that users, and often clients, are resistant to learning a notation in order to be able to comment on a specification's validity. This is not surprising given the perception that it is the analysts' and designers' task to design a system, so why should the users be given the onerous task of checking a specification? The deliverables from task synthesis, particularly the example screen layouts, are a valuable communication aid between designer and user. Users can relate to these immediately and comment on them constructively, particularly when they are presented as dialogue sequences. Thus it is recommended that the deliverables from task synthesis are used to gain acceptance of the design from the clients.

Many design notations have been proposed for the purposes of user interface design. Each has its pros and cons, including whether or not there is tool support for the notation. Within STUDIO two notations are offered. Firstly, the state transition network notation (Woods, 1970), on the basis that this is gaining acceptance among structured system development techniques. Secondly, the statechart notation (Harel 1988) is offered because of its power, brevity and particular applicability to user interface design. This step overviews these two notations and explains how the deliverables from task analysis are used to populate these notations. In 'Formative evaluation' (Step 305), the question of assessing the design from its specification will be addressed.

3.3.1 State transition diagrams

State transition diagramming is often employed as a notation for specifying interactive dialogues. The main elements are nodes and arcs. Nodes are usually depicted as circles representing the states that a dialogue can reach. Different states are connected via arcs that represent directed transitions between states. Nodes are usually given a meaningful label and actions that take place on entering that state are written in close proximity to the node. Arcs are labelled with the events that cause a transition. A small example is shown in Figure 3.21. This specification represents a dialogue for obtaining a user's password. The user is prompted ('password?') and the resulting user input is assigned to the variable T1. On input of a carriage return (CR) the dialogue progresses to node 'check password' where the system checks the password and generates event T1-Ok or T1-Nok depending on whether the password is legal. If the password is accepted, then the dialogue reaches node 'welcome'. At this point in the dialogue the message 'welcome to App X' is presented and after 2 seconds (!2) the dialogue progresses further. Screen positions for placing prompts and messages can also be represented. For instance, 'c2, r11' preceding a message would display the subsequent message beginning at the second screen column in row eleven. The use of variables allows branching in a network to be made conditional. Sub-dialogues can also be represented as labelled rectangles, such as 'Sub-Dialogue Z' in Figure 3.21. Such sub-dialogues can have multiple entry and exit points (Figure 3.22). These can be labelled uniquely such that the exit from the sub-dialogue can be made conditional on the entry arc and can be usefully employed to represent excursions from the main dialogue. It should be noted that sub-dialogues that could happen anytime during an interaction would have to be represented by as many arcs as there are nodes on the diagram.

Tools to support state transition diagram production and interpretation may also include notation for embedding external function calls in the diagrams. For instance, in Figure 3.23 a function call is embedded in a dialogue regarding a person's age. The function takes a person's age in years as input (V1). From this it calculates the person's year of birth (V2), which is presented to the user.

For small, well-determined sequential dialogues state transition diagrams are quite adequate. There are major difficulties in applying state transition diagrams to user interface design, particularly where multitasking in a WIMP style interface is required. For such an interface the use of state transition diagrams is not advised.

In Step 305, the analysis of state transition diagrams for certain properties is discussed briefly. For medium- and large-sized interface developments, particularly those supporting concurrent activities, the statechart notation described in the following section is recommended. Davis (1988), provides a review of various notations, including statecharts.

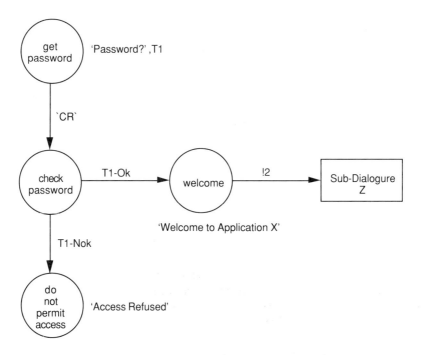

Figure 3.21 *Example state transition diagram for password verification.*

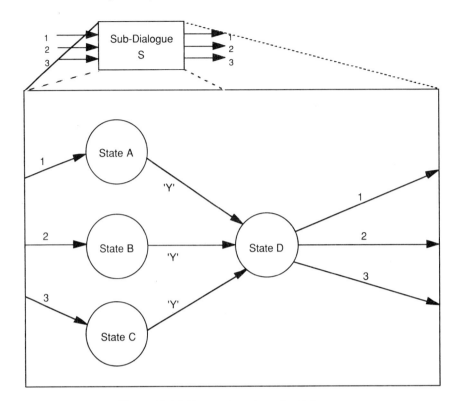

Figure 3.22 *Example of a sub-dialogue.*

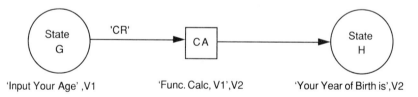

'Input Your Age' ,V1   'Func. Calc, V1',V2   'Your Year of Birth is',V2

Figure 3.23 *Example state transition diagram with an external function call.*

3.3.2 **Statecharts**

The main component of the notation is a blob which represents sets. Two blobs are shown in Figure 3.24. Blobs are usually shown as rectangles with rounded corners but can in fact be any shape. Every set of interest must be represented by a unique blob. By so doing, each set can be given its own unique label. In Figure 3.24 it is not clear whether **A** is labelling the difference between the two sets represented by the blobs or the entire set of the upper left blob. To resolve this situation two further blobs are introduced and uniquely labelled. This satisfies the requirement that all sets of interest be represented by a unique blob. In Figure 3.25 the intersection **A ∩ D** is labelled **C** and the difference **A − D** is labelled **B**.

As each set of interest must have its own unique border the only *real* identifiable sets are atomic sets. Atomic sets are represented by blobs at the bottom levels (not intersected by any other blobs) of the diagram. Blobs, excepting atomic blobs, denote a compound set consisting of the union of all the blobs that they totally enclose. Thus on Figure 3.24 there are no atomic blobs. On Figure 3.25, blobs **B** and **C** are atomic

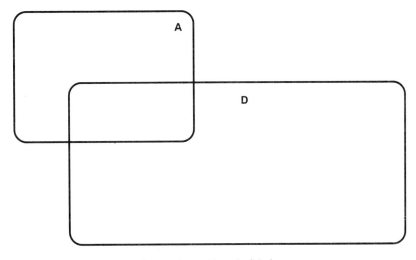

Figure 3.24 *Simple blobs.*

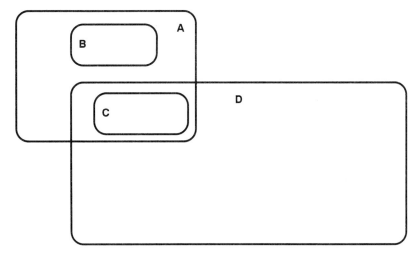

Figure 3.25 *Adding unique blobs for all identifiable sets.*

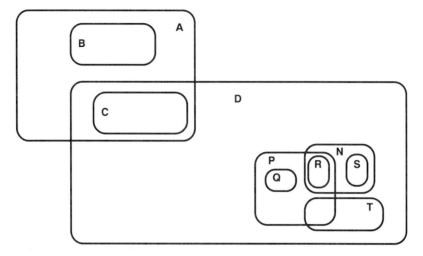

Figure 3.26 *Nesting of blobs.*

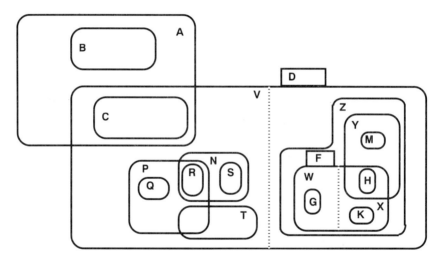

Figure 3.27 *Adding cartesian products.*

and on Figure 3.26, **B, C, Q, R** and **S** are all atomic. In this notation the intersection of two blobs means nothing unless further blobs are added in appropriate places. Empty space in the diagram represents nothing at all.

The first extension to the blobs and labels is a notational construct to represent cartesian products: the result of combining the individual elements of two sets. Cartesian products are represented by dashed lines that bisect a blob. These lines can in theory be in any orientation but perfect horizontals and, more usually, verticals are the norm. Two examples of this notation are shown in Figure 3.27, where the set **F** is the product of **G** and the union of **H** and **K**. Where the cartesian product notation is used, then a label for the blob directly affected is shown in a box attached to the blob's border. In this way the two portions of the cartesian product can also be labelled. Thus blob **F** is labelled as just explained with **W** and **X** being the labels for the partitions.

The above covers the statechart notation sufficiently for the representation of sets and their set-theoretic relationships. Edges (lines) are now introduced as a means of representing further relationships between sets (blobs). An edge can be directed or undirected, and can be labelled or unlabelled. Figure 3.28 shows examples of directed binary edges (i.e. **C** to **G**), and one example of a directed three-way edge (**A** to **C** or **D**). Edges connect sets to sets **not** elements to elements. Figure 3.29 shows an example of an entity-relationship diagram and Figure 3.30 shows its equivalent represented in the statechart notation. The diamond-shaped boxes in Figure 3.30 are labels to describe the relationships and are **not** nodes. The area enclosed by a blob can be used for recording the attributes and properties of the set if so desired. The *insideness* of blobs can thus be used to represent semantics such as inheritance.

Statecharts have been developed to cope with problems encountered when specifying highly *reactive* systems. A reactive system is one which has to react continuously to external or internal stimuli. Examples include communication networks, avionics systems and computer user interfaces. The problem lies in trying to represent reactive behaviour in a manner that is clear, concise and correct. Statecharts succeed in addressing these issues. In addition, statecharts provide a formal (in the mathematical sense) and rigorous representation with rich semantics that can be computerised. In fact, tools exist for the creation and execution of statecharts. The behaviour of reactive systems is provided by sequences of input and output events, conditions (contexts) and actions.

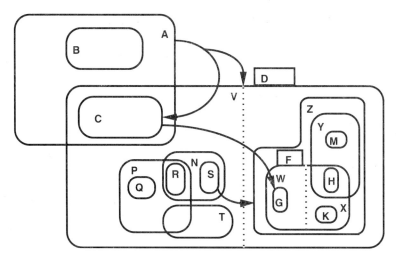

Figure 3.28 *Representing relationships in statecharts.*

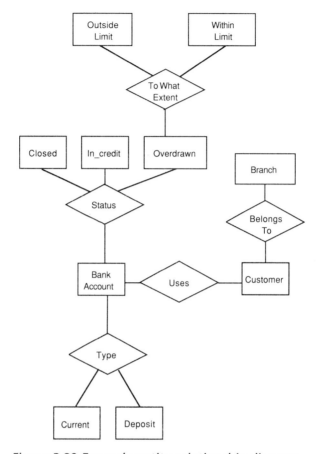

Figure 3.29 *Example entity-relationship diagram.*

In statecharts, as used for user interface specification, the blobs represent states and the edges (arrows) represent transitions:

Statecharts = state diagrams + depth + orthogonality + broadcast communication

Depth or grouping is provided by the insideness of blobs. This is illustrated in Figure 3.31(a, b). The labels on the edges represent events causing transitions. A bracketed part to an edge label such as is illustrated by **j(c)** represents a condition. The event **j** will only cause the transition from **R** to **S** if condition **c** is met. As **R** and **S** do not overlap and are both completely inside **T** it is the case that **R** and **S** are exclusive states. Thus the system can be in state **R** or **S** but not both. While in state **T** the system is in state **R** or **S** but not both. The **k** edge shown in Figure 3.31(a) applies to both **R** and **S**. Using insideness, these two arrows can be replaced by a single arrow (**k**), as shown in Figure 3.31(b). Insideness overcomes two criticisms levelled at state transition diagrams, namely, their inability to provide depth (although recursive state

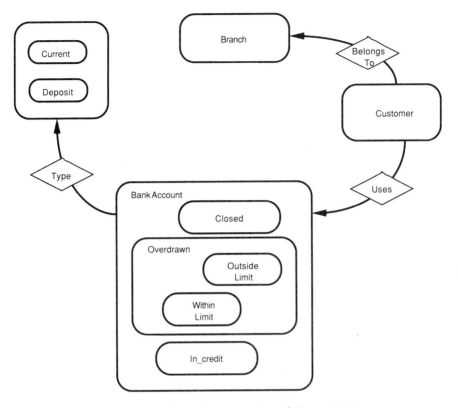

Figure 3.30 *Statechart version of Figure 3.29.*

transition diagrams largely overcome this problem) and their lack of economy due to the need for repetition. Insideness renders statecharts particularly concise when considering systems having many states and levels.

The interpretation of the small default arrows depends on them containing blobs. In Figure 3.31(b) the default is **R** if joining state **T** but the default is **S** from inside **T**. Thus, following event **m** the default would be **S**. The arrow labelled **m** could have been continued through **D**'s boundary to **S**'s contour, but on many specifications it is more readable to use the convention shown in Figure 3.31(b).

Orthogonality is supported by the cartesian product notation introduced earlier. The power of this addition to the notation is demonstrated by comparison of the two specifications shown in Figure 3.32. In Figure 3.32(b) there are two orthogonal states, **G** and **H**. Being in state **Z** means that the system is in states **G** and **H**. Two default arrows are required to indicate the default states within **Z**. Figure 3.32(b) also illustrates the use of special conditions attached to events, the event **q** only causing a transition from state **P** to **T** if the system is also in state **V**.

Comparison of the number of states shown in Figure 3.32(a, b) exemplifies the exponential explosion of states that have to be shown on a normal state transition

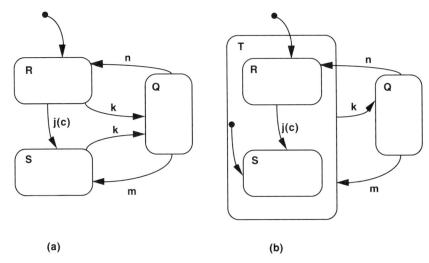

(a)   (b)

Figure 3.31 *(a, b) Example of depth provided by statecharts.*

diagram. The number of states on a 'flat' state transition diagram is the product of the number of states in the orthogonal components of a statechart version plus the number of non-orthogonal states. Further specification power is afforded to statecharts through the inclusion of a broadcast mechanism. This is achieved through the inclusion of output events (also known as actions). External events (cf. Figure 3.32(b) for event **x**) can trigger a number of state changes in the orthogonal components of the statechart. Similarly, output events can cause a chain reaction of transitions through the 'broadcasting' of new events to related components. Output events are depicted by a backslash and label concatenated to the primary event. An example of this is shown in Figure 3.33. If event **q** occurs, then the output event **r** is activated resulting in a transition from state **V** to **S**.

The above provides an overview of the statechart notation. Not all the notation has been covered; more will be introduced in the course of the following example producing a statechart-based specification. A few extra conventions will also be introduced beyond *pure* statecharts that have been found useful, particularly for user interface specification.

Example statechart specification
The dealing room example has thus far produced outline designs, stipulated interaction rules, documented dialogue sequences and established style guidelines. From these inputs a statechart specification has been produced. This specification will be described in part for the task of TRADE IN PRODUCT.

It is worth making the point that in producing the specification, windows do not necessarily map on to blobs. Blobs are states possibly relating to a component of a window, a combination of windows or the overall dialogue. Thus, the designer should begin by establishing the states that the user interface might be in and creating blobs

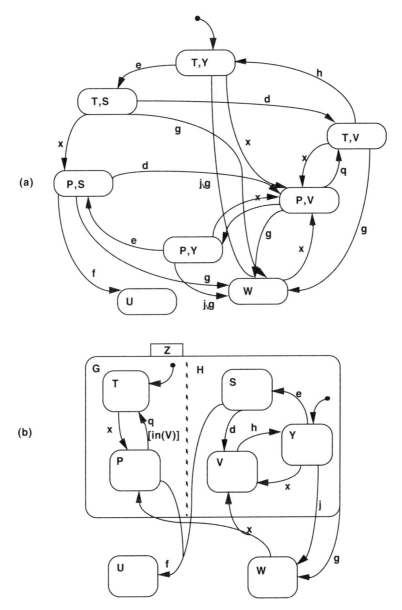

Figure 3.32 *(a, b) Example of depth provided by statecharts.*

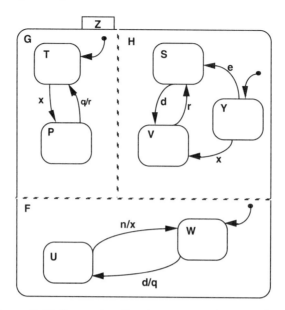

Figure 3.33 *Example of output events in statecharts.*

for these states. The first state might be *waiting for the user to choose a task*; another might be *waiting for the user to enter data*; and yet another might be *waiting for the user to terminate the task*. Thus blobs relate to contexts within which one of a number of user actions can take place. The determinacy of actions, that is, their groupings, map on to blobs. It should not be forgotten that the system may also generate events that change the state of the interface and these also have to be specified.

The full statechart specification for TRADE IN PRODUCT requires a full sheet of A3 paper in order to be readable. For this reason only an outline of the full specification is provided followed by full specifications for some of the states within TRADE IN PRODUCT.

Figure 3.34 shows the specification in outline. There are four partitions to the state TRADE IN PRODUCT. The broadcast mechanism described earlier is employed to propagate actions across the partitions. The WAITING/FINISHING partition specifies the initial state of the interface and the states that cause the task to be terminated. The WINDOWS partition describes the opening and closing of windows. DATA STATES indicates whether the data items required for the successful completion of the task are known or not at any particular juncture in the task. Finally, INPUT STATES depicts the controls and system behaviour as the user interacts with each of the input fields in the display. For example, there is a blob for Customer specifying how the user interacts with the data input field for Customer. Many of the blobs depicted in Figure 3.34 contain other blobs. Some of these will be described in detail below.

Within the statechart examples that follow, mouse operations are indicated as follows:

M v : mouse button release
M ʌ : mouse button depression
M   : mouse movement

Figure 3.35 provides a specification for the state labelled **Cus/M/Input**, which stands for **Cus**tomer/**M**ouse/**Input**. This is a state wholly within **Customer**. Within this state, a user can indicate a particular customer. This example introduces the concepts of **Entry, Throughout** and **Exit** behaviours. These are system behaviours that occur on entering, during or on leaving the state signified by the blob. These behaviours could be associated with the appropriate edges entering, leaving or existing within a blob, but expressing them once as attributes of the blob aids readability. There are two **Entry** behaviours within **Cus/M/Input**, namely, displaying a menu (M1) and changing the shape of the mouse cursor. **Throughout** the state, any menu option under the mouse cursor will be highlighted. On **Exit**ing, the **Entry** behaviours are reversed. It should be noted that as well as a mouse cursor there is an input cursor which is displayed on entry to the **Customer** blob.

Selection by the user is indicated by a circled '**S**'. In the state **Cus/M/Input**, there is a selection from a menu (M1) which is made by releasing the mouse button. Should the user release the mouse button while no menu selection is chosen, then there is no

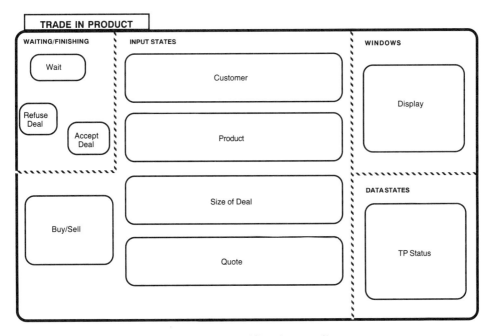

Figure 3.34 *Specification outline.*

INPUT STATES

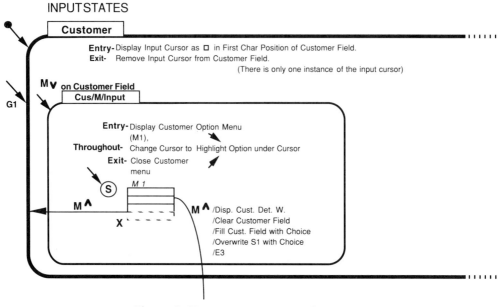

Figure 3.35 *Cus/M/Input specification.*

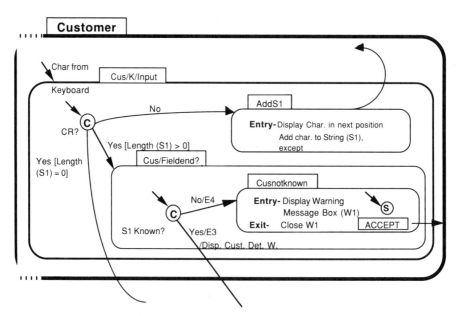

Figure 3.36 *Cus/K/Input specification.*

effect. This non-selection is indicated by the **X** at the base of the arrow leading from the menu.

Checks are often required as to the validity of some data entry, particularly where that entry has been made via the keyboard. In the blob **Cus/K/Input**, which is also wholly contained within **Customer** (Figure 3.36), there are two examples of checks which are each denoted by a circled 'C'. The first is a check of whether the input character is a Carriage Return (**CR**). If it is, then a check is performed to identify whether the **CR** indicates data entry completion or whether the input cursor should move to the next input field. This mechanism permits the user to perform data entry in any order, skipping input fields when required.

Output events have been included in both **Cus/K/Input** and **Cus/M/Input**. For instance, in **Cus/K/Input**, YES/E3 indicates that event E3 should be broadcast and /Disp.Cust./Det.W indicates that the CUSTOMER DETAILS window should be displayed.

A particularly convenient and often used type of blob when specifying GUI-style user interfaces is the **WAIT** state (Figure 3.37). This is a state, as one might suspect, that does nothing but 'observe' for certain events. The **WAIT** state is often used to identify those occasions when the mouse cursor is used to change the input field.

While it might have been thought that the initial design produced during Step 301 was simplistic, the exercise of specifying its behaviour indicates how complex superficially simple graphical user interface designs can be. If the same design had been specified using state transition diagrams it would have been far larger and less readable.

By reviewing a statechart specification the designer can identify all the pieces of text, forms, message boxes, warnings, etc., that will be required. In the full specification from which Figure 3.34 is taken the following were identified:

- W1, a warning message for when the Customer input is not known to the system;
- W2, a warning message for when the Product input is not known to the system;
- W3, a warning message for when the Size of Deal input is deemed dubious by the system;
- W4, a warning message for when the Quote is deemed dubious by the system;
- M1, a menu listing the most frequent Customers;
- M2, a menu listing the most frequent Products;
- M3, a menu listing possible Sizes for Deals;
- EM1, an error message indicating that the user has not supplied all the required information for the Deal to be completed (efforts might be made to refine this message further to indicate which data items are missing),
- Mess1, a confirmation message on Accepting the Deal.

At this point meaningful textual content for these messages should be documented. This should be released to the project as 'Textual content of the dialogue', D303. This should include any Help texts required. These texts should be generated by reference to the style guide produced during Step 302. This guide should provide rules for the content of all Help text, error messages, warnings, etc. For instance, the style guide

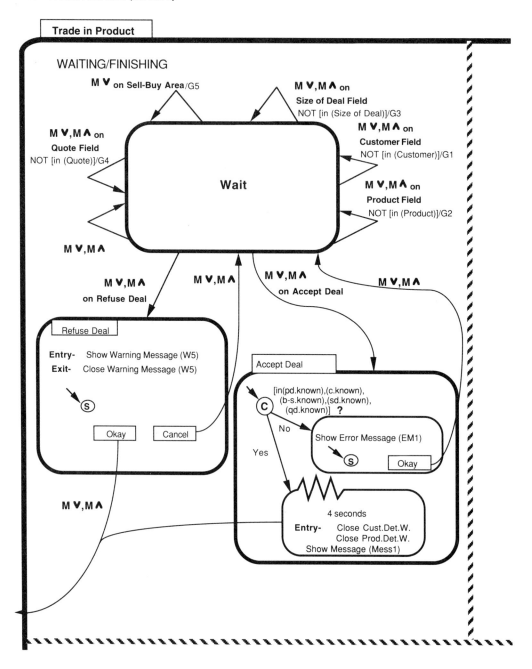

Figure 3.37 *Example of Wait state.*

may stipulate that all error messages must identify the source of the error, provide a solution and suggest sources of further guidance. Also for reasons of consistency, it is good practice to create this document in one pass.

Any historical data values that may need to be held locally, and possibly manipulated, were also identified:

- S1, a string used to identify the Customer;
- S2, a string used to identify the Product;
- S3, a string used to identify the Size of Deal;
- S4, a string used to identify the Quote.

Particularly commonplace operations such as interpretations of keystrokes may be omitted from the specification. For instance, the interpretation of keystrokes such as 'del', and 'backspace' are omitted.

States having a known transient quality can be indicated using a jagged line as part of the state's boundary. An example of this is given by **Accept Deal** in Figure 3.37. On entering this state a message is displayed for four seconds. This is indicated by the jagged line used as part of the boundary of one of the blobs within **Accept Deal**.

3.3.3 **Step summary**

This step has resulted in the production of a user interface specification, the first evaluation of which will take place in the next step. The value of specification should not be underestimated. The argument that prototyping alone is a sufficient means of deriving a design misses the objective of having a specification. Specifications, particularly ones written in powerful notations such as statecharts, demand rigorous attention to detail on the part of the designer. The specification itself provides a basis for assessing the design in a cost effective manner. In addition, because they are unambiguous, specifications aid communication between designers and developers.

The specification should not be made a deliverable until undergoing evaluation (Step 305). The 'Textual content of the dialogue' (D303) should be produced at this step, although it will likely be modified as a result of Step 305 ('Formative evaluation') and Stage 4 ('Usability engineering').

3.4 **User support (Step 304)**

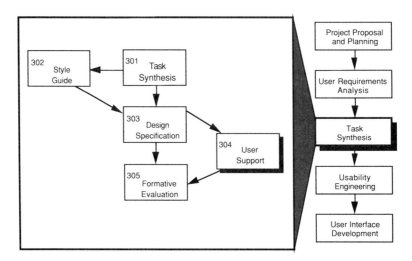

User support (Step 304).

Poor documentation can, and often does, detract from the usability of software. It is common for users to continue to use a sub-set of a system's functionality because they find it daunting to explore new functionality on the basis of available documentation. As a result, sub-optimal interaction occurs, with the system never being utilised fully. One of the main ways in which documentation fails is through being organised by system commands. Often, if a user wishes to know how to perform a given task, then it is necessary for the user to first know the name of the necessary command so that he or she can index into the appropriate section of the documentation. One of the reasons why documentation is often poor is that it is perceived to be of secondary importance compared with other system deliverables. Developers often fail to appreciate that the production of system documentation is a skilled exercise that should be undertaken only by trained persons.

This step provides many guidelines which it is hoped will be helpful to the designer or technical author responsible for the production of user support documentation. The primary guideline, and one that will be re-iterated throughout this section, is that documentation should be organised by task as opposed to command or function. These guidelines are based largely on the 'Draft British Standard recommendations for the design of user documentation for software products for text and office systems' (1991), which provides a framework for the production of documentation. This framework dictates that users' requirements for documentation are established first. These requirements then allow a realistic timetable for completing the documentation to be produced. Any existing corporate policies or documentation standards are then reviewed before a structure for the documentation is determined. These activities are followed by the creation of a logical and then physical design for the documentation prior to any text or illustrations being drafted. The documentation is then reviewed and amended before the release of copies for evaluation. On the basis of brief evaluations, changes are made to the documentation prior to the release of the first version proper. A further evaluation of the documentation will take place during Stage 4 in the context of the prototype system.

3.4.1 Outline the user requirements

During user requirements analysis much evidence will have been collected that is germane to the provision of documentation. Among this evidence will be user characteristics such as the literacy of the intended users, their previous experience of information technology, the context in which the new system will be used and their expected training with the new system. All these factors affect the design of documentation. It is worth recording these factors separately by reviewing the deliverables from Stage 2, particularly the contextual information. A document entitled 'User requirements for documentation' (W304a) should be produced. It will be a short document clarifying the following:

- the media for documentation, i.e. on-line, tutorials, reference manuals;
- contextual factors that might impact the documentation, i.e. one manual per user, tailored to or by individuals, likelihood of being mislaid, required portability;
- user knowledge that can be assumed;
- terminology/symbology that can be taken for granted.

As with software-based aspects of the user interface, documentation can also be subjected to usability criteria. Some criteria may already be listed in the usability issues document (W202). The technical author should review the user requirements analysis and establish further criteria by liaison with the analysis team and users where possible. These criteria may include such statements as the following:

- Users will be able to access a designated section of hardcopy documentation within two minutes.
- Users will not be required to have prior knowledge of system commands in order to access documentation.
- Users will be able to cross-reference any interactive state to the accompanying hardcopy documentation within two minutes.
- The hardcopy documentation alone will provide users with sufficient guidance that they will be able to perform useful work after four hours of study.

In conjunction with the project planners a timetable for the production of the documentation should be created. This timetable (W304b) should marry with the timescales for software prototyping so that documentation evaluation can be conducted in concert with prototype evaluation. It is important to account for the time overheads in issuing documentation, particularly if it is to include graphics or make use of colour.

3.4.2 Check standards

The technical author should take account of available standards. Sources include the following:

- corporate policies;
- house style;
- industry standards.

It is not uncommon for organisations to have policies on the provision and style of documentation. Such policies may stipulate standards of presentation and syntax to which documentation must conform. Where this is the case the policy should be reviewed for adequacy and applicability. Where it is considered wanting, the technical author should propose alternatives or exceptions to be applied for the purpose of the present project. Any such modifications must be agreed with the client in advance of documentation preparation.

Where the client has no policy, the developer may have a ready-prepared style/policy that is deemed suitable. Again, this must be agreed. Alternatively, an industry standard may be acceptable. Consideration might be given to Government standards such as BS 5515:1984 ('Code of practice for documentation of computer-based systems') and BS 4899:1990 ('Guide to the user's requirements for technical manuals').

3.4.3 Make decisions about the overall structure of the documentation

The technical author must determine the type of information to be provided. The main categories are *guidance*, *reference* and *training*. Guidance material provides much background information. It can be thought of as documentation that a naïve user might like to peruse in order to understand the support to be provided by the system. Reference material is intended for users who wish to corroborate or learn how to perform some task/operation with the system. Training material is intended as a course of self- or tutored education. Whatever types of documentation are chosen, a further decision as to whether they are provided on-line, off-line or both should also be determined. This may have been determined during user requirements analysis.

Another consideration should be the use of further aids such as quick reference cards.

Ease of consultation of documentation is vitally important. The technical author should satisfy himself or herself as to the general characteristics of the intended users. For instance discretionary users tend to forget what they have learned and are often best served by a quick reference aid. All documentation should include well-ordered content, meaningful section headings, comprehensive indexes and contents list, and a good numbering scheme.

3.4.4 Logical design

The logical structure of documentation is important for purposes of navigation. The structure should be consistent with the order in which tasks are performed. Therefore, the major influence on the structure of the documentation should be the task hierarchy diagrams. These provide the logical task sequence which will be reflected in the interaction system and should be embodied in all supporting documentation. The top-level tasks identified in the task hierarchy diagrams provide the main sections of the documentation with related tasks grouped together as in the task hierarchy diagrams. Sub-sections of the documentation should then be chosen to relate to sub-tasks as in the task hierarchy diagrams. Where the documentation will be extensive, then it should be partitioned, possibly in a way that reflects the tasks associated with different user roles. For instance, in the context of financial trading, separate volumes of documentation might address the requirements of gilts, foreign exchange and equities traders. This may necessitate the inclusion of redundant information between volumes. The objective should be one of providing documentation that has relevance to its user and does not appear daunting because of its physical size. Page layout, including margins, column widths running headers/footers, etc., should be used consistently throughout. Each section should begin with an overview to help orient the user to the material. Task-descriptive terms should be used for section headings. Thus sections cover what the user wants to do rather than describe the hardware or software. A numbering system should be adopted. It is recommended that a decimal approach to numbering only be applied to three levels. Illustrations should also be numbered. The documentation should be indexed alphabetically showing the main terms and alternative names for terms. The use of prose should be tempered with alternative formats such as questions and answers, graphics, lists, and keywords. The logical design should be recorded as a document (W304c, 'User support: Logical design').

3.4.5 Physical design

Physical design refers to the material form of the documentation. The technical author must decide page size, paper quality, page orientation, methods of binding, line length, text justification, and typeface size and font. These decisions should be based on the requirements and contextual factors documented in Stage 2. For instance, it might be anticipated that documentation is going to be heavily annotated by individual users, the documentation should be portable, possibly pocket-sized, so that users can carry it with them, or it has to be extremely durable because of the environment in which it will reside. These decisions should also take account of the likely life expectancy of documentation. It may be reasonable to assume that documentation will be re-issued every year to accommodate system modifications or replacement of pages. These factors will affect the choice of physical design.

3.4.6 Draft text and illustrations

As the design specification for the user interface (Step 304) becomes available its content can be drafted. In general, the documentation should be written for the lowest common denominator, namely those users with the lowest technical and reading abilities. Other guidelines for documentation include the following:

Text

- Use the second person ('You') where reasonable but do not be patronising.
- Documentation should explain why the user has to perform certain tasks in the way prescribed. Users are more forgiving if they at least understand why things are done in a particular way.
- Avoid making the system appear easier than it is.
- General principles that apply throughout the system should be explained upfront. This will help the user to create an accurate and generalisable mental model of the system.
- Where many possible outcomes depend on a limited set of parameters, consider using tables to represent the options.
- Avoid unnecessary words such as 'clearly', 'obviously' and 'in fact'.
- Use sentences of varying lengths to help retain the user's attention. Average sentence length should be in the range 15–20 words but no longer than 30 words. Short sentences help to reinforce crucial points.
- Each sentence should convey just one main point.
- Clauses and sub-clauses should be minimised.
- Repeat material rather than have users cross-refer to other sections for explanations.
- Technical terms should be included in a glossary.
- Avoid using potentially ambiguous words.
- Slang and colloquialisms should be avoided.
- Each concept should be referred to by the same name throughout.
- Write in the active rather than the passive voice. So, 'you must click the mouse button', is better than 'the mouse button must be clicked by you'. The general grammar is subject ('you'), then verb ('click'), then object ('mouse button').
- On the whole avoid using negatives. None the less, they can be helpful for stressing points such as in warnings.
- If metaphors are used they should be drawn from a domain with which the user is likely to be familiar.

Graphics

- Graphics should be tested with users to ensure that they convey the appropriate meaning.
- The role of graphics is to enhance the meaning of text.
- Graphics of physical objects should have a perspective consistent with the user's likely angle of view.

■ Each graphic should attempt to convey only one concept.

■ Where colour is used, the potential for confusion by colour-blind users should be taken into account.

Warnings

■ Warnings should be highlighted in some way so that they stand out from the rest of the text. White space is, paradoxically, an effective highlight.

■ Warnings should be given before the point at which they are of importance.

■ Different levels of warnings might be indicated using the terminology, 'Warning', 'Caution' and 'Danger'.

■ The state of the interactive system can be indicated using screen dumps.

Errors

■ Ideally, all error messages should be self-explanatory and should not require further documentation.

■ Error messages should explain how and why the error has occurred and how the user should proceed.

Tutorials

■ Tutorial material should be structured in accordance with task and sub-task sequences.

■ Worked examples for common tasks should be included.

■ Memory aids such as analogies and mnemonics should be included where possible.

3.4.7 Apply design specification

Having produced draft content for the documentation the technical author should apply the logical design specification as stipulated in W304c ('User support: Logical design').

3.4.8 Review content

The proofs should be checked for consistency with the software design specification. All documentation should be checked for mutual consistency. Thus, tutorials, reference guides, user manuals and on-line documentation should all be consistent.

3.4.9 Produce evaluation copies

It should now be possible to produce copy in readiness for evaluation as part of the system prototyping. This should be released to the project as 'User support documentation' (D304). While this version will fall short of the quality of the final copy it should be as close as is cost effective. Change control procedures should be established at this point. Document versions should be released in tandem with new software releases.

3.4.10 Refine test criteria

The documentation usability criteria established in W304a ('User requirements for documentation') should now be re-visited. These will provide a basis for assessing the adequacy of the documentation. Where possible, preliminary evaluations should be performed to identify inefficiencies. These can be conducted quite briefly by asking users to tell you, by reference to the documentation, how particular tasks are accomplished. Where users are experiencing difficulty in finding the necessary guidance or in finding the appropriate documentation or are still unclear as to what they have to do, then the documentation is inadequate. Such deficiencies should be rectified before proceeding to user evaluations.

3.4.11 Step summary

The importance of documentation as an aspect of a system's user interface and a determinant of overall usability should not be underestimated. Writing quality documentation is a skilled undertaking. The guidelines given above will help but there is no replacement for the skills of a trained technical author in deciding what will be successful in practice and how material can best be presented to meet usability criteria.

The first release of the documentation ('User support documentation', D304) should be produced by following the guidelines as stated above. The main structure of all documentation should be guided by the task hierarchy diagrams as produced in Stage 2. In this way both the software and the documentation will have a consistent structure that matches user task requirements. The first release of the documentation should be of a quality that permits it to be evaluated during Stage 4. In anticipation of necessary modifications, a change control procedure should be instantiated in accordance with the quality plan for the project.

3.5 Formative evaluation (Step 305)

The very process of producing a specification helps the designer to improve the design by imposing rigour and adherence to consistent practices. In addition, having produced a specification it makes sense to evaluate it as far as practically reasonable. Rectification of poor design decisions at this juncture will save effort during subsequent stages. The specification itself then provides a systematic basis for evaluation.

The term *formative evaluation* is used here to distinguish this process from prototype evaluation and summative evaluation which take place in later stages.

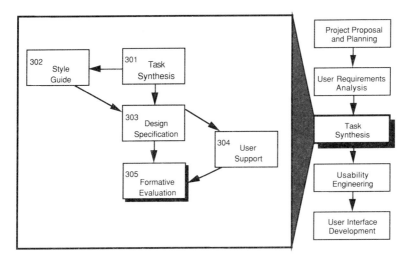

Formative evaluation (Step 305).

3.5.1 Formative evaluation of state transition diagrams

State transition diagrams do not offer as much scope for evaluation as statecharts. None the less, some useful examinations of state transition diagrams can be made. The designer should certainly assess the following:

- Is each state in the specification reachable?
- Are any parts of the dialogue particularly complex and could they be simplified?
- Are all possible sequences of user input catered for?

It is possible when generating state transition diagrams to include non-reachable states. The designer should check for reachability by taking each node in turn and tracing a path back to some base state. In this way the designer should be assured that each state is reachable.

Where a state transition diagram looks complex it is likely that the resulting implementation will also be complex, that is, where there are many interconnecting arcs and nodes the resulting dialogue is likely to be complex. The number of options open to the user may be such that a bewildering dialogue results. The designer should seek to simplify such situations.

It can be a useful exercise for designers to list the various events that a user can invoke. The designer can then select sequences randomly and apply these given the various start states. This procedure, while rather a blunderbuss approach, can be very effective in identifying oversights in the specification.

3.5.2 **Formative evaluation of statechart specifications**

With a statechart specification the designer can make many checks as to the sufficiency of the specification:

- Are all default states appropriate?
- Are all states reachable?
- Do all output events have an effect?
- At every point in the dialogue does the user have sufficient feedback to know the state of the system?
- Are all input sequences catered for?
- For common sequences the designer can perform analyses to estimate the time the sequence will take to complete.

The following will briefly discuss each of the above and will offer some examples from the case study specification. These evaluations are best performed as independent reviews and not by the specifier, who is less likely to identify inadequacies.

Default states

The designer should satisfy himself or herself that all default states are appropriate in the specification, for instance when entering a state or partitioned states are all the defaults as required? On entering the state TRADE IN PRODUCT what happens?

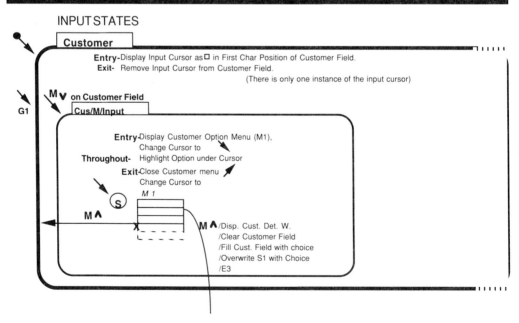

Figure 3.38 *Cus/M/Input specification.*

In the partition INPUT STATES (Figure 3.35, reproduced here as Figure 3.38 for convenience), the default is to enter the state Customer as indicated by the arrow with the rounded end. This is as required. Checking back to the task hierarchy diagrams it can be seen that the first thing the dealer normally identifies is who the customer or counterparty actually is. On entering the partition DATA STATES (Figure 3.39) there are a number of partitions in the state TP Status. An inadequacy in the specification can be identified here in that there are no defaults signified for entering states c, b-s, pd, qd or sd. These should be added. Within each of these states the default is the state 'Unknown'. This is correct given that no data has yet been provided by the dealer. A small inadequacy can be found in the partition WAITING/ FINISHING (cf. Figure 3.37) as no default is shown. In fact, the default should be the Wait state. In summary, the initial default states include opening two windows, awaiting input of customer details and initialising data states.

The designer should check all defaults, particularly those resulting from entry and exit events.

Reachability

It is important that each state is reachable. Specifications can be generated that obviate the possibility of even attaining certain states. The designer should check that this has not occurred by backtracking from states. This is difficult to perform rigorously but it should be attempted. For instance, if we examine the state 'TP Status /pd/ Known' (Figure 3.39), it can be seen that the only means of reaching this state is by event E5 occurring. The designer should identify whether this event can occur and then backtrack from the states that can cause E5 to ensure that those states can be reached.

Sufficient feedback

In line with the general design principles of STUDIO the user should always be given sufficient feedback regarding the state of the system. Thus the interface should always provide sufficient cues to inform the user of what has been accomplished, what remains to be accomplished and what options are available at present. The present input field is always shown in the specification, that is, an input cursor marker is placed in the first character position of the present active field. The only exception to this is when the dealer is determining whether the deal is a buy or sell (Figure 3.40). Having done this, no input cursor is shown. This raises a question as to whether the dealer is to be given more feedback at this point. Unfortunately, there are insufficient grounds for defaulting to any particular field after choosing buy/sell. On the up side, indicating whether the deal is a buy or sell is probably the last piece of data input that the dealer will make apart from confirming the deal. Implicit in the specification is the display of a mouse cursor at all times, in addition to the input cursor.

Input sequences

The designer should check the effects of various input sequences. Working on the principle that if something is possible then the user will make it happen, the designer

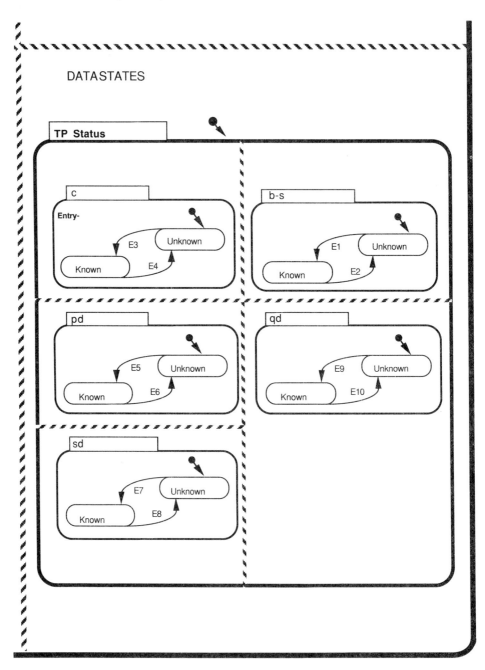

Figure 3.39 *Data states.*

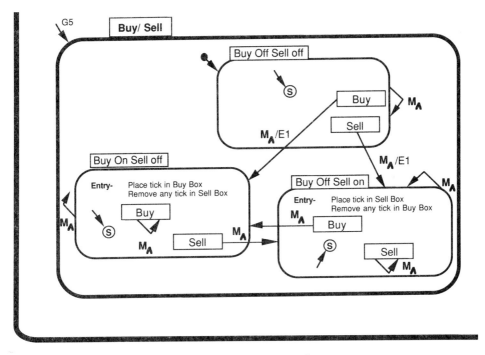

Figure 3.40 *Buy or Sell.*

should generate unlikely sequences from the possible inputs and trace their effects. For instance, what happens if the dealer types in the following sequence from within the state **Prod/K/Input** (Figure 3.41):

K (Character from keyboard), CR, $M_\wedge$, $M_\wedge$, $M_>$, $M_\wedge$, $M_\wedge$ (in Own Position Window), CR, CR

The system would take the CR and check whether the string in the product field was known. On finding that it was not (a string of length 1 is unlikely to be a unique identifier), a message box (W2) would be displayed. The following two mouse presses would be ignored as only a clicking on the ACCEPT button is recognised in this dialogue state. The CRs following this would also do nothing unless the specification intended CR to be interpreted as ACCEPTance by default. This should be clarified. If the CR was taken as an ACCEPT, then the next CR would again display the Message Box (W2).

This exercise should identify unusual sequences of interaction that may produce unusual dialogues. Even in the above example, the sequence and subsequent analysis has suggested that a decision is necessary as to whether a CR is a legitimate way of selecting a push button (ACCEPT) by default. On close examination it also raises the question of whether the Product input field should be reset following the entry of an unknown identifier.

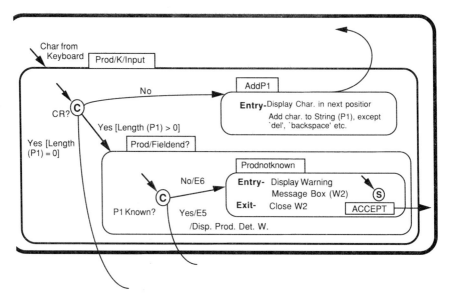

Figure 3.41 *State Prod/K/Input.*

Common sequence

The main objective of this design work is ultimately to render the system usable. A powerful means of checking the likely speed of interaction with the system can be applied at this time. This is called the Keystroke Level Model (KLM) (Card *et al.* 1980). This model basically applies a number of constants to certain operations which can then be summed to give a time for completion of a dialogue sequence. The constants are as follows:

K: a keystroke from the keyboard, or a mouse button press;
P: pointing to a target on the display with a mouse;
H: placing a hand on the keyboard or mouse;
M: performing a mental operation;
R: system response time.

The values associated with these constants are as follows:

K 0.2 secs (based on an average typing level);
P 1.1 secs (based on Fitt's law (Fitts and Posner 1973));
H 0.4 secs (empirically-based estimate);
M 1.35 secs (empirically-based estimate);
R t (system specific).

Specification estimates of the time required to complete tasks can be provided by a statechart. For instance, how long will it take a dealer to Give a Quote? In the requirements established in Stage 2, a usability target of 25 seconds on average for quoting a price was established. A modal time of 20 seconds was also quoted. Given that the KLM only applies to error-free interaction it is to be hoped that the prediction it provides for Quote a Price is 20 seconds or less. If it is not, then the design may have to be re-addressed or the targets relaxed.

Table 3.3. provides an example of KLM as applied to the case study. The specification assumes that the user will use the mouse where possible.

Obviously, the calculation of 15.75 seconds for Quote a Price is only an estimate. None the less, the model has predictive validity as proven over a number of studies. The estimate is significantly better than the target of 20 seconds. It should be remembered that this estimate takes no account of any errors such as might occur if the user chooses the wrong option from a menu. None the less, the analysis has been applied cautiously. For instance, the mental operation time for Calculate Quote has been doubled to reflect its relative complexity. It also includes the typing of the quote which might happen after the quote has been announced to the customer. Indeed, the times associated with the other mental operations are also generous given that the customer will be offering these to the dealer in unambiguous terms. Generous system response times have also been included.

Table 3.3 *Keystroke-level-model worked example*

Operation	Operator	User action (keypresses)	Time (elapsed)	Cumulative (secs)
Decide to Deal	M	–	1.35	
System Response, Windows	R	–	2.00	3.35
Locate and Grasp Mouse	H	–	0.40	3.75
Point at Option	P	M>	1.10	4.85
Press Mouse Button	K	M∧	0.20	5.05
Release Mouse Button	K	M∧	0.20	5.25
Identify Source (Customer)	M	–	1.35	6.60
Point at Source on Menu	P	M>	1.10	7.70
Press Mouse Button	K	M∧	0.20	7.90
System Response, Window	R	–	1.00	8.90
Release Mouse Button	K	M∧	0.20	9.10
Ascertain Product	M	–	1.35	10.45
Press Mouse Button	K	M∧	0.20	10.65
Release Mouse Button	K	M∧	0.20	10.85
System Response, Window	R	–	1.00	11.85
Calculate Quote (Complex)	M	–	2.70	14.55
6*Quote Characters	K	AAAAAA	6*0.20	15.75

Performing this analysis can result in the designer identifying potential inadequacies that need to be rectified. Alternatively, the analysis can provide reassurance that the design will meet the performance usability criteria set for the interface.

Given that the analysis is time-consuming it is suggested that it is applied only to a sample of the dialogues, preferably those for the most crucial tasks, and those with associated productivity usability targets.

Because evaluations of specifications can save significant effort in the long term, it is recommended that effort be made available for the above exercises. All inadequacies in the specification should be addressed and an updated specification produced. This specification should be documented as 'user interface specification', D305a.

3.5.3 Establish function requirements

The specification provides an opportunity to stipulate the functions required of the system that are not directly catered for by the user interface software. These normally include such things as database retrievals and updates. Given a statechart-based specification these are easily identified.

All check points in the specification are potentially points in the dialogue at which the system, other than the interface, will have to perform some function. Many of the Entry and Exit events associated with states will be function calls, and some of the output events will have to be supported by functions. Each of these should be documented, including the input and output parameters. For some functions, a decision will have to be made as to whether the function can or should be performed by the interface software or is in fact a function call on the *back-end* (back-end is used here to refer to all software other than user interface).

The potential functions identified from the complete specification for TRADE IN PRODUCT are:

- Provide data for Customer Details Window;
- Provide data for Product Details Window;
- Provide data for Own Position Window;
- Provide data for Deal Window;
- Check Customer Identifier;
- Check Product Identifier;
- Check if Quote Acceptable;
- Check if Size of Deal Acceptable;
- Provide Options for Product Menu;
- Provide Options for Customer Menu;
- Provide Options for Size of Deal Menu.

All other events are user interface software functions. None of the above functions include any formatting. Formatting should always be the responsibility of the user interface software. A number of the functions listed could be performed by the user interface software. For instance, if the menus are static rather than dependent on a transient factor, then they may as well be provided statically by the interface software.

Similarly, where a truly finite set of legal options exist as input, then these, too, could be checked by the interface software. In fact, Deal Window does not require anything from the back-end. All that is required is *time*, which is a general function.

With regard to the case study, the decision could be made that only the functions shown in Table 3.4 will be required of the back-end software.

Table 3.4 *Functions required*

Function name	Input parameters	Output parameters	Exceptions
Provide Own Position Data	Dealer Identifier	Dealer Name, P/L Value [Last Six Deals (Customer, Product, Size (M), Quote, Date/Time of Deal)], Exposure $, Exposure £, Exposure Yen	
Provide Date/Time Now	–	Date (DD/MM/YY), Time (HH:MM)	
Provide Customer Details	Customer Identifier	[Last seven deals by customer (Product, Size (M), Quote, Date/Time, Limit per Deal, Limit on Position)]	'Customer Not Known'
Provide Product Data	Product Identifier	Spot Rate Reuters, Spot Rate Telerate, Spot Rate In-house [Last 120 Spot Rates from Telerate (xx,xx, . . . , xx)]	'Product Not Known'
Quote Acceptable?	Product Identifier, Quote value	Okay	'Quote not acceptable'
Size of Deal Acceptable?	Dealer Identifier, Product Identifier, Quote	Okay	'Not Acceptable'
Submit Deal	Dealer Identifier, Customer Identifier, Product Identifier, Quote, Size of Deal, and Buy/Sell		

It should be noted that the checking of Customer and Product Identifiers have been bundled with the larger functions of providing data for the Customer Details and Product Details Windows. The reason for this is that the only times when the Customer and Product are checked is for purposes of producing these windows. As stated above, the Deal Window is not populated with data so it can be produced without recourse to the back-end. Functions for checking the Quote and Size of Deal are included. Because the acceptability of Size of Deal is dependent on the individual dealer and the Product, both of these are supplied to the back-end as input parameters to the function.

It is worth noting the self-contained nature of these functions. Atomic functions are bundled together as far as is possible so that a minimum number of functions are required. This is achieved by only having functions for those points in the dialogue at which the interface actually requires some data or clarification. This approach to generating functions is efficient at establishing the data that the user interface software should maintain for itself. It is often the case that at the beginning of a task a number of functions can be performed, the results of which are then stored locally. In this way subsequent system response times during the remainder of the task can be minimised.

This function set should be documented as 'User interface function catalogue', D305b. Its content should be discussed and agreed with the development team. It is an extremely important document that should subsequently be reviewed regularly. This may necessitate amendments which should also be agreed with the development team. It provides a level of agreement and independence between user interface and back-end (database) developers.

3.5.4 INteraction POints Analysis (INPOA)

The following provides a method (INPOA) for estimating the effort required for user interface developments. The author would not have the temerity to suggest that this method will provide reasonable estimates – yet. None the less, through refinement over a number of projects this method has the potential to become a valid estimating tool.

The general framework is based on the function point analysis method (Symons 1991).

In order to make estimates it is first necessary to gain an appreciation of the amount of work at hand. This is referred to as system sizing.

System sizing is performed by counting – if applied following design specification, or by *guestimating* if performed prior to specification – the major user interfacing components. This count is then normalised.

In INPOA the proposed interfacing components are as follows:

- N_{IW} = total number of Input Windows (character-based);
- N_{DW} = total number of Display Windows (non-interactive data displays, not graphical);
- N_{PW} = total number of Pop-up Windows (i.e. for errors, warnings, help);
- N_{PB} = total number of Push Buttons or stable interactive icons;
- N_{OP} = total number of OPerations (i.e. delete, find, refresh). These are usually menu items;

- N_{GW} = total number of Graphic Windows;
- N_{XGW} = total number of eXceptional Graphic Windows (Interactive).

The total number of Unadjusted INteractive OPerations (UINOP) is calculated thus:

$$UNIOPs = (3*N_{IW}) + (1.5*N_{DW}) + (0.8*N_{PW}) + (1.1*N_{PB})$$
$$+ (0.8*N_{OP}) + (5*N_{GW}) + (10*N_{XGW})$$

The weightings applied to the various interfacing components, for instance 3 * the Number of Input Windows N_{IW}, is based on the relative effort required to develop instances of each of these components. As experience of using INPOA grows and as tools, such as visual programming tools, become available, these weightings will be adjusted.

General characteristics of projects are now considered and used to adjust the UINOPs. The Interactive Complexity Ajustment (ICA) is calculated by considering nine factors as listed below. A score is awarded on the basis of each factor. The sum of these scores is the ICA value.

The nine factors and their associated scores are as follows:

User interface style:

    0 = question answer
    1 = form-filling
    2 = windows, icons, mouse, pointers (WIMP)
    3 = direct manipulation
    4 = multimedia, including interactive graphics

Functionality:

    0 = minimal, no requirements for productivity functions
    1–3 = reversible actions, cut and paste facilities, etc.
    4 = context-sensitive dialogues, sophisticated UNDO/REDO
    5 = dynamic data exchange, tailorable dialogue

User base:

    0 = supports just one type of user
    1 = supports various job functions
    2 = users are variable in their computer literacy
    3–4 = many job functions and heterogeneous user population
    5 = general population is target user base

Usability requirements:

    0 = no usability criteria established
    1 = minimal usability requirements such as productivity
    2 = general usability criteria set for whole system
    3 = criteria set specific to system functions
    4–5 = criteria setting and usability engineering are clearly the responsibility of
          the contractor

Organisational issues:

> 0 = not influenced by other systems
> 1–3 = should be consistent with other interfaces existing at the workplace
> 4–5 = should be consistent with other interfaces presently under development

Style guide:

> 0–1 = must comply with an 'industry standard' guide
> 2–3 = an existing in-house style should be applied
> 4–5 = a new style guide should be developed and applied

Evolvability:

> 0–1 = no stated requirement for evolvability
> 2 = interface should be evolvable in terms of surface factors such as changes to the command language
> 3–4 = interface should be evolvable in terms of offering increased functionality (i.e. new data presentation mechanisms)
> 5 = interface should be evolvable but in yet unstated ways. For instance, new applications might be added

Training

> 0 = no requirement for on-line Help
> 1 = user manual to be provided
> 2–4 = user manual and on-line Help to be provided and in a consistent fashion
> 5 = standalone on-line tutorial to be provided

Display factors

> 0 = no graphics
> 1 = business graphics
> 2–3 = scrollable graphics
> 4–5 = interactive graphics

$$INOP = UINOPs \times ICA \times F$$

F is a constant, which at present is taken to have value 1. As experience is gained and data is collected from projects this F factor may be used to calibrate the equation to improve estimation.

System size is taken to be the adjusted (normalised) figure given by INOP.

To calculate the effort (in man hours) an estimate of productivity is required. This can only be gained from experience and should be stated as the number of INOPs delivered per hour. So:

$$\text{Effort} = \frac{\text{System size (INOP)}}{\text{Productivity}}$$

Given the present calibrations, productivity has been assumed as 1 INOP per hour, thus simplifying calculations until sufficient data is available to permit calibration of constants. Making this assumption means that, for the time being:

Effort (man hours) = System size (INOP)

The reader is invited to perform this calculation for the case study material, deal capture only. The calculation should give an answer in the region 400–450 hours, depending on the complexity factors chosen. This is not an unreasonable estimate given that the case study covers a new piece of functionality, requiring the application of modern user interfacing techniques to provide a user interface demonstrating high-quality usability.

This value for effort can now be divided proportionally between the stages of STUDIO, thus:

User requirements analysis	= 0.15 × Effort
Task synthesis	= 0.15 × Effort
Usability engineering (prototyping)	= 0.20 × Effort
Coding/integration	= 0.40 × Effort
Acceptance testing	= 0.10 × Effort

As stated previously, INPOA is at present a framework for estimating. Its validity will only be known once it has been applied on a number of projects and calibrated accordingly. In the fullness of time, all the constant values suggested may change and as yet unconsidered factors may be found to be of importance in sizing a project.

None the less, users of STUDIO are strongly encouraged to collect the data and apply the formulae retrospectively on projects so that successive projects can benefit from experience gained.

3.5.5 Step summary

The value of formative evaluations should not be underestimated. Time expended on this activity can provide significant savings in the long term. If at all possible, the designer should seek independent evaluations of the specifications. This is recommended on the basis that the producer of a specification is the least able person to review it. Having completed the formative evaluations of the specifications, the designer should have sufficient confidence in the deliverables with regard to usability that the development can progress to the production of a prototype. Where it becomes clear that usability targets are not going to be met, the designer should enter discussions with the client.

A framework for estimating effort has also been introduced at this point. While this framework has no predictive validity at present, the designer is encouraged to collect the appropriate metrics for the benefit of estimating subsequent projects.

3.6 **Stage summary**

Task synthesis is one of the most demanding activities for a user interface designer. It requires the most design experience. STUDIO provides a suitable structure and set of techniques for performing design. These include techniques for specifying user interface behaviour and estimating effort. On completion of Stage 3 of STUDIO a first pass fully specified design should exist for the user interface. Any external interfaces to supporting back-end software should have been documented. The style of the user interface should be known and documented. In addition, a first proof of the user documentation should be available. The next stage is to prototype the design and assess it by user evaluation.

The main deliverables to the next stage are:

- General user interface decisions (D301)
- User interface style (D302)
- Textual content of the dialogue (D303)
- User support documentation (D304)
- User interface specification (D305a)
- User interface function catalogue (D305b)

The project can now progress to the stage of usability engineering featuring prototyping techniques.

Further reading
Nielsen, J. (ed.) 1989. *Coordinating User Interfaces for Consistency* San Diego, CA: Academic Press (an excellent collection of papers largely discussing industrial experiences).

Trademarks
OSF/Motif is a trademark of the Open Software Foundation Inc.
CUA is a trademark of the IBM Corporation in the United States.
OPEN LOOK is a trademark of AT&T.
X Window System is a trademark of Massachusetts Institute of Technology.

4 Usability engineering (Stage 4)

This stage of STUDIO applies two techniques in order to engineer the usability of the developing system. The term *engineering* is apt as used here. If reflects the iterative process of improving the definition and construction of a system given the constraints of finite resources. The two main techniques are prototyping and impact analysis, together referred to as usability engineering.

Prototyping is a well-recognised and often applied technique for the testing of designs (Wilson and Rosenberg 1988). The power of prototyping can, however, be undermined simply because it is inappropriately planned and managed. The benefits of prototyping are only fully realised when associated with an evaluation exercise that is properly conducted and its results fed back into the engineering process. The second technique is impact analysis, as applied to usability, which involved the rank ordering of difficulties, estimation of the costs of changes and allocation of resources to the generation of solutions on the basis of cost-benefit analysis. By applying these two techniques in the framework described below, developers can avail themselves of a powerful and manageable method for usability engineering. The framework is shown in Figure 4.1.

'Usability engineering planning' (Step 401), and 'Prototype build' (Step 402) are normally conducted in parallel. These steps provide a detailed plan and a prototype on the basis of deliverables from Stage 3. 'Design audit' (Step 403), aims to eliminate the most salient design inadequacies prior to hands-on evaluation by users. During 'Prepare evaluation materials' (Step 404) all the necessary infrastructure materials for running the prototype evaluations and collecting data are prepared. 'Prototype evaluation' (Step 405) is performed with users under realistic conditions for the purposes of assessing the adequacy of the design and gaining feedback that can be fed into 'Impact analysis' (Step 406), which prioritises the inadequacies of the prototype and allocates resources to finding and implementing improvements. A number of cycles through Steps 405 and 406 may be performed depending on usability levels achieved and available resources. The final step, 'Update specifications' (Step 407), ensures that all relevant documentation is brought up to date in accordance with changes to the prototype.

Usability engineering is, to all intents and purposes, the last opportunity to refine the user interface design. Subsequent to Stage 4, changes will be significantly more costly to implement, possibly prohibitively so (Whiteside *et al.* 1988). Usability engineering also applies to the user documentation produced in Stage 3.

Throughout this stage of STUDIO the HCI specialists are referred to as *evaluators*. The users participating in the evaluation are usually referred to as *subjects*.

STAGE 4: Usability Engineering

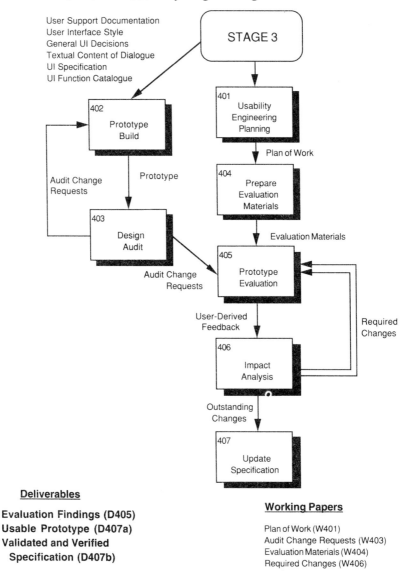

User Support Documentation
User Interface Style
General UI Decisions
Textual Content of Dialogue
UI Specification
UI Function Catalogue

STAGE 3

402 Prototype Build

401 Usability Engineering Planning

Audit Change Requests

Prototype

Plan of Work

404 Prepare Evaluation Materials

403 Design Audit

Evaluation Materials

405 Prototype Evaluation

Audit Change Requests

User-Derived Feedback

Required Changes

406 Impact Analysis

Outstanding Changes

407 Update Specification

Deliverables

Evaluation Findings (D405)
Usable Prototype (D407a)
Validated and Verified
  Specification (D407b)

Working Papers

Plan of Work (W401)
Audit Change Requests (W403)
Evaluation Materials (W404)
Required Changes (W406)

Figure 4.1 *Overview of Stage 4.*

4.1 Usability engineering planning (Step 401)

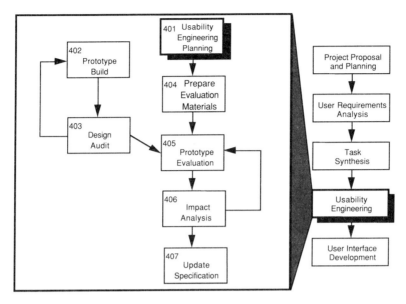

Usability engineering planning (Step 401).

Prototyping is an iterative process and as such it requires careful management. STUDIO provides the necessary framework to support the management and tracking of prototyping exercises. It achieves this by using the usability criteria established earlier in STUDIO as a basis for deciding when prototyping has accomplished its aims. If such criteria were not applied, prototyping could be continued indefinitely in the pursuit of improvements. The framework provided by STUDIO facilitates the production of a plan that addresses the following:

- user involvement;
- realism of the prototype evaluation conditions;
- populating the prototype with data;
- user documentation;
- evaluation scenarios;
- PLUME usability measures;
- plan of work;
- management of expectations.

These aspects of the plan are discussed below.

4.1.1 **User involvement**

Evaluation of any system is most enlightening when performed under realistic conditions. Realism is contributed to by the participants. Too often, developers and designers offer themselves as subjects in evaluations. This is of limited value given that they know far more about the system under development and far less about existing working practices than does the expected user population.

For these reasons it is essential to enlist a representative sample of users for evaluation exercises. The task allocation charts produced in Stage 2 identify the job roles to be supported by the new system. Individuals who will be expected to fulfil these job roles or who are similar in terms of computer experience and educational background should form the subject panel for evaluations.

For most systems it will be impossible to perform evaluations with all potential users. None the less, the larger the sample the more typical the results will be. Typically, eight users would be involved, providing a cross-section of the user population. Given that user involvement may be restricted because of other day-to-day commitments, early agreement and assignment to the evaluation should already have been agreed when the project was planned (Step 102). To this end, the evaluators should confirm both the users who will take part in the evaluations and their availability.

4.1.2 **Realism of prototype evaluation conditions**

It is not unusual to find that evaluations provide misleading data because they have been conducted under unrealistic circumstances. For instance, an evaluation of a prototype air traffic control system that only handled one aircraft at a time would be inadequate if the controllers were expected to handle twenty aircraft an hour. Good evaluations are performed under realistic conditions. Evaluations should be treated as dress rehearsals. Everything should be as it will be when the system goes *live*. The difference is that you can make mistakes during a rehearsal and it doesn't matter.

The problem is that users will not behave in a representative, and thus predictive, manner if they are not in a realistic situation. To achieve an amount of realism may require preparation above and beyond the provision of software. The physical situation in which the prototype will be evaluated may need to be prepared. Resources required to achieve this realism should be estimated for planning purposes.

4.1.3 **Populating the prototype**

Populating the prototype with realistic data is extremely important. Most developments will have a readily available data set that can be used for evaluation purposes. The aim is to ensure that subjects in the evaluations feel that they are using a real system. Created data is less suitable than data plagiarised from an existing system. Where there is no existing system then the developers are left with no option. The importance of using realistic data should not be underestimated. Users have a *feeling for what is right* and may spend more time in criticising the data than in interacting with the prototype. Usually, the quantity of data can be more limited than would be the case with the final system but even this difference should be minimised. Data volumes can affect system response times adversely and, in turn, user response times.

The evaluators should identify data requirements and estimate the time to collect and populate the prototype.

4.1.4 User documentation

During Step 304 a proof of the user documentation will have been prepared. This should now be made available for evaluation. While some evaluation of the documentation will already have taken place, a more realistic and demanding test comes when it is used in conjunction with hands-on prototype evaluation. During the prototype evaluation sessions the documentation will be evaluated as rigorously as the prototype itself. As such, evaluation of the documentation needs to be planned in just as much detail. Documentation will usually include user manuals but may also include training materials. The latter should be evaluated in the manner in which they are ultimately expected to be used.

The quantity of documentation required, a date for its availability and a schedule for training should all be documented.

4.1.5 Evaluation scenarios

Benchmark tests should be established for use during the evaluation sessions. These will usually require the user to perform some tasks, identified through task analysis, with the system. Normally, these will be stated at quite a high level. For instance, *create a mail message stating your availability today and send it to your boss*. Alternatively, *create a pie chart representing last month's sales by sector*.

Such tests are sufficiently open that the user has to make decisions, yet are sufficiently specific that the end of the test is quite clear. Benchmark tests should be chosen to give sufficient coverage of the system's range of functionality, provide data with which the usability targets can be checked and offer experience of those tasks that are most crucial to the users' successful performance of their duties.

Materials such as instruction sheets may need to be prepared for the purpose of administering these tests.

4.1.6 PLUME usability measures

The usability criteria, documented earlier in STUDIO, now take centre stage. These criteria provide targets that the system should meet. The prototype will be evaluated against these targets. To be able to test, one needs to be able to quantify and measure. Means of quantification for the PLUME usability categories are discussed below. It should not be forgotten that other categories of usability, such as *accessibility*, may be of equal or greater importance to a particular development.

Productivity

Productivity is dependent on the time spent on a task, the percentage of the task completed and the time allocated to the task (Whiteside *et al.* 1985). The following formula captures the relationship between these factors:

$$P = \frac{1}{T}(\%C \times AT)$$

where:

P = a productivity score
T = the time required to complete the task
$\%C$ = the percentage of the task completed at time T
AT = length of time allocated for task completion

The units for T and AT must be the same and are usually in seconds or minutes. Thus if a user completes a task in 2 minutes and the time allocated for the task was five minutes, the productivity score would be 250, as calculated below:

$$P = \frac{1}{T}(\%C \times AT)$$
$$P = \frac{1}{2}(100 \times 5)$$
$$P = 250$$

If only 80 per cent of the task had been completed in the time available, then a score of 80 would result. Where feasible, the constant AT should be the same as any usability target set for the task at hand. In this way, if the average productivity rating is 100 or higher, then the target is being met. Where productivity targets have not been set for the task at hand it is advisable to choose a value for AT that will allow most subjects in the evaluation to complete the task. This will avoid the need for, or reduce the inaccuracies associated with, estimation of the percentage of the task completed.

Absolute time measurements can be used where it is felt that they are more appropriate than a percentage task complete measure.

Productivity measures are task-specific. Normally, evaluations will only collect data on task completion for the most central or critical tasks as identified during task synthesis (Step 301).

Learnability

Learnability is the time and/or effort required for a user to reach an agreed level of proficiency. Thus, to measure learnability requires that a level of proficiency in relation to the system be determined. For instance, users could be considered proficient once they can complete a certain task without referring to any documentation. The time in terms of training and hands-on experience to achieve this would then provide the measure of learnability of the system.

Learnability may well be task-specific. For instance, it might take a user two hours to become proficient at sending electronic mail messages but four hours to become proficient at using a business graphics application.

User satisfaction

User satisfaction is a subjective measure. The most frequently used means of quantifying satisfaction is attitude questionnaires based on semantic differential scales. With this technique, users provide ratings for the system or prototype on a five-point scale anchored on the extremes by bipolar adjectives. An example is shown below:

Prototype

Understandable	—	—	—	—	—	Mysterious
	1	2	3	4	5	
Predictable	—	—	—	—	—	Unpredictable
	1	2	3	4	5	
Simple	—	—	—	—	—	Complex
	1	2	3	4	5	
Clear	—	—	—	—	—	Confusing
	1	2	3	4	5	
Familiar	—	—	—	—	—	Unfamiliar
	1	2	3	4	5	

For comparative purposes the questionnaire can be administered to users before exposure to the prototype in order to assess satisfaction with the present system. Then a comparative evaluation can be made by administering the same questionnaire with relation to, and following hands-on exposure to, the prototype.

Alternatively, a usability target can be set as an average rating score over the various scales. Given the scales above, it would be reasonable to expect an average score in the region of 2 for a well-designed user interface.

The number of scales can be as numerous as is felt necessary. Indeed batteries of scales can be administered for different aspects of the prototype if these are warranted. Thus a set of scales could be used for rating the on-line tutorial, another for the spreadsheet and another for the word processing facilities of a particular prototype.

Memorability

Memorability is the most difficult usability metric to quantify. For many applications it is not of particular importance, while for others it is very important. If customers experienced difficulty in remembering how to use an Automatic Teller Machine every time they wished to withdraw cash, then this would severely impact the usability of the machines. Memorability is a major issue when the system is to be used by infrequent users. Persons who only interact with the system irregularly or at regular but long intervals may have trouble remembering how to interact.

The best means of measuring memorability is to replicate the frequency of interaction and take measurements of error rates or productivity. For instance, if a productivity rate of 120 was achieved on a benchmark test of a particular task at the end of the user's first session with the system, then after a two-week absence the user's productivity rating dropped to 40, this would indicate a problem in memorability. Ideally, a system should be just as usable at the beginning of a new session as at the end of a preceding session. Ideals are rarely achieved but targets can be set and if deficiencies are identified, then actions can be taken to improve matters.

Errors

Errors can be reported as rates or ratios. An error rate is the percentage of inputs that are erroneous. If in typing 10 000 characters 125 are in error, then an error rate of 1.25 per cent would be reported. If reported as an error ratio, then the measure would be 1 : 80; put another way the user is making one error every 80 inputs. Reporting errors as ratios is preferable because it gives a better feel for size than do small percentage values (Bailey 1982).

When measuring and reporting errors, evaluators need to be specific in regard to the errors' level. For instance, errors can be reported at the character, field or record levels. To reinforce this point, consider error ratios for the task of filling a form. If a ratio of 1 : 120 is reported at the character level, then this might be thought quite reasonable. If the form had six characters per field, then the ratio at the field level might be 1 : 25. Again, this might seem quite acceptable. If each form has twenty fields, then it might be found that greater than 1 : 2 records were in error, which might be totally unacceptable. (NB the ratios at the different levels are not simple multiples of each other because errors are rarely distributed evenly.)

When reporting error statistics the evaluator must be careful to state the level of the error and it is preferable that ratios rather than rates are provided.

With regard to error recovery the evaluator must be careful to stipulate whether the error rates are for data input to the system for processing, or keying errors that may or may not be rectified before submitting the data for processing. Normally, only errors in data submitted for processing should be reported. The exception to this rule is when, for the purposes of usability engineering and impact analysis, it is felt that design changes might be made in order to reduce *keying errors* as opposed to *commit errors*.

Baseline data

The usability targets for the system will have been documented in W202. These targets are rarely mutually exclusive. For instance, a change in a productivity measure may have been achieved at the cost of a more error-prone interaction. Thus, it is worth establishing and maintaining a range of targets during the evaluations. By so doing, the evaluators can ensure that improvements to one aspect of the prototype are not affecting other aspects of the system's usability adversely.

4.1.7 Plan of work

Sufficient time must be allocated to data collection and analysis if the benefits of prototyping are to be attained. All too often, time is allocated to users interacting with a prototype but little time is allowed for reflecting on that interaction let alone using the data to plan and make improvements. The following exercises, to be conducted during Steps 404 ('Prepare evaluation materials') and 405 ('Evaluation'), all need to be planned and timetabled:

- training;
- pilot evaluation;
- briefing/de-briefing sessions;
- data collection;
- data analysis;
- impact analysis;
- iterating impact analysis;
- producing a plan.

The effort allocated to evaluation is warranted given the comparable cost of overlooking usability at this stage. The costs of rectifying poor design decisions at the time of implemention, and the costs in terms of training, poor throughput, etc., would likely be much greater than those required to conduct usability engineering.

Training

In order for subjects to be able to use the prototype, they are likely to need some introduction to its capabilities, command language, etc. This training should be similar to the training that users will be expected to receive in preparation for use of the final system. Therefore, this training may require a formal lecture course or the use of an on-line training aid, for instance. Thus the training materials must be available in sufficient time. In addition, the evaluators should not forget that the training material is as much a part of the user interface as any software. As a result it is as open to scrutiny and improvement as the software. This material will contribute most to any usability targets under the heading of 'Learnability'.

Pilot evaluation

However confident the design and development team are regarding the appropriateness of their deliverables, it is essential that a pilot evaluation precedes evaluation proper. The purpose of pilot evaluations is to ensure that nothing major has been overlooked and to provide some reassurance that the evaluation will run to schedule and without difficulties. The pilot evaluation is not performed with any great rigour. On this occasion the subjects can be part of the development team, but are preferably individuals with little experience of the user interface. Hardcopy materials and training aids should be as they would be in the actual evaluation. The pilot evaluation should be timetabled to be completed well in advance of the actual evaluation so that obvious modifications to the system or supporting materials can be made.

Briefing/de-briefing sessions

At the outset of an evaluation it is worth briefing subjects as to the purpose of the exercise, that is, their involvement and time is for purposes of rendering the system more supportive of their requirements and it is in their own interest to be helpful and critical.

At the end of an evaluation it is worth de-briefing subjects. This will normally include a discussion of the difficulties encountered and give subjects an opportunity to voice their misgivings or even thanksgivings.

These sessions can be extremely important for managing the expectations of users.

Data collection

Depending on the usability targets to be analysed, different data collection techniques will need to be employed. For instance, subjective satisfaction ratings would have to be conducted as part of the de-briefings. If the data gathered by this technique were to be used as part of a comparative evaluation with an existing system, then a similiar set of ratings would have to be gathered in advance of hands-on experience of the prototype. Time-based data is collected ideally by embedded software. Often, this cannot be achieved so evaluators must define the simplest yet least intrusive means of taking timings, even possibly through the use of hidden cameras making time-stamped recordings.

Errors may be collected on-line by having the system collect a log of the interaction for later analysis. Where this is not feasible the evaluator may need to sit with subjects. Preferable to the latter is to have access to a video output from the user's screen that can be viewed independently (Green and Wei-Haas 1985).

Evaluators should seek the least intrusive means of collecting data. The very fact that an evaluator is in attendance can be sufficient to detract considerably from the reliability of the data collected. Where the evaluator must sit with the subject, then strict protocols should be established and followed in regard to how much assistance the evaluator offers, particularly when the subject encounters difficulties.

Data analysis

Organising data collection and evaluation is not as straightforward as might at first appear. Even after determination of the targets to be met and having ensured that users, documentation and prototype availability are scheduled, there still remain some very important considerations. Not least of these is how the data itself will be analysed and reported. The evaluators should produce tables depicting usability targets and actual performance under test conditions for each task. The evaluators should consider how data is going to be collapsed over a number of subjects and should specify exactly what will be deemed acceptable. Table 4.1 provides an example.

In Table 4.1 the usability issues column was taken from the dealing room case study. During user requirements analysis these issues will have been documented in W202 ('Usability issues').

The 'Measuring concept' column is a statement of how the usability issue is to be assessed. The most frequently used assessment methods include the following:

Table 4.1 *Usability targets*

Issue	Measuring concept	Measure	Target	Present level
Errors (in documenting deals)	Deal scenarios	Log of deals	1 in 1000	1 in 500
Speed (of quoting)	Deal scenario	Stopwatch timings	25 secs average	30 secs average
Learnability	Range of deal tasks with prototype	Time taken before dealers stop asking questions	One day	Ten days
Durability (of visual display units)	Extended use of prototype	Count of screen scratches and estimate of life expectancy	Life expectancy of 18 months	Life expectancy of 8 months
User dissatisfaction	Attitude questionnaire	Semantic differential score	2 (highly positive)	?

- user performance on specific tasks (with prototype);
- monitoring user during undirected interaction;
- questionnaire;
- user interviews;
- interaction logging;
- critical incident analysis.

The 'Measure' column states what the actual metrics are to be. Many types of measure can be taken. For instance, each task might be assessed in terms of time to complete or percentage of task completed in a given time. Time spent rectifying errors and accessing help and documentation may also be recorded. Other measures to be considered that can also be indicative of problems include the number of regressive behaviours in a given time period and the number of audible complaints made by users.

The 'Target' column lists the usability criteria, that is, targets that should be achieved through the process of usability engineering.

The final column provides base-level measures for each usability issue. It is not always possible to provide this data. If no system exists at present or the new system is providing novel functionality, then there may not be a baseline.

During impact analysis Table 4.1 will be extended to incorporate data on usability levels achieved during prototype iterations. This will provide a record of improvements.

Having determined how the data is to be collected and analysed, it is now possible to estimate the effort required to perform the evaluation. Estimates of effort required for data analysis should be produced as input to the plan.

Impact analysis

The data collected from the evaluations should relate to training, the documentation and to the interactive components of the system. Input may come from observations, logging data, interviews, etc. From these inputs the designers and evaluators will seek to make design changes that will improve the usability of the system. This exercise, of generating and implementing design improvements, is conducted as part of impact analysis. It should be included in the plan of work.

Iterating/impact analysis

As a rule of thumb, three iterations of prototype evaluation should be planned. These iterations should be allocated resources in the ratios of 5 : 3 : 2. Thus half of the available resources will be allocated to the first iteration. This is reasonable given that most usability problems should be identified during the first iteration. Impact analysis will prioritise how these resources are deployed following the first prototype evaluation.

Producing a plan

The activities described above have to be planned. Elapsed time to complete and resources required to complete, along with milestones and deliverables, must be documented. An example deliverables list is shown in Table 4.2. These plans, together with supporting text, should be documented in W401. In addition, all those responsible for deliverables should be informed of deadlines at the earliest possible time. All subjects involved in the evaluations should be formally notified of their anticipated contribution.

Table 4.2 lists each of the deliverables produced during Steps 402–406. The list is organised from top to bottom in the sequence in which their availability is required. As the 'Order of completion' column indicates, a number of deliverables can become available in any sequence. The major milestones are completion of the implementation of the prototype at which time it can be populated with data, all of the evaluation materials becoming available, the prototype being ready for pilot evaluation, the prototype being ready for full evaluation and prototyping complete (for that iteration).

4.1.8 Management of expectations

One of the most noted failings of prototyping exercises is the creation of unreasonable expectations among the subjects of the evaluation. For this reason it is important that subjects are kept informed. Subjects, following an evaluation of a realistic prototype, often believe that the system is almost complete and will be available for their use in a very short period of time. They should be given an idea of expected delivery

Table 4.2 *Deliverables from Steps 402–406*

Step	Products	Milestone	Order of completion
402	Version I of prototype		T1
403	Required audit changes		T2
404	Evaluation scenario documentation		T3
404	Data for populating prototype		T4
402	Audit compliant prototype	Prototype ready for populating with realistic data	T4
404	User documentation		T5
404	Instruction material		T5
404	Training materials		T5
404	Briefing/de-briefing material		T5
404	Data collection materials		T5
404	Documented data analysis techniques	Evaluation materials fully prepared	T5
404	Populated prototype	Prototype ready for pilot evaluation	T6
405	Findings from pilot evaluation	Prototype ready for full evaluation	T7
405	Raw evaluation data		T8
405	Analysed data	End of prototype evaluation	T9
406	Problems listing		T10
406	Rank-ordered list of problems		T11
406	List of design improvements		T12
406	Estimates of resources required for implementing improvements		T13
406	Documented design changes to be progressed	End of impact analysis	T14

timescales and an explanation of the implementation work remaining. Such information is best provided during de-briefing sessions held after evaluations.

During the briefing and de-briefing sessions, subjects may make many suggestions for changes to the prototype. They may expect unequivocally to see those changes in the final system. Because of this the evaluation must ensure that subjects are given reasons why only some of their suggestions may be incorporated. None the less, the evaluators should ensure that subjects realise that their feedback is most important and that the design is based on their input.

Where the users are not the purchasers (the usual case), then the purchasers' expectations must also be managed. They must be convinced of the value of the usability engineering stage. The usability measures provide the evidence for the evaluator's assertions. The procurers may also need to be convinced that the evaluators are in control of the prototyping process and will curtail the process within agreed timescales or sooner if adequate usability is achieved.

4.1.9 Step summary

The iterative nature of prototype evaluation and impact analysis requires in-depth planning. The above provides a basis for producing a plan. This should ensure that deliverables and resources are available when required. In addition, it should not be forgotten that the expectations of users are open to both positive and negative influences during these steps. These expectations should be managed carefully.

The main deliverable from this is a plan of work with associated products and milestones (W401).

4.2 Prototype build (Step 402)

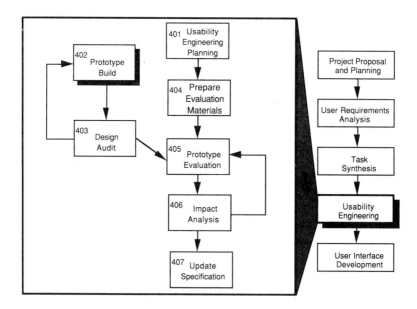

Prototype build (Step 402).

It would be naïve to predict that an implemented design will meet all usability criteria. For this reason prototype evaluation and modification are usually necessary. Prototyping is attractive because it permits design inadequacies to be rectified in a cost effective manner. Design changes following full implementation are usually prohibitively expensive.

4.2.1 Throw-away or evolvable prototype

The first major decision to be made is whether the prototype is to be a true 'throw-away' or something that will be evolved (Hekmatpour 1987) into the delivery system. This decision should be based on the expected delivery vehicle and whether it can support rapid prototyping (Wilson and Rosenberg 1988). The decision will affect the effort assigned to prototype build significantly. With a throw-away prototype much less effort should be expended on software engineering and achieving robustness. With a throw-away it must be remembered that the goals are to obtain a system that gives an impression of being complete and is sufficiently robust that an evaluation can be performed.

With an evolvable prototype the goals are different. An evolvable prototype should have sufficient structure that it can be extended into a fully fledged system. It must also be sufficiently flexible that rapid changes can be implemented following evaluations.

4.2.2 Managing expectations

It is also important that the expectations of the procurers are realistic. If a throw-away prototype is to be built, then it must be made clear that, following evaluation, implementation will begin anew, that is, a period will pass during which the client will have nothing but the prototype. It must also be made clear that even though the throw-away might look complete, substantial development effort is still required.

Given that prototypes can be so influential it is important that users who are party to the evaluations are left with a positive impression. Sometimes the mistake is made of allowing users to have hands-on experience of a prototype too early. Users must never be exposed to a prototype that *falls over* or operates too slowly. While user involvement is desirable, its timing must be tempered by the consideration of creating a favourable impression.

Resistance to change can also be managed during a prototyping activity. Users often find it easier to retain proven methods for realising their job aims and resist changes to these methods. When this type of resistance is encountered the evaluator must be patient and allow sufficient time for end-users to appreciate the benefits being offered. The following quotation may help to remind evaluators of how procedures, however inappropriate they may be, can become common practice and resistant to change.

Husband to wife: *Why do you cut the end off the ham before you bake it?*
Wife: *I don't know; my mother always did it that way.*

Husband to wife's mother: Why do you cut the end off the ham before you bake it?
Mother: I don't know; my mother always did it that way.
Husband to wife's grandmother: Why do you cut the end off the ham before you bake it?
Grandmother: I never owned a pan large enough for a whole ham.
Potosnak 1988.

4.2.3 Managing resourcing

The effort allocated to prototype build should be commensurate with the needs of prototype evaluation. The effort is being expended so that the changes required can be identified and implemented. If too much effort is expended on building the prototype, then there will be resistance from developers to make changes. The basic principle to be applied with throw-away prototypes is that the software be provided by the quickest means possible such that a system that is sufficiently robust for users interaction is provided, but no more. Even though this might upset some purists, there is absolutely no point in expending effort on software engineering for a prototype that has a very limited life expectancy.

4.2.4 Choosing tools

Many tools exist for producing prototypes. These range from screen painters to notation-based prototypes or base languages, possibly with classes of re-usable interface widgets. The choice of prototyping tool should be made on the basis of a number of factors. If the prototype is to be evolvable, then the final delivery vehicle determines the choice of prototyping tool. The design for the interface will determine a number of constraints on the prototyper. For instance, in the case study design the prototype should support windows, mouse interaction, the presentation of trend lines on graphs, field-level validation and choosing from data lists (menus), but it does not have to support interactive graphics or an Undo mechanism as these are not required by the design. The hardware delivery platform may also restrict the set of appropriate prototyping tools. Having considered these factors only a shortlist of possibles is likely to remain. The main determining factor, then, is likely to be the productivity of the various options, that is how quickly can the prototype be implemented and changes be incorporated?

In making the choice, the requirements set for populating the prototype with realistic data should not be forgotten. This may require that access be made available to some sort of database, either supplied with the prototyper or accessed via some base language.

4.2.5 Defining scope

It is often the case that a prototype only supports a sub-set of the anticipated final system, that is, the decision has been made that only a portion of the final system's functionality is to be engineered for purposes of usability. When this is the case, then the most central and critical tasks as identified in Step 301 define the scope of the prototype.

4.2.6 Build

At the outset of prototype development a meeting should be held between the designer(s) and developers, the objective being to ensure that the developers obtain an overview of the design and its rationale, and get up to speed as quickly as possible. It can be disconcerting for developers to have a partial understanding of a design, especially where responsibility for development is further partitioned. The designer can play a major role in ensuring that all developers are adequately briefed.

Stage 3 of STUDIO provides the specification to which the prototype should comply. 'General user interface decisions' (D301), 'User interface style' (D302), 'Textual content of the dialogue' (D303), 'User support documentation' (D304), 'User interface specification' (D305a) and 'User interface function catalogue (D305b) provide the specification for the desired system.

Where, for whatever reasons, the developers cannot meet the specification, they should document their difficulties and arrange to discuss them with the designer. Decisions to change the design should be made by the designer and not by a developer.

While Step 403 provides an opportunity for the designer to verify the prototype against the specification, it is often worthwhile checking the build as it progresses. By so doing, misunderstandings of the specification can be identified and remedied earlier rather than later.

4.2.7 Step summary

Very important decisions have to be made during this step which relate to the life expectancy of the prototype and its scope. During this step designers and developers should work closely to ensure that the spirit as well as the specifics of the design are taken forward into the prototype. Care must be taken to ensure that unrealistic expectations are not established.

4.3 Design audit (Step 403)

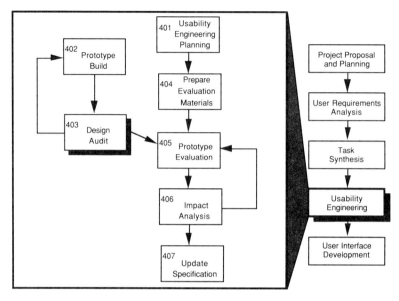

Design audit (Step 403).

The purpose of this step is twofold: firstly, to ensure that the design specification has been followed; secondly, to check some of the usability aspects of the prototype that are less than easy to check from a specification. This step is to be performed expediently and with a minimum of effort. There is no provision for, and there should be no need to iterate through, design audits and prototype modifications. The evaluation proper is the time when most change requirements will be identified.

4.3.1 Verification

There is no substitute for hands-on experience of the prototype by the designer for purposes of verification. The designer should walk through the statechart specifications in order to check that the implementation has applied them accurately. Similarly, the screen layout, textual components and available documentation should be reviewed for accuracy of implementation. In particular, the documentation and prototype should be cross-checked for mutual consistency.

4.3.2 Audit

It is not possible to check all aspects of the design adequately at the specification stage. For this reason it is valuable to perform an audit of the prototype.

An example audit is provided in Appendix C. This audit describes a number of interface attributes, some desirable, some undesirable. The audit provides the means for checking for these attributes and noting down their impact and possible improvements. Appendix C only provides an example; it can be modified to suit the needs of individual projects.

By way of example, two of the audit tests are described here. It is desirable, on returning to a system after some time away – for instance after a visit to the coffee machine – that users be able to proceed with the dialogue without needing to remember the history of their previous interaction with the system. This is referred to as the coffee break test. Failures on this test are not drastic of themselves but are frequently symptomatic of the more fundamental problem of poor user feedback. A second example involves dead-ends. Users should never be able to reach a point in the dialogue from which they cannot progress except by performing some exceptional keying sequence such as 'Ctrl Alt Delete'. The design should always permit the user to curtail a dialogue gracefully. Some of the audit tests are best performed with users, preferably potential users who have been involved with the design but who are not going to be required during evaluation.

The task scenarios to be used in the evaluation should be used as the basis for conducting the audit.

4.3.3 Reporting the design audit

Failures on the design audit should be recorded, together with recommended changes in 'Audit change requests' (W403). Given the numerous considerations impacting the implementation of changes, it is advisable that the original designer also be the proposer of changes, or at least be a party to any changes. On occasions, the scope of the prototype may impact its success during an audit. For this reason the auditor should be made aware of such planned limitations.

4.3.4 Implementing audit recommendations

Before proceeding to evaluation, the changes resulting from the design audit should be incorporated into the prototype. Completion of changes should be recorded and documentated in W403. An example form for recording the changes is illustrated in Table 4.3. The auditor should countersign the changes once satisfied that they have been completed satisfactorily. This auditing and checking process should never be allowed to consume large amounts of resources.

Table 4.3 *Form for recording usability problems*

Dialogue component	Problem	Specification source	Suggested change	Implemented? Yes/No (Date)
On-line Help	Access	W305	Provide an index with acronyms	

4.3.5 **Step summary**

Design audit is a quick verification and validation step applied to the prototype prior to user involvement. Change requests are recorded and tracked in working paper W403, 'Audit change requests'.

4.4 **Prepare evaluation materials (Step 404)**

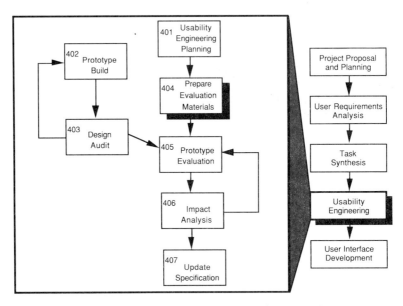

Prepare evaluation materials (Step 404).

A distinct step is included in STUDIO for the production of evaluation materials. This is in recognition of the significant level of effort often required for this exercise. The materials required have been discussed in Section 4.2. During Step 404 the evaluators must ensure that these materials are made available and are of the required standard.

4.4.1 **Users**

The most central resource for evaluations consists of the users or subjects. The timetable for their involvement and their commitment must be confirmed. It should be remembered that the subject panel should provide a representative sample, covering a spread of roles.

4.4.2 **Prototype evaluation conditions**

It may be necessary to establish a laboratory-style setting for performing the evaluations. For instance, where the system is an office system it may be necessary to include phones, message pads, etc. In fact, the evaluation scenarios may include the actual use of telephones, as would be the case with the dealing room scenario.

4.4.3 **Populating the prototype**

It is often required that the prototype be populated with realistic data. Once a possible set of data has been identified it is worth confirming with prospective users that it is actually representative.

4.4.4 **User documentation**

User documentation, including manuals and training materials, must be available for the pilot evaluations. The evaluators should ensure that this will be the case.

4.4.5 **Evaluation scenarios**

During this step the evaluators should prepare a set of evaluation scenarios for use during the evaluations. Rather than just have subjects use the prototype in an undirected fashion, it is important that objectives are set, for instance, to *create a spreadsheet for use in a monthly report*. Scenarios can be quite complex and necessitate a lot of preparation on the part of the evaluator. For the dealing room example, it might be necessary for the evaluators to have *brokers* phone the dealer and request quotes.

The evaluators should assure themselves that the tasks that subjects will be asked to complete are suitable. In addition, any instruction sheets, scripts or other materials for use during the evaluations should be prepared.

4.4.6 **PLUME usability measures**

The evaluators should confirm precisely those measures which are going to be taken during the evaluation. In addition, any requirements for measuring tools should be identified and fulfilled. For instance, attitude questionnaires may need to be prepared for use during briefing and de-briefing sessions.

4.4.7 **Pilot evaluation**

Most importantly, this step should perform a pilot evaluation. This is in addition to the audit performed in Step 403. This evaluation can only be performed once the prototype is complete, but it must take place well in advance of the evaluation proper so that particular problems with the evaluation materials can be resolved.

The pilot evaluation should be an accurate, scaled-down version of the planned evaluation, the main difference being that far fewer subjects are involved. Usually one or two subjects will suffice. These subjects should be trained, briefed, perform the task scenarios, and be de-briefed. Data should be collected as in the case of the true evaluation.

The pilot evaluation provides an opportunity to identify and rectify problems before expending resources, including finite user resources, on a real evaluation.

4.4.8 Step summary

This step should not consume significant amounts of resources. None the less, it is important that it is performed in a rigorous fashion. All too often, evaluators embark on work without being adequately prepared. This can lead to embarrassment and, in the worst cases, the production of poor data that are of little value for impact analysis. Provided that Step 404 is conducted in a rigorous manner, these difficulties should be avoided.

All evaluation materials should be collated and made available as 'Evaluation materials', (W404).

4.5 Prototype Evaluation (Step 405)

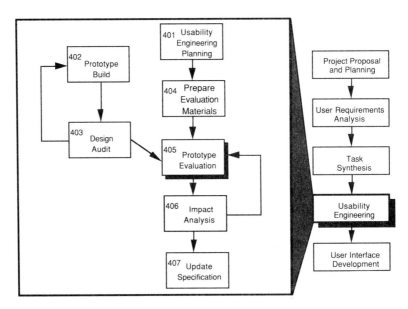

Prototype evaluation (Step 405).

Realisation of the power of prototyping requires that objective evaluations are performed and that the results are fed back into the development process.

4.5.1 Data collection and analysis

The basic rule of evaluation is to be non-intrusive. The fact that an evaluation is taking place should have a minimal effect on what is observed.

The data collection exercise should provide timings, error rates, etc., that now need to be analysed. Raw data must be prepared for analysis by collating similar data items and providing descriptive statistics for use during 'Impact analysis' (Step 406). The major categories of data items should be in accordance with the usability criteria. Thus, all problems encountered by users that contribute to a particular usability issue should be reported together. Problems encountered on particular tasks should also be grouped together.

4.5.2 Reporting

A problem is defined as *any aspect of interaction that causes users to divert their attention away from performing the task at hand*. Thus, seeking help, opening an inappropriate window, filling a field with the wrong data would all be problems. Errors made are obviously symptomatic of a problem. In addition, points in the interaction where the user seeks guidance from a manual or has to ponder for a significant length of time on how to proceed should also be noted. As the definition stated, anything that diverts the user's attention from progressing the task is a problem. Tables 4.4 – 4.8 provide examples of problems. Each table applies to one of the five main categories of usability (PLUME).

As Tables 4.4–4.8 show, the problems must be documented in terms of their impact. Thus, time spent on resolving the problems, their impact on error rates, the

Table 4.4 *Productivity problems*

Problem	Productivity Impact Average per deal (secs)
Re-positioning of Deal Capture window	0.5
Typing of Quote in Size Of Deal field	0.7
Not knowing how to remove warning message from the screen	2.4
Loss of menu and experiencing difficulty popping it up again	3.1
Trying to click on label for Buy field rather than the sensitive area indicated by the box	3.4
In Product Details window attempting to scroll the graph to see earlier trends	1.7
Difficulty identifying where in the Customer Details window the customer limits are displayed	2.6

Table 4.5 *Learnability problems*

Problem area	Learnability Impact
Mouse usage	5 minutes
Identifying required information in Own Position window	On third attempt went straight to the required information
Identifying required information in Customer Details window	Experienced difficulty in aligning data with labels
Identifying required information in Product Details window	Never became confident that the spot rates were up to date
Data Input by choosing from menu	10 minutes (fifteen entries) before dealer kept finger down on mouse button after appearance of window
Indicating Buy/Sell	On the first two attempts dealer failed to do this without error
Interacting with pop-up messages	On the third occasion dealer removed the message without having to ask what to do
Finding required information in user manual	Completely failed to use the index provided, and refused to read text
Starting up the visual display unit	Asked where the on/off switch was

Table 4.6 *User satisfaction problems*

Interaction area	User satisfaction Average for six subjects (rating: 1 – v.good)
Deal capture facility	2.4
User documentation	1.8
Presentation of Customer Details	1.6
Presentation of Product Details	2.0
Presentation of Own Position	1.9
Use of mouse	1.7
Data entry facilities	1.5

Table 4.7 *Memorability problems*

Problem area	Memorability
Data Input from keyboard	Continually reached for the numeric keypad in order to type in a data item
Switching on visual display unit	Each time a new evaluation session started the subject asked where the on/off button was
Data entry	For each session: forgot how to get a pop-up menu for a data entry field
Data entry	For each session: forgot how to move from field to field when performing data entry via keyboard

Table 4.8 *Error problems*

Problem	Errors
Lost menu	13:132
Clicked on label for Buy field rather than the mouse-sensitive area indicated by a box	3:5 Okay thereafter
In Product Details window attempted to scroll the graph to see earlier trends	Once only
Tried to perform data input using the numeric keypad	First five times only
Typed Quote in Size of Deal field	1:10
Clicked on background to try to get a window	Twice only
Chose wrong item from menu	1:15

effect on learning to use the system, etc., must be noted. At this point, all problems, however trivial, are recorded and analysed. In some instances the same problems may contribute to a number of the usability categories.

4.5.3 Step summary

The results of the evaluation should be reported in as objective a manner as possible and should be self-explanatory. The results of the evaluation should be documented formally in a report entitled 'Evaluation findings' (D405).

4.6 Impact analysis (Step 406)

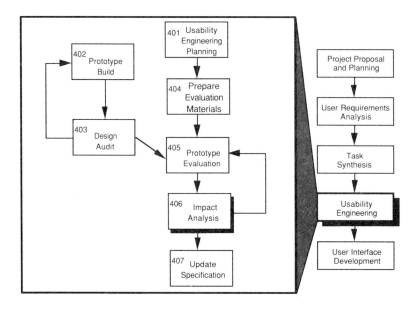

Impact analysis (Step 406).

Impact analysis provides a means of prioritising areas for further effort and assigning limited resources to making improvements. The objective is to gain the most positive result given the resources available. The major inputs are the results of prototype evaluation, the usability criteria and resource availability. The major activities undertaken within impact analysis are as follows:

- Analyse interaction problems with respect to usability criteria.
- Rank-order problems.
- Generate design improvements.
- Provide estimates of resources to achieve improvements.
- Decide on changes to be made.

The purpose of impact analysis is to direct resources to those areas where most resources are required and will have greatest positive impact. To this end, the next activity is intended to analyse the impact of problems encountered.

4.6.1 Analyse interaction with respect to usability criteria

The evaluators should first provide themselves with an overview of the usability of the prototype. This is obtained by tabulating the observed levels of usability by each subject for each of the usability criteria (Gilb 1984, Good *et al.* 1986). An example is shown in Table 4.9, based on the usability criteria established during user requirements analysis for a set of six subjects.

In addition, to the criteria given in Table 4.9, further criteria may also have been assessed that can only make sense when presented as a metric for all subjects. For instance, the durability of visual display equipment is best assessed cumulatively for all dealers participating in the evaluation. It might be reported as the total number of scratches on the visual display units used in the evaluation. A system test might also have indicated that the information update rate was of the order of thirty seconds – well within the criterion set.

It can be seen from Table 4.9 that the learnability of, and user satisfaction with, the system have both met their criteria. Users needed less than one day's training to meet the criteria stipulated. On administering the post-evaluation questionnaire the subjects gave favourable ratings that, on average, were better than the criterion of '2'.

Error ratios have been reported, that is, the number of errors per number of occasions on which an error could have occurred. Insufficient data was collected to make a definite statement on the error rate for documenting deals, but initial indications are that the very strict criterion have been fulfilled.

The prototype apparently failed on productivity for the task of quoting deals. Dealers in the evaluation took, on average, a little over thirty seconds to make quotes. This is significantly higher than the criteria set.

Thus far, only overall ratings have been provided. Analysis might have been taken to a far greater depth in order to demonstrate the usability of smaller task fragments, for instance, the learnability or error rates for data entry alone. The level of detail of the analysis depends on the specificity of the criteria. Thus, if criteria are set for particular tasks, then the analysis should provide findings at the task level. Depending

Table 4.9 *Usability by subject*

Dealer number	Errors in documenting deals (errors : deals)	Speed of quoting (seconds)	Learnability (days)	User satisfaction (scale of 1–5, 1 is very satisfied)
D1	0 : 35	32.5	<1	1.8
D2	0 : 42	28.7	<1	2.1
D3	0 : 57	22.6	<1	1.4
D4	0 : 36	35.1	<1	2.0
D5	0 : 44	28.9	<1	1.9
D6	0 : 35	33.2	<1	1.8
Target	<1 in 1000	<25	<1	<2
Now	0 : 249	30.2	<1	1.83

on the size of the subject panel and the resources made available, evaluators may consider performing statistical analyses to assure themselves of the reliability of data collected.

4.6.2 Rank-order problems

The problems now need to be rank-ordered in terms of their impact on usability. Users may be solicited to help with rank-ordering. For instance, they may be requested to make paired comparisons in order to establish the relative impact of different problems.

The list of problems should not be shortened at this time. Because the objective of impact analysis is to generate the best possible results given the available resources, it is not necessarily the case that the most profound problems or those that are easiest to solve will actually be resolved. There simply may not be solutions to some of the problems. Therefore, it is best to generate a lengthy list so that cost–benefit analyses can then be used to determine the most suitable set of problems to be addressed.

From the case study material, only the usability criterion for productivity has not actually been met. Therefore, the evaluators would seek to provide solutions to problems that impact positively on productivity. Indeed, following the true spirit of usability engineering and impact analysis, no further effort should be directed towards those areas of usability that are already at, or better than, criterion.

The list of problems for the dealing room case study are shown in Table 4.10.

Table 4.10 *Usability problems*

	Problem	Impact
1	Clicking on label for Buy field rather than the mouse-sensitive box	Reduced productivity by 3.4 seconds on average per deal
2	Difficulty in getting menus to stay in view (Having to keep mouse button depressed)	Reduced productivity by 3.1 seconds on average per deal
3	Identifying Customer Limits in Customer Details window	Reduced productivity by 2.6 seconds on average per deal
4	Not knowing how to remove warning messages from the screen	Reduced productivity by 2.4 seconds on average per deal
5	Typing data into the wrong field	Reduced productivity by 1.7 seconds on average per deal
6	Tried to perform data input using the numeric keypad	Short-term reduction in productivity
7	Forgetting where the on/off button for the visual display unit was	Minimal effect on productivity for Quote a Deal

A further aid to assessing impact is the use of Pareto charts (Deming 1982). An example chart is provided in Figure 4.2. Problems are listed along the horizontal axis. The left vertical axis shows the percentage of the total task time attributed to each problem. For instance, problem 1, on average, accounted for approximately 11 per cent of total task time. The right vertical axis represents the total time spent in problem resolution. For the task Quote a Deal, over 50 per cent of the total task time was spent resolving problems. Such Pareto charts provide a useful representation for discussing the significance of problems and prioritising them.

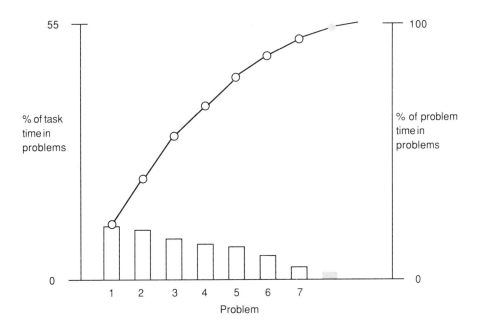

List of problems

1. Clicking on label for Buy/Sell field
2. Menus disappearing
3. Identifying customer limits
4. Removing warning messages
5. Typing data into wrong field
6. Using numeric keypad for data input
7. Forgetting whereabouts of on/off switch

Figure 4.2 *Usability impact analysis represented as a Pareto chart.*

4.6.3 Generate design improvements

Design improvements that will resolve or at least contribute improvements must now be generated. It is not the case that the most salient problems will necessarily be the most difficult to resolve or, indeed, that the least significant problems will be the easiest to resolve. The only means of assessing the cost–benefit trade-off for design improvements is to generate possible solutions/improvements and estimate the cost of implementing them.

Design improvements should be generated, where possible, for each of the problems on the list. There may be more than one proposed solution for some problems, as shown in Table 4.11.

Table 4.11 *Proposed problem solutions*

Problem	Solution	Solution description
1	1a	Permit the label as well as the bounded box to be mouse-sensitive
	1b	Extend the bounding boxes to enclose the 'buy', 'sell' labels
2	2a	Alter the operation of menus (thoughout the interface) so that they are selected by a mouse button down, but do not disappear until a further mouse button down and release operation is performed
3	3a	Enlarge the font for the Customer Limits in the Customer Details window
4	4a	Extend the 'close' button label on warning messages so that it reads 'press here to continue'
5	5a	No solution offered: the fields are already presented in the most suitable order. Colour coding the fields, closing the gap between label and input field or making the labels more salient might have a small effect
6	6a	Permit data entry via the numeric keypad in addition to the keyboard
7	7a	Add on/off labels to the front of visual display units indicating where the on/off switch is located

4.6.4 Provide estimates of resources to achieve improvements

The cost, in terms of effort to implement each of the improvements should then be estimated through discussion between the evaluators, designers and development team.

Costs, as considered here, refer to the resources required to modify the prototype. The developers of the prototype are best placed to make such cost assessments given their existing experience. Therefore, they need to be involved in the costing process.

An example listing of problems, solutions, their impact and the associated costs and benefits of the proposed solutions is provided by Table 4.12.

4.6.5 Decide on changes to be made

Having determined the costs and benefits associated with each solution, decisions should be made as to which solutions to implement. These decisions should be made by the evaluators but will necessarily be constrained by the resources available. They should also be tempered by any requirement for resources to be made available for further iterations around the *evaluate and modify loop*.

Figure 4.3 depicts an updated version of the Pareto chart. It shows that if it were decided that solutions to problems 1, 3, 4, 6 and 7 were to be implemented, then approximately 65 per cent of the time presently spent in problem solving would be eliminated. It is predicted that resolving these problems would speed the task of Quote a Deal by over nine seconds and bring the overall task time below the criterion of 25 secs.

The changes required and their associated costs should now be used to produce a plan of work for implementing the changes and conducting further evaluations. These changes should be documented along with an updated plan of work, 'Required changes' (W406). This document should include sufficient explanation of why the changes are necessary such that they are not reversed subsequently. The evaluators should provide a history and background for the changes so that the evolution of the prototype and, subsequently, the system can be traced.

Table 4.12 *Solutions, impact and costs*

Problem	Solution	Cost (man days)	Estimated benefit (productivity)
1	1a	0.5	3.4 secs per deal
1	1b	0.5	3.4 secs per deal
2	2a	2.5	2.0 secs per deal, after consideration of the need for an extra mouse click
3	3a	0.5	2.0 secs per deal
4	4a	0.5	1.0 secs per deal
5	5a	—	—
6	6a	1.0	Minimal
7	7a	0.5	Minimal

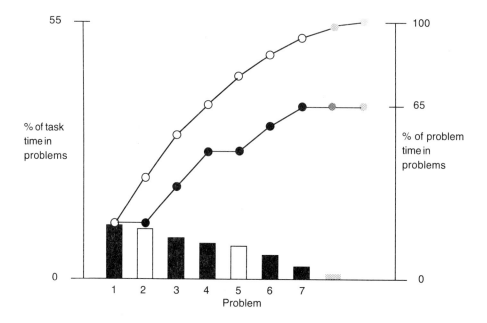

List of problems

1. Clicking on label for Buy/Sell field
2. Menus disappearing
3. Identifying customer limits
4. Removing warning messages
5. Typing data into wrong field
6. Using numeric keypad for data input
7. Forgetting whereabouts of on/off switch

Figure 4.3 *Usability impact analysis represented as a Pareto chart.*

4.6.6 Step summary

Impact analysis provides a means of prioritising modifications to the prototype. In this way limited resources can be deployed in the most cost effective manner.

4.7 **Update specifications (Step 407)**

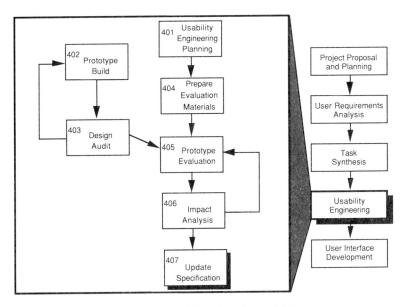

Update specification (Step 407).

The specifications for the user interface are an important deliverable to the next stage of STUDIO. It should not be thought that the prototype alone will suffice as a deliverable to the development stage. For various reasons, access to the prototype may be difficult and often more troublesome than gaining access to the documentary specification. In addition, it is often easier to implement from a specification than from an existing implementation, particularly where the final delivery vehicle differs from the prototype delivery vehicle. Therefore, it is paramount that the design specification be updated to reflect changes made during usability engineering.

The deliverables constituting the specification for the prototype should now be updated. The documents concerned are as follows:

- 'General user interface design decisions' (D301);
- 'Textual content of the dialogue' (D303);
- 'User support documentation' (D304);
- 'User interface specification' (D305a);

Depending on the gravity of the changes it may also be necessary to update the following:

- 'User interface style' (D302)
- 'User interface function catalogue' (D305b).

Where changes are made to these documents they should be cross-referenced to the appropriate section of 'Required changes' (W406). This will then provide an audit trail that should avoid the difficulties associated with identifying the source of modifications.

4.8 Stage summary

Proactive planning reduces the risks often associated with prototyping. For this reason a distinct step (401) for the planning of evaluations has been included. Many checkpoints are also embedded in Stage 4. Before an evaluation takes place the prototype is audited (Step 403) by the design team and a pilot evaluation (Step 404) is performed. 'Prototype evaluation' (Step 405) and 'Impact analysis' (Step 406) are also planned as iterative steps in a controlled fashion.

The final result is a prototype (D407a) and specification (D407b) that have been tested under realistic conditions and have been shown to meet required usability levels.

The specification should be produced as a single document (D407b) at this point. This will be an amalgam of the updated versions of the following:

- 'General user interface design decisions' (D301);
- *Optional*: 'User interface style' (D302);
- 'Textual content of the dialogue' (D303);
- 'User support documentation' (D304);
- 'User interface specification' (D305a);
- *Optional*: 'User interface function catalogue' (D305b).

This document may also be supplemented with example screens which may be generated manually or, where possible, screen dumps from the prototype should be used.

Usability engineering ensures that the potential of prototyping is harnessed to best effect. It ensures that development resources are deployed to best effect in tackling the most significant usability problems.

Further reading
Nielsen. J. (1992). *Usability Engineering*. San Diego, CA: Academic Press (very readable overview of usability engineering).

5 User interface development (Stage 5)

At the commencement of this stage the developers should have assured themselves of the following:

- that the user requirements are fully understood;
- that the design will provide the required level of usability;
- that the specification is valid with respect to both the requirements and the design.

Given these assurances, development should progress satisfactorily. The concerns that might be voiced at this stage include the following:

- comprehension and appreciation of the specification by the development team;
- outstanding high-level architectural issues;
- integration of the user interface software with the remainder of the system;
- final acceptance of the system.

This stage begins with the 'Hand over of the specification' (Step 501). During this 'Hand over' a number of activities can be performed to help communicate the specification to the development team and provide some context for the development. Following development, the user interface will have to be integrated with, or at least interfaced to, the application software. Application software is used here to mean all software not provided for purposes of user interface provision, but usually including a database management system. 'Integration/interfacing' (Step 502) is the point in STUDIO at which all software developments are brought together. Following integration a final evaluation takes place as part of 'Acceptance testing' (Step 503). The last and also a very important management step is 'Termination reporting' (Step 504). During this step the experiences from, and data collected during, the project are collated and documented for use by subsequent projects. The sequence of these steps is shown in Figure 5.1.

This stage of STUDIO docs not deal with specific implementation or software engineering issues arising from the choice of any particular delivery environment.

5.1 Hand over specification (Step 501)

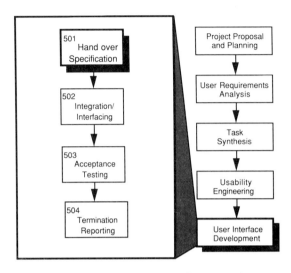

Hand over specification (Step 501).

Developments of significant size involving many individuals must support good communication and common understanding in order to be successful. STUDIO deals at length with the issue of designers and evaluators working with end-users and provides many techniques to help with this channel of communication. It is now necessary for the user interface designers to pass the specification over to a development team. While the designers may be on-hand to answer questions arising from the documentation and to act in a supervisory role to validate the development, the ideal scenario would be one where the specification was so rigorous that the designer could simply return at the end of the development in the knowledge that if the specification were implemented unerringly, then the final system would be as required. Unfortunately, it is rare for specifications to be interpreted as intended. Where development teams work independently to the same specification it is likely that the final results will differ somewhat. Because of this fact it is necessary for designers to support the implementation of their specifications.

STUDIO includes a specific step for the hand-over of the user interface design. The objective of this step is simply for the designers to convey the design to the development team. This requires that the reasoning underpinning design decisions, as well as the logic of the design, is discussed. Designers should aim to share their ideals for the design with developers. Where developers understand and share these ideals, they are more likely to implement the design as intended.

Where the development team is large, possibly with separate teams working on distinct aspects of the design, it is important that each team has a common

STAGE 5:   User Interface Development

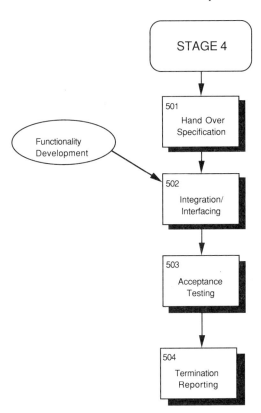

Figure 5.1 *Overview of Stage 5.*

understanding and appreciation of the whole design and how their part fits into the whole. Without this synergy there is a possibility that the final deliverable will look like a number of separate developments *stitched* together.

Step 501 should include the following activities:

- a design walk-through;
- an introduction to the relevant documentation;
- established protocols for raising and resolving design issues.

5.1.1 **Design walkthrough**

A design walkthrough is often the best way of moving from design to implementation. The designer(s) should provide an overview of the system required in terms of the tasks that it is to support, the usability factors and criteria to be met, and the major design decisions such as the user interface style chosen. It is also advisable that the designer conveys the process by which the design has been produced; this will help to convey the effort and reasoning behind the design. The walkthrough can begin by describing the main tasks to be supported using the task hierarchy diagrams. It can then progress to describing how these tasks will be supported using example screen layouts.

The audience for the walkthrough should not be restricted to project leaders and other senior staff members. The purpose of the walkthrough is to provide all developers with a knowledge of the end-users and the context within which the system will operate. It is helpful for everyone to have a context and an appreciation for where the system will be used. Indeed, where possible, it may be worthwhile arranging a site visit to see the present equivalent of the new system. The walkthrough should also introduce the findings from the usability engineering activities.

At the end of the walkthrough the audience should understand the issues that have guided the project to this stage and the tasks to be supported by the new system. A further benefit of the walkthrough is that developers should be able to trace the reasoning behind the design.

5.1.2 Introduction to documentation

Where the development team is unfamiliar with the chosen specification notation, then time should be planned to teach the notation. This might, for instance, require a one-day course on the statechart notation.

Some of the specification is likely to be mandatory reading. For instance, it might be vital that a style guide be read and understood. This might require time to be set aside to ensure that it is not overlooked.

The development team should be made aware of all supporting documentation from the detailed specification and design document to the style guide and user documentation. While developers will be provided with personal copies of some of the documentation, means should be established whereby they can obtain all necessary documentation at short notice.

5.1.3 Resolving design issues

It is inevitable that design issues requiring resolution will arise during the development. Protocols should be established whereby designers and developers can adjudicate on such issues, possibly with end-user cooperation to resolve design issues. This protocol might be as simple as asking the designer for an answer or as formal as filling forms and submitting these to the designer. Such formality may be required where it is necessary to track the progress of design issues and where their resolution might necessitate design changes that will have side-effects requiring the supporting design documentation to be updated.

5.2 Integration/interfacing (Step 502)

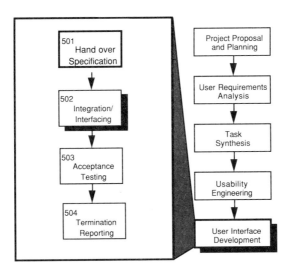

Integration/interfacing (Step 502).

On many projects, existing systems may create requirements that impose particular constraints on the architecture of the system. While the architecture of the system will usually have been finalised prior to this stage it is included at this point in STUDIO because it is closely related to integration. The architecture of the system referred to here means the major high-level issues of separation of responsibilities within the code and location of processing.

Increasingly, it is the case that systems will be developed such that user interface software is resident on personal computers (PC), while the storage and management of data, together with processor-intensive computations, are performed on mainframes. This is increasingly referred to as client/server computing. The objective of client/server computing is that hardware is configured and processing is distributed in order to optimise the use of available hardware resources and, in turn, to optimise system performance. The large storage capacity and raw computing power of mainframes can be balanced against the potential of personal computers to support graphical user interfacing and the use of personal productivity tools.

The reasons behind selecting such configurations are often historic. Traditionally, mainframes have been the corporate choice for the storage and distribution of data. Personal computers began to appear on the desks of executives seeking to benefit from their usability. In many cases, this led to a scenario where dumb terminals sat side by side with PCs. The dumb terminals provided access to corporate data and the PCs provided productivity tools such as spreadsheets, personal organisers, word-processing and business graphics capabilities. Unfortunately, the down side of this scenario is that direct access to the data held on the mainframe could not be achieved with the PC. The executive was forced to download or even transcribe data between dumb terminal and PC. This highlighted a requirement for mainframe access from the PC, enabling the dumb terminal to be dispensed with. This architecture is referred to as client/server computing, where the client is the PC and the server the mainframe. The potential advantages of this architecture are numerous. At the very least, the IT footprint can be decreased (less desk space is occupied by hardware); the load on shared central processors can be reduced; and users have to perform less data transfer activities. Unfortunately, these advantages are often the only ones actually achieved, even though far more is possible. Users may still be required to work with numerous command languages (one for each mainframe-based application); they may still have to appreciate and work with various file structures; and they may have to perform much user interface navigation, including log-in routines, in order to access required data, etc.

Ideally, users should be able to work with the productivity tools available on their PCs without needing to understand different mainframe communications, protocols and data structures. Users should be given a seamless and consistent interface and STUDIO supports this ideal. Stages 1 through 4 have paid little attention to the requirements posed by the need to communicate with existing or to-be-built mainframe-based applications. This is not an accident. The ethos of STUDIO is that user requirements drive development (Figure 5.2), rather than the traditional approach of having technology determine design.

While the above discussion has concentrated on IT solutions requiring PC to mainframe communication, it is equally applicable to developments that are wholly PC-based. The issue is one of separation of user interface software.

The above view of computing does raise a number of questions regarding architecture design and allocation of function. For instance, where within the code should responsibility for error trapping reside? The user interface code can probably trap most syntactic errors, but where should semantic errors be trapped? Where the user tries to delete a non-empty mailbox, should the user interface have sufficient data stored locally to trap the error or will the transaction have to be sent to a remote mail server in order to trap the error? Many issues such as these will exist and need to be resolved. Many scenarios may be considered, including the batching of data input or requests to be sent to the application software and the loading of application models locally to speed processing.

To achieve separation requires that an interface be established between user interface software and applications software. Stage 3 of STUDIO provides a set of function calls that need to be supported by application software. In the financial dealing room example, a number of calls for data were identified that were outside the functionality of the user interface software. These calls were documented separately in the 'User interface function catalogue' (D305b). This catalogue made no attempt to state how the functions would be serviced, for instance in terms of which database or network would be used. These decisions are *back-end* software considerations, but STUDIO can provide requirements for the software interface.

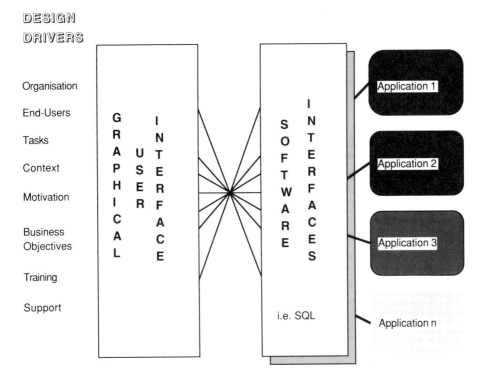

Figure 5.2 *Integrated interface architecture.*

On many projects, user interface software (client) must be interfaced to server software. STUDIO keeps user interface concerns separate from server or database issues. None the less, STUDIO supports the specification of the communication interface between user interface (client) and server during stage 3. Where parallel development of user interface and server software takes place, the interface can and should be validated in preparation for integration.

5.3 Acceptance testing (Step 503)

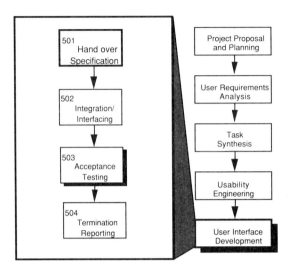

Acceptance testing (Step 503).

It is always necessary to perform acceptance testing. Even where a design has been engineered for usability and then implemented faultlessly, the client will wish to test that the final implementation meets the requirements and performs as expected when installed. Acceptance testing usually takes the form of a written script of tests to be undertaken, along with a set of criteria to be met. This is very similar to prototype evaluation. In fact, the same scripts may be re-applied. This testing is often referred to as 'summative evaluation' to distinguish it from 'formative' or 'prototype evaluation', which only test a sub-set of required functionality or a partially implemented sub-set. From the client's perspective it is the final opportunity to ensure that the supplier has provided everything that has been agreed and to the standard required.

The activities to be undertaken are as follows:

- Establish acceptance test criteria.
- Agree a timetable and resources.
- Carry out system demonstrations.
- Administer acceptance tests.
- Review results.

The acceptance test criteria are established by reference to those criteria generated during the project. Even at this stage, it is worthwhile reviewing the criteria established for the project at the time of its inception. As with all testing, a timetable should be created which identifies all persons who will conduct the tests and when the tests are to take place. The tests should be administered and the results collected on prepared sheets. Such sheets may classify failures in various ways, such as minor and major failures. The results should then be analysed. How failures are to be dealt with should be agreed with the client.

Of all the evaluations undertaken, acceptance testing will be the most realistic. Where possible, the designers and evaluators should re-evaluate the system with regard to usability criteria. In this way the accuracy of the predicted usability levels can be gauged.

5.4 Termination reporting (Step 504)

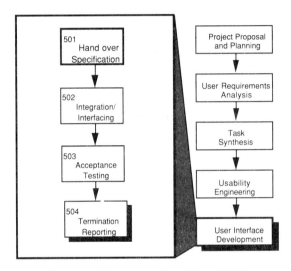

Termination reporting (Step 504).

The contents of the termination report were determined during Stage 1 and documented in the quality plan. During the development, data should have been collected as planned. Normally, three categories of data will have been produced.

The first category is an estimate of the size of the user interface development. One means of estimating the size of the system depends on function points as used in function point analysis (FPA). STUDIO introduces a variant on FPA called INteraction POint Analysis (INPOA). If the project has employed INPOA, then a retrospective analysis of its accuracy should be performed with a view to tuning it for future use. At the very least, the project should offer some statistics in terms of the number of interface widgets indicating the user interface's size. The main widgets will be windows but dialogue boxes, actions as provided on menus and number of graphics should also be included.

The second category of data refers to the manpower consumed by the project. This should be sub-divided by development activity. In this way measures can be obtained for the relative number of resources required per stage and step.

Finally, data should be provided for the amount of code produced. This can simply be in terms of lines of code, as is often quoted. More useful measures are provided when account is taken of how much of the code is re-used code.

The termination report (W505) should also detail useful experiences from the project. These may include techniques developed or extensions made to existing techniques. Negative experiences are also worth noting as they can help to prevent mistakes being repeated.

5.5 **Stage summary**

STUDIO provides advice on how to progress from specification to implementation. In addition, some important considerations are raised with regard to the separation of the user interface from other application code. Finally, STUDIO addresses the important point of providing a legacy for future projects in the form of project data. The diversity of tools/delivery vehicles and the abundance of literature on good programming practices precludes discussion of program design and programming methods.

6 Conclusion

The productivity of office workers has not increased as a result of greater expenditure on information technology during the past thirty years. While the reasons for this may be argued indefinitely, my own conjecture is that the poor usability of information technology has been the major factor precluding significant gains. Laboratory studies (Temple, Barker and Sloane 1990) have demonstrated that productivity gains can result from the application of modern user interfacing technology.

Systems demonstrating quality usability provide business benefits including increased productivity, reduced training overheads, more accurate operation and more satisfied users. Therefore, it is logical that projects should expend resources in an effort to meet user requirements and provide more usable systems. To date, the necessary techniques for delivering usable systems have largely been disparate and thus difficult to apply. STUDIO has brought the necessary techniques together to form a single, coherent and industrial-strength method.

STUDIO has proved itself commercially both on projects that are exclusively concerned with user interface design and on projects for developing total systems. For instance, STUDIO has been used for the analysis and design of a system to support a telephone enquiry service operated by a major transport company. The data analysis and modelling aspects of this project were performed using SSADM. A corporate style guide was generated for a large automotive manufacturer. This has since been made a standard for their Windows 3 developments. A major law firm has applied STUDIO to the analysis, design and usability engineering of the user interfaces to its new applications. STUDIO has also been applied to the production of a corporate style guide for use with the NeXTStep user interface which is the delivery vehicle for these applications.

Undoubtedly, technology will continue to advance in ways that impact user interface delivery; examples include multimedia products and pen-based technology. STUDIO will evolve and respond to these advances. It is also intended that STUDIO will be broadened to address such issues as business process redesign.

Appendix A
Documents Produced

Deliverables

Deliverable	Description	Produced	Updated	Used
D101 Business case/ cost–benefit analysis	A written case for financing the project or at least the user interface design aspects of a project	101		
D102 Quality plan	A set of statements establishing the practices to be followed during the project, possibly including standards to be applied	102		Throughout
D201 Scoping document	Outline of the roles to be analysed, areas of concern and scope of the study	201	(203)	Throughout
D202 Problems/ requirements list	Requirements including functional requirements, noted during evidence collection and subsequent analysis	202		
D205 User requirements analysis report (client)	A selected sub-set of all deliverables suitable for presentation to the client	205		

Deliverable	Description	Produced	Updated	Used
D301 General UI decisions	Dialogue rules and presentation rules	301		303
D302 User interface style	Style guide documentation	302		303
D303 Textual content of the dialogue	Texts for help, messages, etc.	303	405, 406	402
D304 User support documentation	User documentation such as manuals, text for on-line help, cue cards, etc.	304	405, 406	Stage 4
D305a User interface specification	Specification provided as statecharts, state transition networks or other notation	305	407	402, Stage 5
D305b User interface function catalogue	List of all the calls the user interface will make on the back-end (database)	305	405, 406	502
D407a Usable prototype	Fully tested interactive prototype	403, 405, 406, 407	405, 406	Stage 5
D407b Validated and verified specification	Specification for the user interface that has been updated in accordance with changes resulting from the prototype evaluations	407		Stage 5
D407c Evaluation findings	A record of the results of the evaluations	406, 407	405, 406	406

Working Papers

Working Paper	Description	Produced	Updated	Used
W201 Timetable for analysis	An agreed timetable of analysis activities	201		Stage 2
W202 Usability issues	Notable usability issues that are noticed during analysis	202		Stage 3, 4
W203a Task hierarchy diagrams	Task analysis findings as documented using THDs	203		303, 304
W203b Knowledge representation grammar sentences	Task analysis findings as documented using KRG sentences	203		303, 304
W203c Action lists	Task analysis findings documented as action lists	203		303, 304
W203d Object list	Task analysis findings documented as object lists	203		303, 304
W203e Context data	A record of relevant contextual data identified during analysis	203		303, 304
W203f (opt) DISCs	Dichotomy scoping charts	203		Stage 3, 4
W203g (opt) TACs	Task allocation charts	203		Stage 3,4
W205 User requirements analysis report	A complete record of all deliverables from stage 1	205		Stage 3
W304a User requirements documentation	Record of requirements for user support such as on-line help	304		Stage 4

Deliverable	Description	Produced	Updated	Used
W304b Timetable	Timetable for the production of user support deliverables such as manuals	304		
W304c User support: Logical design	Logical design for user support deliverables	304		
W401a Plan of work for usability engineering	Plan of work for iterative evaluation and impact analysis. Will include a list of deliverables, milestones and resources	401		Stage 4
W404a Evaluation materials	Collected examples of the materials to be used during evaluation. These will include user documentation, training materials and data collection aids	404		405
W405a Evaluation findings	Problems identified and their impact on the usability of the prototype	405		406
W406a Required changes	Listing of the changes required to be made to the prototype and a plan of work for their implementation and subsequent evaluation	406	406	405

Appendix B
Quick Reference Guide

The following provides a breakdown of STUDIO. This serves as a quick reference guide to the stages in STUDIO, the steps within each stage and, finally, the activities undertaken within each step.

Stages

Project Proposing and Planning
Usability Requirements Analysis
Task Synthesis
Usability Engineering
User Interface Development

Stage 1 **Project Proposing and Planning**

Cost–benefit analysis	(101)
Quality planning	(102)

Stage 2 **User Requirements Analysis**

Preparing the groundwork	(201)
Evidence collection	(202)
Task analysis	(203)
Validating the evidence	(204)
Reporting the findings	(205)

Stage 3 **Task Synthesis**

Task synthesis	(301)
Style guide	(302)
Design specification	(303)
User support	(304)
Formative evaluation	(305)

Stage 4 **Usability Engineering**

Usability engineering planning	(401)
Prototype build	(402)
Design audit	(403)
Prepare evaluation materials	(404)
Prototype evaluation	(405)
Impact analysis	(406)
Update documentation	(407)

Stage 5 **User Interface development**

Hand over specification	(501)
Integration/interfacing	(502)
Acceptance testing	(503)
Termination reporting	(504)

Stage 1 **Project proposing and planning**

Step 101 Cost-Benefit analysis

Quantify the benefits and put a value on them
Identify the cost of performing UID activities
Analyse the relationship between costs and quantified benefits

Step 102 Quality Planning

Define QA standards
Identify user interface design guidelines
Define baseline data collection
Specify contents of design documentation
Provide pro-forma examples of QA documents
Outline project termination report contents
Provide hardware/software acquisition list
Decide on project library procedures
Define management and tracking procedures
Identify process for establishing usability criteria
State how usability criteria will be used during acceptance tests
Establish change procedures
Specify resource commitment for user involvement
Specify major review points, property rights, security procedures, staffing duties and contingent liabilities

Stage 2 User requirements analysis

Step 201 Preparing the groundwork

Planning/gaining an overview
Obtaining access to users

Step 202 Evidence collection

Review project documentation
Decide on assessment methods
Carry out data collection
Update usability issues list and problem/requirements list

Step 203 Task analysis

Establish task hierarchy diagrams
Identify contextual information
Formulate KRG sentences for tasks
Identify generic actions
Complete action and object lists
Allocate tasks (TACs) to system and users
Scope the system (DISCs)
Revise requirements list
Define usability requirements

Step 204 Validation

Clarify ambiguities, omissions and misunderstandings
Use scenario generation and question reframing techniques to confirm data
collection results
Confirm analysis with users – TACs and DISCs
Carry out peer review – walkthrough

Step 205 Reporting findings

Document results of analysis for library
Produce document set for users

Stage 3 **Task Synthesis**

Step 301 Task synthesis

Identify crucial tasks
Perform PLUME analysis
Investigate logical screen design
Generate outline designs
Assess alternative designs
Assess practicality of the design
Re-apply PLUME analysis
Document new functional requirements
Draw general conclusions
Derive the command language
Determine the interface syntax
Determine the window layouts
Determine rules for window management
Consider exceptional circumstances
Document style implications
Repeat for all tasks

Step 302 Style guide

Principles
User interface options

Step 303 Design specification

Define statecharts for interaction

Step 304 User support

Identify usability criteria
Define timetable
Respect house styles
Decide on overall structure
Structure for logical design
Define physical design
Draft the text
Apply logical design
Review contents
Produce evaluation copies

Step 305 Formative evaluation

Evaluate statecharts for default states
Evaluate for reachable states
Evaluate for feedback
Evaluate input sequences
Establish function requirements
Perform interaction point analysis

Stage 4 **Usability Engineering**

Step 401 Usability engineering planning

Plan user involvement
Establish realistic evaluation scenario
Identify data requirements, resource requirement to collect and construct
data set for prototype
Define documentation set, availability, training materials and schedule
training sessions
Define task performance benchmark criteria, particularly in relation to
usability criteria
Identify timetable and resource requirements
Define process to manage user expectations

Step 402 Prototype build

Select type of prototype required
Manage user expectations
Decide on resourcing levels
Select toolset for construction of prototype
Initiate prototype build
Scope the prototype system
Build prototype

Step 403 Design audit

Verify design of prototype
Review interaction procedures
Carry out audit
Report results of audit
Review audit results and modify prototype

Step 404 Prepare evaluation materials

Confirm user resource commitment
Define evaluation conditions
Confirm prototype data set with users
Check availability of user documentation and arrangements for training
Prepare evaluation scenarios
Confirm PLUME measures to be used
Conduct pilot evaluation
Document evaluation materials

Step 405 Prototype evaluation

Carry out user training and scenario briefing
Perform data collection and analysis
Report evaluation results

Step 406 Impact analysis

Analyse interaction problems with respect to usability criteria
Rank-order the problems
Generate design improvements
Estimate resource requirements
Review and determine changes to be authorised

Step 407 Update specification

Document changes
Finalise specifications

Stage 5 User Interface Development

Step 501 Hand over specification

Design walkthrough
Hand over relevant documentation
Devise protocols for raising and resolving design issues

Step 502 Integration/Interfacing

Review user interface implementation options

Step 503 Acceptance testing

Establish acceptance test criteria
Agree timetable and resources
Carry out system demonstrations
Administer acceptance tests
Review results

Step 504 Termination reporting

Review development process
Analyse and record effectiveness of techniques
Submit documentation to library in accordance with quality plan

Appendix C
Testing/Auditing

Usability audit

The following audit outline provides a set of questions that can be asked of a user interface. The purpose is to identify the possible shortcomings of a design. It is not necessarily the case that any inadequacies will be rectified. The audit provides a record of ways in which a system's usability might be improved. It is a project management decision as to whether any remedial action will be taken.

Not all questions will be applicable to all systems. It is not the responsibility of the auditor to decide whether the results are of consequence.

The audit should be conducted in the light of the following high-level principles for user interface design:

- Always strive for usability.
- Strive for consistency.
- Group actions logically.
- Reduce short-term and working memory requirements.
- All actions should be reversible.
- Errors should be designed out.
- Provide information not data.
- Use the terminology of the user.
- Provide feedback at all times.
- Modes should be avoided, operations should have the same effect wherever they are invoked.
- Support contexts.

The format

The following format will be used to outline the motivation and mechanisms for administering the tests.

- An explanation of the possible failure.
- Examples of the failure.
- How to apply the test.
- The ramifications of the failure.
- How to document the failure.

A user interface audit of _ _ _ _ _ _ _ _ _ _ _ _

Author _

Date _

The Coffee Break Test

It should be possible for the user to curtail interaction at any point, for instance in order to have a coffee break, and on returning to the system be able to identify exactly how to continue interacting with the computer. In fact, any user approaching the system at any time, should be able, from the information available on the screen, to continue interacting with the system. Basically, users should never be dependent on having a knowledge of their (recent) past interaction with the system in order to continue interacting effectively.

A simple example of this would come from a system offering you only the options to 'delete', 'copy' or 'replace'. If that is all the guidance available to the user, then there are no means of knowing, except through human memory, what will actually be copied, deleted or replaced.

Ask a colleague or user to interact with the system. The auditor requests the user to stop interacting at intervals. The screen is then viewed and the auditor has to decide whether it would then be possible to continue interacting effectively with that system without a knowledge of the user's past interaction. The auditor should assure himself or herself that continuing the interaction is possible.

Failures on this test indicate that an unnecessary load is being placed on the user's working memory, that is, the user is being expected to remember rather than recognise pertinent information. An example is provided by the delete function. If you can invoke a delete without being informed of the object of the deletion, then the system has failed the Coffee Break Test. A means of avoiding this particular instance of the problem is to employ context-sensitive dialogues. For instance, the legend indicating the delete could also provide an identifier for what will be deleted.

Systems that fail the Coffee Break Test often do so in many ways. The audit should record the point in the interaction where the failure occurred and the historical information that was not available. The auditor might also make suggestions for remedial changes.

Location of failure	Information not available	Comment suggestion	Usability issue
Screen 102	Document identifier	Display document identifier at top of text processing window	User has to check document identifier before progressing dialogue. This takes upwards of 20 seconds and can lead to lost work

Data overload

When data screens are being presented, how much of the data is relevant? It is often the case that all related data is shown together, even though the user may only have a requirement for a small proportion of that data. This is to be avoided.

Database enquiries often provide an example of this failure. A simple enquiry can result in tens of items of data being displayed. While all of this data may be related to the item of interest, it is rarely the case that the user wishes to view it all.

Ask a user to identify some data requests that s(he) may perform during the course of his or her work. Then ask that user to simulate one or more of those tasks. Once a data screen is produced, enquire of the user as to the relevance of each item of data to present needs. Document the task, the data items displayed (including continuation screens) and identify those that were and were not relevant. For completeness, and as a reliability check, ask the user how he/she would be affected by the removal of the 'never used' data items from the screen.

Data overload is very common. Its affects on usability are often subtle. It is likely to cause users to spend more time searching data screens and wasting effort. Users are also more likely to utilise the wrong item of data mistakenly. One way to ameliorate the problem is to provide default screens that supply the data necessary to satisfy 90 per cent of tasks with an option to view the remaining data at the press of a single button.

The failure should be documented under the headings of task (enquiry), location of failure, associated irrelevant data items, and any other comments.

Task	Location of failure	Irrelevant data items	Comment	Usability issue
Retrieve sales figures for inclusion in report	Window: 'Sales Data'	Stock code, date of batch delivery	Place data item in a second (obscured) window that can be accessed via a push button	Searching for required data is slowed

Engineering model: underlying functionality

On occasions, underlying implementation details emerge at the user interface. Those responsible for the implementation may be able to offer plausible reasons as to why this has happened, but these are unlikely to impress the user.

The 'mv' command in UNIX is a classic example of engineering model failure. While the command effectively renames a file, the acronym mv suggests movement. The 'movement' is actually the re-directing of a pointer from one place to another. This is of little importance to users of UNIX unless they are dedicated systems people.

This test is best applied with the auditor keeping an open mind while working with the system, possibly taking guidance from a user. Openmindedness is required because the auditor must actively search for things that are of little or no interest to the user. Engineering models can 'show through' at the interface as unusual content, form or behaviours. For instance, error messages such as 'FRSAPR' or 'core dump' contain information that is irrelevant to the user, although the auditor might understand their meaning explicitly. An example of a problem of form is given by systems that always display monthly data in columns running from January to December, even though the most recent month might be March, and the April data is actually the most out of date, even though it appears near the centre of the display. Unusual behaviours could include the user being required to 'load', 'compile' and 'execute' a procedure, even though the user is never voluntarily going to want to pause after the load or compile step.

While knowledge of a system's underlying model is sometimes of value for maintenance purposes, most end-users would prefer to be offered, and would benefit from being offered, a system model that mirrored their tasks. When this is not achieved, users will resort to sub-optimal interactive behaviours, their tasks will be complicated and a feeling of 'lack of control' may result.

Test failures should be documented by example. Attempt to document failures under one of the headings: content, form and behaviour. By so doing, the depth of the problem will be better understood.

Location of failure	Type of failure (Content form behaviour)	Description	Usability issue
Window: 'Sales Data'	Form	Most recent month is not at the beginning of the sequence	User has to discriminate most recent month each time

Help: a task in itself

In order to access Help, does the user need to know the answer first? Most requirements for Help occur when a user does not know a command or where to find it. Many Help systems are organised by command, that is, in order to obtain Help on a command the user has to know the command name first. This is to be avoided if Help is to be useful.

Suppose a user wants to erase a document. There is an on-line Help system. The user types Help and is requested to indicate what it is that he or she requires Help with. To support the user, a list of topics is displayed. Unfortunately, it is ordered alphabetically and contains 300 items. There is no entry under 'erase'. What does the user do? The user is fortunate enough to stumble on an entry called 'delete' and recieves an explanation of how the command works and how it is to be used. The user exits the Help system and types 'delete' but cannot remember the rest of the syntax. The user then has to retrace his or her steps all over gain. A worse scenario still would be where the 'Help system' does not prompt the user but asks 'Which command would you like help on?>'

By using the Help system for solving simulated problems the auditor should be able to identify obvious shortcomings.

Problems with Help systems often result in their disuse. Whilst this is not a problem in itself it does have some side-effects. It is likely to contribute to sub-optimal interactions, because users do not learn the most suitable interaction strategies. When users do get into difficulties they do not know how to go about resolving the problem. Thus any difficulties are more likely to become minor catastrophes.

It is sufficient to document problems with Help systems in free-text. This can be structured under such headings as 'Access to Help', 'Structure of Help entries', etc.

General problem with Help (i.e. access)	Description	Comments/ suggestions	Usability issue
Structure of Help index	The Help provided is insensitive to the user's present interaction stage	Provide Help that is sensitive to the active window	Help is rarely relevant so will be disused

Mode test

Does the system operate in more than one mode, each of which interprets the same set of keystrokes in different ways?

This failure is apparent wherever the same keystroke, set of keystrokes or command invocation can have more than one meaning. It is related to the 'predictability' of interaction. At any point in an interaction it should be possible to state what the effect of an input will be without having prior knowledge of the interaction so far. This is a rule of thumb. Valid exceptions can be identified but for most systems this is both achievable and desirable.

In some word processors there is both a 'typeover' and 'add-in' mode for creating/editing text. This can be useful but it can also lead to confusion. When the user terminates text editing in order to carry out a task such as printing or saving a document, the modes do not apply in the same fashion. For instance, invoking 'save' may prompt the user with a default filename. To alter the filename one might expect to be able to type over the default if the system is in the typeover mode. Incongruently, the default disappears completely as soon as one starts typing. Such errors can be frustrating for users. What is happening from an interaction point of view is that the user is forming a conceptual model of how the system operates which is inaccurate under certain conditions. Had the system followed a guideline that said 'typeover' will operate in all conditions where the user provides input, then the interaction problem would not have arisen.

The mode test can be applied on at least two levels: firstly, by identifying whether modes exist, whether they are consistent in operation and whether the current mode is always apparent to the user, as it should be; more refined testing requires observation of user interaction over an extended period of time to identify errors resulting from the modal nature of the system, that is, users interacting as though the system were in a different mode from the one it is actually in.

Failures of this kind lead to short-term errors, possibly long-term dissatisfaction and sub-optimal interactions such as using one mode exclusively.

The problem can be documented simply as a description of the modes, the tasks they impact and the observable usability problems that they create.

Location of failure	Modes	Description	Usability issue
Throughout text editing	Update view	The same window ('Sales Data') is presented in exactly the same way with no indication of whether it is 'Read Only' or updatable	User gets frustrated when trying to update a 'Read Only' window

Dead ends

The problem of 'dead ends' can be identified as any reachable point in a dialogue at which the user resorts to invoking escape sequences, possibly even re-booting the system. Basically, users should never be able to reach a point from which they cannot gracefully return.

As an example, users should never reach a point where entering a valid data item is the only means of progressing the dialogue.

The only means of testing for this attribute is to interact exhaustively with every part of the interface. Of course, if appropriate guidelines have been adopted and adhered to, such as every window has a cancel button, then there should not be a problem.

Where a system does fail the test the opportunity exists for users to experience serious difficulties, one of the worst being loss of work, possibly as a result of a frustrated user powering down the system.

Any dead ends should be noted, stating where and under what circumstances they can be encountered.

Location of failure	Circumstance	Comment suggestions	Usability issue
All input windows	Cannot 'save' a part completed form	Each window should have a 'save' function	Leads to loss of work

Unable to complete

It is possible for the user to reach a stage in a task, possibly over the course of a number of minutes, and then realise that he or she needs one more piece of information that cannot be obtained without unwinding some or all of the work already completed?

Examples of this exist in data processing applications. A user traverses four enquiry screens in order to identify the last occasion on which Mr Jones received a delivery.

On reaching the appropriate enquiry screen the system insists on having Mr Jones' account number. The user then has to retrace through the four enquiry screens, diverge into account records and re-navigate to the appropriate screen. The system is failing the user by not permitting a context to be maintained. In human–human communication it is common for conversation to take major departures and return smoothly, without re-counting previous conversations.

Unfortunately, there is no brief test for this failure. The auditor must traverse the system exhaustively to establish whether any 'unable to complete' scenarios will occur. It will help if the auditor has a ready-made set of representative tasks to perform.

Unable to complete scenarios are frustrating for users. They can impede throughput and cause mistakes.

Failures should be documented by identifying where the dialogue may break-down and the ramifications for the user. An indication of how many extra steps, keystrokes, and time required to return the dialogue to the required context should be noted.

Location of failure/task	Point in interaction	Usability issue
Checking date of delivery	Account details screen	User has to backtrack four screens and re-input all navigation commands again. Time-consuming and error prone

Stupid questions

Does the system behave as though it is trying to conserve CPU time? For instance, does it ask questions or request data that it could obtain unambiguously for itself.

An example is offered by automatic teller machines. Having successfully keyed in your PIN number, the system poses the question, 'How much money would you like?' You answer, only to be informed that you cannot have so much and are requested to indicate a lesser amount. This set of questions can be repeated until you are finally requesting the minimum amount (usually £10) that the machine can physically deliver. The machine might then inform you that this is still too high. Further examples are offered when systems request a piece of data and then make a supplementary request. The answer to the first request actually obviates the need for the second, but the system asks it anyway.

Testing for this quality in an interface has to be performed exhaustively.

Such failures are rarely catastrophic. More usually, they are just irritating for the user. They can slow a dialogue and offer an opportunity for mistakes to be made. On occasions, they are desirable for purposes of cross-checking.

Such failures have to be documented exhaustively. It can be helpful to note data dependencies, even if they exist only in the perceptions of the user.

Location of failure/task	Point in interaction	Data dependencies	Usability issue
Cash withdrawal	Enter withdrawal amount that is higher than present limit	Withdrawal amount (input), withdrawal limit	User gets frustrated. Time is wasted

Jotting test

It is often the case that users have to resort to making notes on pieces of paper for use later in the dialogue. This is necessary because the data items cannot be remembered and will not be in view when required. For instance, a number of reports or files are to be printed but the report generation window obscures all other windows. Thus the user resorts to writing a list of all the reports.

A brief search of the area immediately around the keyboard may reveal scribbled notes indicating the existence of this problem. The auditor can also generate task scenarios and perform them to identify whether pen and paper are necessary tools for effective use of the system.

Failure on this test is an inconvenience, will adversely affect throughput and may cause errors.

Again, examples of the failure should be documented for subsequent review.

Location of failure/task	Description	Data to be Remembered	Usability issue
Printing multiple files	When providing a print instruction the user cannot provide file names	File names	Productivity is slowed, possibility for errors is increased because of transcription

Standalone test

This is a very simple test. Do users provide their own add-ons to the system, such as a keyboard overlay, because they cannot remember the operation of function keys accurately? Do they press 'Post-it' notes on or by the screen as *aides-memoire*?

In financial institutions it is common to find plastic cards listing the short-codes for information pages.

The test is made by noting the use of *aides-memoire*, notes, keyboard overlays, etc., and identifying their function.

The failure is indicative of a failing in the user interface. The user is being asked to remember too much, or the information required is difficult to access.

Such failures should be noted in full, describing the user's attempts to ameliorate the situation and the user interface failure that necessitates it.

Location of failure/task	Description	User's solution	Usability issue
Throughout	The user cannot remember all the functions associated with the function keys	A paper overlay has been placed above the function keys	The user has to survey the overlay to identify the appropriate keypresses for a command

Maintenance test

One assumption of user interface auditing is that users wish to complete tasks that contribute to the execution of their jobs. This assumption excludes users from performing any interaction that is necessary simply for the maintenance of a dialogue with the system. Often it is not easy to identify such dialogue maintenance. Another way of considering this overhead is any input from the user which is not data input or task clarification.

One set of examples are window maintenance activities. For instance, opening, closing, sizing, bringing to the foreground, etc., are all maintenance activities that do not contribute directly to the user's job-related tasks. Other such tasks might include the creation of directories or the deletion of old copies of files.

The test is applied by having someone, possibly yourself perform tasks. In this way you should be able to identify all the maintenance activities that are necessary.

The ramifications of this failure are that the user is distracted from productive work. Having to learn such maintenance facilities will also add to the training time for a system.

Examples of the failure should be documented as fully as possible as free-text descriptions.

Location of failure/task	Description	Comments/ suggestions	Usability issue
All windows	The user is expected to perform all window maintenance operations	Could a set of rules be devised for opening and closing windows depending on the state of the dialogue?	Users spend an inordinate amount of time on window management activities

Consistency test (to be applied with look and feel guides such as CUA, OSF/MOTIF, the Apple Desktop Interface and Open Look

All systems developed with the express intention of adhereing to a particular standard should do so unerringly, the exception to this being when a justifiable and documented reason exists.

Where a standard has been adopted it should apply throughout the user interface. For instance, if Help is always obtained by pressing 'F1', then this should always be so. In fact, 'F1' should never be able to invoke anything other than the presention of a Help screen.

The test can only be applied by exhaustively listing the standards to be applied and checking each part of the dialogue to ensure compliance.

Failures will lead to an inconsistent interface that does not allow users to generalise between different aspects of the interface. This means that they will commit errors as their preconceptions are found to be inaccurate.

Examples of the failures should be noted and, where possible, cross-referenced to the appropriate section in the standards.

Location of failure	Place in standards	Usability issue
Pull-down menu from 'Special'	Section 3.2.13	There are no options for short keys rather than menu choice

Reversibility

It is desirable that every operation the user invokes can be reversed. The benefits of this include the fact that the user is more likely to investigate new functionality and will work faster in the knowledge that any mistakes can be rectified. Undo/Redo functionality can be variously sophisticated but the user should at least be able to Undo the last operation invoked.

There are many examples of this, for instance, a user may wrongly delete a file and wish to retrieve it but not be able to do so. The user might make an enquiry and in retrospect realise that it is not what he or she wished to know, and that it will take a significant length of time to complete for no pay-off.

The auditor should decide on a number of tasks and commands to complete. As each command is invoked, the auditor should ensure that the effects of that command can be reversed.

The problems associated with a failure in reversibility range from the negligible to the significant. Lost work and poor use of functionality can be side-effects of interfaces that do not support reversibility.

The failure can be recorded as general descriptions of inadequacy or specific examples of the failure.

Location of failure/task	Description	Suggestions	Usability issue
Deleting a file	Whenever a file is deleted there is no way of getting it back	Files should only be marked for deletion during a session. The actual deletion should not take place until the user logs out	Loss of work. General slowing of interaction as users take a lot of care

Functionality test

It is often the case that, even after extended use, only a small percentage of a system's functionality is actually used. The reasons for this can be numerous. The system might simply be overengineered. Alternatively, it can be a sympton that the system is 'unforgiving', that is, the risks to adventurous users are too high in terms of lost work or expended effort.

A persuasive example is offered by telephones. Many new telephones have numerous functions, i.e. for transferring calls and conferencing. Surveys have shown that few users avail themselves of more than two or three of these functions.

To identify how much system functionality is being used and with what frequency can be time-consuming. It requires the auditor to obtain a list of the functions. Users can then be interviewed directly to ascertain which of the functions they are familiar with. Data gathering in this manner can be quite inaccurate and more valid results are obtained by observation of actual interaction. The ultimate data capture method is through automatic logging of user interaction. This has the advantage of being minimally disruptive, accurate and cost effective.

There is no definitive answer as to what constitutes failure on this test. None the less, there is an inadequacy in any system that lulls users into sub-optimal interaction. The implication is that means must be sought to encourage users to explore the system, for instance by making exploration risk-free through the use of powerful recovery procedures. With the telephone example, means would have to be found whereby in-coming calls were always recoverable.

The findings of this test can be documented at a number of levels of detail. At the very least, there should be an indication of how many functions (commands) are never used, or are used infrequently. At the end of the day it might be acceptable for 10 per cent of commands to account for 90 per cent of all interaction. What are more enlightening are interaction sequences requiring numerous commmands that could be performed with a single function.

Commands used/ sequences	Alternative command/ sequence	Usability issue
Copy FileA FileB DELETE FileA	RENAME FileA FileB	More error-prone sequence, and takes more time

Knowledge of completion

It is not always made obvious during an interaction that the system has completed a processing request. This is another issue of user feedback. The user should always be kept informed of the state of the system. That is, the user should always be made aware of whether the system is processing, has completed processing successfully, or has completed processing but something went awry.

This can happen when the user requests some information. If the system cannot find the requested information it may leave the user wondering whether the system is still processing or waiting for more input. Printing a document to a remote printer provides an example of where the user may fail to be informed of completion. The user could wait for a long time expecting some kind of feedback, or start new tasks believing the printing has finished. Either scenario can have undesirable side-effects.

The test for knowledge of completion requires that the auditor have a set of tasks to perform (preferably long-running tasks). The auditor performs these tasks and checks that the system indicates at all times whether it is processing and when it has finished.

This failure can leave users feeling that they have little control over the system.

They can waste time waiting for feedback and can lose work by starting new tasks without waiting for a still-running task to complete.

The documentation for the failure should note the task, a description of the lack of feedback, the impact on the usability of the system and, possibly, a suggested improvement.

Location of failure/task	Description	Suggestions	Usability issue
Print a document	User is never sure if the printing process has finished	When printing finishes display a message to that effect	The user waits for a long time to ensure that printing has finished before exiting the application

Summary

The audit described above is intended to provide feedback on the adequacy of a user interface design. STUDIO recommends that the audit be conducted as Step 403 immediately following prototype build. It can in fact be applied at any time once a prototype or initial implementation of the system is available. For obvious reasons the earlier it is performed the better.

Depending on the style and nature of the system under consideration, some of the tests may not be applicable and others not listed above may be more appropriate. The auditor is at liberty to extend or modify the audit as required.

The auditor should not feel constrained by the tests. Any problems of usability encountered while applying the audit should be recorded so that they can be addressed as early as possible.

Appendix D
Standards Organisations

Addresses for Standards Organisations

International Organisation for Standardisation (ISO)
Central Secretariat
1, rue de Varembé
Case postale 56
CH-1211 Geneva 20
Switzerland

International Electrotechnical Commission (IEC)
Central Office
3, rue de Varembé
CH-1211 Geneva 20
Switzerland

Comité Consultatif International Télégraphique et Téléphonique (CCITT)
Place des nations
CH-1211 Geneva 20
Switzerland

European Computer Manufacturer's Association (ECMA)
Geneva
Switzerland

Comité EuropÞEen de Normalisation (CEN)
rue Bréderode 2, Boite 5
B-1000 Brussels
Belgium

The European Telecommunications Standards Institute (ETSI)
BP 152-F-06561
Valbonne
Cedex
France

Dr L J. Besse
Chairman CEN/CLC/AMT/ERG-WG
Information Technology Advisory Expert Group – Manufacturing (ITAEG-M)
Université Catholique de Louvain
c/o Marc C. Lobelle
Place Ste Barbe, 2
B-1348 Louvain-la-Neuve
Switzerland

The Health and Safety Executive (HSE)
Baynards House
1 Chepstow Place
London
W2 4TF

The British Standards Institution (BSI)
2 Park Street
London
W1A 2BS

Glossary

Accelerator A specialised interaction technique that is a speedier alternative to a more common technique. Commonly used for frequently required commands. An example is a key or combination of keys that invokes a menu option without requiring the user to display the menu.

Action list A catalogue of the operations invoked by users.

Active window The window presently receiving input.

Alert box A window normally used for providing warning messages. Following creation of an alert box the user normally has to perform a particular act in order to resume interaction.

Blobs Normally a rectangle with rounded corners representing a user interface state in a statechart specification.

Cascading menu A sub-menu from a menu. The sub-menu's options are displayed when the cursor location is over a parent menu option. The existence of a sub-menu is often indicated on the parent menu, possibly by the presence of an arrow.

Check button A type of control used for setting options that are not mutually exclusive. Selection is indicated by highlighting.

Client area The area within the borders of a window's frame, excluding the menu bar, title area and any other areas reserved for controls.

Command language The actions that the user can invoke when interacting with the system.

Control panel A reserved area within a window used to display controls such as check boxes and radio buttons.

Crucial tasks Those tasks most frequently performed or most central to business effectiveness.

Cursor An on-screen graphical image indicating where user input will appear.

Default An object or action that is taken to be the required selection if an alternative is not chosen.

Design specification A specification of the behaviour of the user interface, normally documented in state transition diagram or statechart notation.

Desk accessory A readily accessible application that may be of use at any time in an interaction. Examples are clocks and calculators.

Dialogue box A display area generated by the system which permits a user to input parameters. It may also contain data, possibly default values and buttons for continuing or curtailing the dialogue.

Discrimination The cognitive act of delineating an item of interest from many possibles.

Do-wells The tasks that are most central to a business's success.

Drag To press and hold down a mouse button while moving the mouse.

Edge A link between two states in a statechart specification. Represented as a curved or straight line with arrows to indicate direction of transition. Also, usually labelled with an event identifier.

End-user A user of the system which is to be replaced or a person considered to be representative of the eventual user population. Developers are unsuitable as end-user representatives. Indeed, procurers are usually unsuitable.

Entry box An area within a window reserved for text entry.

Formative evaluation A set of analysis procedures applied to a user interface specification with the intent of removing poor design decisions in advance of any implementation or prototyping.

Greyed selection A selection that is not currently available and has been dimmed to indicate its unavailability.

Group box A rectangle with a thin border drawn around a set of controls to indicate that they are related.

Highlighting A means of singling out an item from many items. Means of highlighting including the use of colour, shading and flashing.

Icon A graphical symbol representing a user interface object such as a file, application or window.

INPOA An acronym for INteration POint Analysis. This is a framework or the beginnings of a method for estimating the effort required for the development of a user interface.

Insertion cursor A symbol indicating the point at which user input will appear.

Interaction syntax Rules governing the operation of the interface, for instance, how the user can make a choice from a menu.

List box A type of control that displays a selectable list of options.

Location cursor A symbol indicating where keyboard input will be directed.

Maximise button A control, usually displayed towards the top right-hand corner of a window, which when invoked displays the window at its maximum size.

Menu A list of objects or actions from which a user may make a selection.

Menu bar A reserved area, usually towards the top of a window, used to display topics for menus. Sometimes called the action bar.

Message box A type of dialogue box used to present information, issue a warning, etc.

Minimise button A control button, usually situated towards the top right-hand corner of a window. It is used to shrink a window to its minimum size or icon.

Mnemonic A short label for an action or object, often a single character that can be used to invoke a menu item from the keyboard.

Mode A system state in which user actions are interpreted in a particular way distinct from the interpretation they would be given in a different state.

Object list A catalogue of the entities associated with a system that have meaning for users.

PLUME analysis The investigation of the main usability factors of Productivity, Learnability, User satisfaction, Memorability and Errors.

Pop-up menu A menu that is normally invisible but appears under certain conditions at a pre-determined screen location or in a position relative to the currently active window or cursor position.

Primary window The first or top-level window of an application.

Pull-down menu A menu that appears when a menu bar option is chosen.

Push button A graphical image mimicking a real-life button and used to invoke an action.

Radio button A graphical image, sets of which are used to represent mutually exclusive selections.

Requirements list A catalogue of the needs of users. These can include functionality but, importantly, include needs for information, guidance, access, etc. An example would be a need for fast paths of interaction for experienced users.

Re-size border An outer border of a window that can be used to modify the size of a window.

Screen-button An on-screen facsimile of a button. Screen-buttons usually relate directly to the user's current activity.

Scroll bar An image, usually rectangular, used to control the content of a window either on the horizontal or the vertical axis.

Slider The visually movable component of a scroll bar that can be dragged.

Statechart A notation for describing user interface behaviours. It is based on state transition diagrams, higraphs and venn diagrams.

State transition diagram A notation for user interface design that describes dialogues in the form of nodes representing states, and arcs representing events causing transitions between those states.

Style guide A document produced during task synthesis which provides a set of guidelines to be applied during user interface design. For instance, a guideline might be that no menu have more than eight items.

Task allocation charting A method to facilitate the allocation of tasks to roles and provide support for job design (Ip, Damodaran, Olphert and Maguire 1990b, pp. 289-94).

Task analysis A set of methods for establishing the requirements of users and tasks. Task analysis would typically provide information on the frequency of task performance, acceptable performance rates, dependencies between tasks , the relative importance of tasks, necessary communication channels, prior experience of users, etc. For instance, a task analysis might establish that off-the-job training was not infeasible, yet users would need training, thus there is a requirement for on-the-job training, possibly in the form of an on-line training package. Alternatively, a task analysis might identify that end-users are likely to be wearing gloves when interacting with the system, thus increasing the likelihood of keying errors and creating a requirement that keying be kept to an absolute minimum.

Task hierarchy A notation for describing the sequencing of tasks.

Task synthesis Stage 3 of STUDIO during which the deliverables from Stage 2 are used to produce a design specification.

Tile pane Individual panes of a window that do not overlap.

Tiled window A window or windows arranged without overlaps.

Title area A rectangular area situated at the top of a window. It contains the title of the window and may be used to relocate the window.

Usability An assessment of the 'ease of use' of a system based on the quantifiable and qualifiable attributes of a user's interaction with that system. Usability is similar in kind to maintainability, portability or reliability.

Usability criteria Levels of usability set by the client or with the client. These criteria may be used for acceptance testing and possibly as contractually binding targets.

Usability metric A quantifiable measure contributing to usability. For instance, error rate would be a usability metric. All such metrics have to be qualified in terms of the users, conditions and tasks for which they are assumed to generalise.

User interface All aspects of an IT solution and its environment that impact users' effective completion of their job requirements. Thus, documentation, seating, job design, lines of sight, etc, could all be part of a user interface.

User interface function catalogue A document listing all the requirements for processing posed by the user interface on the back-end of the system.

User interface style A style refers to the general method of interacting with a system. Examples include form-filling, question/answer and direct manipulation.

User interfacing principles A set of guiding lights and targets to aim for in all user interfacing endeavours.

User requirements analysis The first stage of user interface development during which a logical view of the existing system is developed – the first stage of STUDIO.

Window management rules A set of rules defining the opening, closing and general management of windows. This should include statements of who is responsible for window management.

Window A reserved area of the screen within which a user can undertake some predefined tasks.

WIMP A style of user interfacing employing Window, Icon, Mouse and Pointer technology.

WYSIWYG A user interfacing attribute. A What You See Is What You Get (WYSIWYG) interface maintains a one-to-one relationship between what appears on-screen and what will be produced as hardcopy.

References

Aetna Life Insurance Co. (1986), 'Software usability guidelines techniques for achieving "normal to use" systems. People/technology issues and programs', The Aetna Casualty and Surety Co.

Apple Computers Inc. (1987). *Apple Human Interface Guidelines: The Apple Desktop Interface*, Cupertino, CA: Addison Wesley

Ashworth, C. and Goodland, M. (1990). *SSADM: A practical approach*, Maidenhead: McGraw-Hill

Bailey, R. W. (1982), *Human Performance Engineering: A guide for system designers*, Prentice Hall, Englewood Cliffs, N.J.

Boyle, L. S. and Mylam, H. M. (1989). 'Improved human–computer interface for HOLMES feasibility study', *Home Office, SRDB, 2/89*.

British Standards Institute (BSI 92/35512 DC) (1992). *Draft for Safety of Machinery: Ergonomic design principles: Part 1 : Terminology and General Principles*.

British Standards Institute (BS 4899) (1990). *Guide to the User's Requirements for Technical Manuals* (based on the principles of BS 4884).

British Standards Institute (BS 5515) (1984). *Code of Practice for Documentation of Computer-based Systems*.

British Standards Institution (1991). *Draft British Standard Recommendations for the Design of User Documentation for Software Products for Text and Office Systems*. IST/18.

Browne, D. P, Mylam, H. M. and Woods, A. J. (1990). 'User-centred Design: Experiences from a commercial project', In Hall, P V. (ed.), *Proceedings of Software Engineering '90*, Cambridge University Press, Cambridge, pp. 467-488.

Browne, D. P, Summersgill, R. and Stradling, P. (1992), 'The user interface: The poor relation in structured methods', in H. R. Hartson and D. Hix (eds.), *Advances in Human-Computer Interaction Volume 3*, Norwood, NJ: Ablex Publishing, Ch. 2.

Browne, D. P., Totterdell, P. and Norman, M. A. (eds.) (1990). *Adaptive User Interfaces*, London: Academic Press.

Cameron, J. R. (1986) 'An overview of JSD', *IEEE Transactions on Software Engineering, 12*, (2), 222–40.

Card, S. K. Moran, T. P. and Newell, A. (1980). 'The keystroke-level model for user performance time with interactive systems', *Communications of the ACM, 23*, (7), pp. 396–410.

Council Directive of 29 May 1990 on the minimum safety and health requirements for work with display screen equipment (fifth individual Directive within the meaning of Article 16(1) of Directive 87/391/EEC (1990), *Official Journal of the European Communities*, **33**, 14–18.

Cox, B. (1987). *Object-Oriented Programming: An evolutionary approach*, Reading, MA: Addison-Wesley

Davis, A. M. (1988). 'A comparison of techniques for the specification of external system behaviour', *Communications of the ACM*, **31**, (9) 1098–115.

Deming, W. E. (1982). *Quality, Productivity, and Competitive Position*, MIT Center for Advanced Study, Cambridge, MA.

Digital Equipment Corporation (1988). *XUI Style Guide*, AA-MG20A-TE, Maynard, MA.

Ericsson, K. A. and Simon, H. A. (1980). 'Verbal reports as data', *Psychological Review*, **3**, 215–51.

Fitts, P. M. and Posner, M. I. (1973). *Human Performance*. London: Prentice Hall

Gentner, D. R, and Grudin, J. (1990). 'Why good engineers (sometimes) create bad interfaces', *Proceedings of CHI'90 Human Factors in Computing Systems*, Association for Computing Machinery, pp. 277–82.

Gilb, T. (1984). 'The "impact analysis table" applied to human factors design', *Proceedings of Interact '84, First IFIP Conference on Human–Computer Interaction*, September 4–7, vol. 2, pp. 97–101, Amsterdam: Elsevier.

Good, M., Spine, T.M., Whiteside, J. and George, P. (1986). 'User-derived impact analysis as a tool for usability engineering', *CHI'86 Proceedings*, pp. 241–6.

Green, P. and Wei-Haas, L. (1985). 'The rapid development of user interfaces: Experiences with the Wizard of Oz technique', *Proceedings of the 29th Annual Meeting of the Human Factors Society*, pp. 470–4.

Harel, D. (1988). 'On visual formalisms', *Communications of the ACM*, **31**, (5), 514–30.

Health and Safety Executive (1992). *Display Screen Equipment Work: Guidance on regulations*.

Hekmatpour, S. (1987). 'Experience with evolutionary prototyping in a large software project', *ACM Sigsoft Software Engineering Notes*, **12**, (1), 38–41.

Hutchings, D. (1990). *In Pursuit of Quality: Participative techniques for quality improvement*, London: Pitman Publishing.

International Business Machines Corporation (1991). *Systems Application Architecture. Common User Access Guide to User Interface Design*, SC34-4289-00.

Ip, K. W., Damodaran, L. and Olphert, C. W. (1990a). 'Task allocation and job design in IT system design', In K. Noro and O. Brown (eds.), *Human Factors in Organizational Design and Management – III*, Elsevier, North Holland.

Ip, K. W., Damodaran, L., Olphert, C. W. and Maguire, M. C. (1990b). 'The use of task allocation charts in system design: A critical appraisal', D. Diaper *et al.* (eds.), In *Human–Computer Interaction – INTERACT '90*, Elsevier, North Holland.

Jackson, M. A. (1982). *Systems Development*. Englewood Cliffs, NJ: Prentice Hall.

Karat, C.-M. (1990). 'Cost–benefit analysis of usability engineering techniques', In D. Diaper *et al.* (eds.), *Human–Computer Interaction – Interact '90*, Elsevier, Amsterdam, pp. 351–6.

Karat, C.-M. (1991). 'Cost–benefit and business case analysis of usability engineering', *Tutorial presented at CHI'91. Conference on Human Factors in Computing Systems*, Association for Computing Machinery.

Leintz, B. P. and Swanson, E. B. (1981). 'Problems in application software maintenance', *Communications of the ACM*, **24**, (11), 763–9.

MacIntyre, F., Estep, K. W. and Siebuth, J. M. (1990). 'Cost of user-friendly programming', *Journal of Forth Application and Research*, **6**, (2), 103–15.

Mantei, M. M. and Teorey, T. J. (1988). 'Cost/benefit analysis for incorporating human factors in the software lifecycle', *Communications of the ACM*, **31**, (4) 428–39.

Myers, B. A. (1984). 'The user interface for Sapphire', *Computer Graphics and Applications*, **4**, (12), 13–23.

Myers, B. A. (1988). 'A taxonomy of window manager user interfaces', *IEEE Computer Graphics and Applications*, September 1988, pp. 65–84.

Open Software Foundation (1990). *OSF/ Motif: Style guide*, Englewood Cliffs, NJ: Prentice Hall.

Potosnak, K. (1988). 'Setting objectives for measurably better software', *IEEE Software*, Vol. 5, no. 4, pp. 89–90.

Rosenberg, D. (1989). 'A cost benefit analysis for corporate user interface standards: What price to pay for a consistent look and feel?' In J. Nielsen (ed.), *Coordinating User Interfaces for Consistency*, San Diego, CA: Academic Press, pp. 21–34.

Roethliesberger, F. J. and Dickson, W. J. (1939). *Management and the Worker: An account of a research program conducted by the Western Electric Company Hawthorne Works, Chicago*. Cambridge, MA: Harvard University Press.

Shackel, B. (1986). 'IBM makes usability as important as functionality', *The Computer Journal*, **29**, (5), 475–6.

Shneiderman, B. (1987). *Designing the User Interface*, Addison-Wesley.

Smith, S. L. and Mosier, J. N. (1984). *Design Guidelines for User-System Interface Software*, The Mitre Corporation.

Sun Microsystems, Inc. (1986). *NeWS Preliminary Technical Overview*, Mountain View, California.

Sun Microsystems Inc. (1989). *Open Look: Graphical user interface functional specification*, Addison Wesley.

Symons, C. R. (1991). *Software Sizing and Estimating: Mk II FPA (function point analysis)*, Chichester: Wiley.

Teitelman, W. (1984). 'A Tour Through CEDAR' *IEEE Software*, **1**, (2), 44–73.

Temple, Barker and Sloane Inc. (1990). *The Benefits of the Graphical User Interface: A report on new primary research*, prepared by Temple, Barker and Sloane Inc., Lexington, MA.

Whiteside, J., Jones, S., Levy, P. S. and Wixon, D. (1985). 'User performance with command, menu, and iconic interfaces', *Proceedings of CHI'85*, pp. 185–91.

Whiteside, J., Bennett, J. and Holtzblatt, K. (1988). 'Usability Engineering: Our experience and evolution', In M. Helander (ed.), *Handbook of Human–Computer Interaction*, Elsevier, North Holland, pp. 791–817.

Wilson, J. and Rosenberg, D. (1988). 'Rapid prototyping for user interface design', In M. Helander (ed.), *Handbook of Human–Computer Interaction*, Elsevier, North Holland, pp. 859–75.

Woods, A., Browne, D. P. and Friend, J. (1991). 'Helping the Police with their enquiries', In D. Diaper and N. Hammond (eds.), *People and Computers VI, Proceedings of the HCI'91 Conference*, 20–23 August, pp. 347–58.

Woods, W. A. (1970). 'Transition network grammars for natural language analysis', *Communications of the ACM*, **13**, (10), 591–606.

Index

STUDIO Update

'STUDIO Update' will keep the reader informed of developments in STUDIO and the discipline of Human-Computer Interaction.

To register for free copies of 'STUDIO Update' simply complete the following form and return it to Dermot Browne or Steve King at KPMG Management Consulting, PO Box 695, 8 Salisbury Square, London, EC4Y 8BB. Telephone 071-236-8000.

Alternatively, copy the form and FAX it to:
        Dermot Browne
    Fax No: 071-955-6910

Name: _____

Title: _____

Company: _____

Address: _____

City: _____

County/State: _____

Post/Zip Code: _____ Country: _____

Telephone: _____

Yes, I would like to be kept informed of STUDIO developments and events ☐